THE
STORY OF THE RUSSIAN CHURCH

THE STORY OF
THE RUSSIAN CHURCH

BY

HUGH Y. REYBURN, B.D.

KIRKINTILLOCH

AUTHOR OF "JOHN CALVIN: HIS LIFE, LETTERS, AND WORK"

ANDREW MELROSE LTD.

LONDON & NEW YORK

1924

PRINTED IN GREAT BRITAIN BY MORRISON AND GIBB LTD., EDINBURGH

PREFACE

THE Russian Church may be looked at from many points of view, but the following pages are confined for the most part to one of them. Their purpose is to outline in its nature and results the connection which has subsisted between Church and State during the thousand years separating Ruric and the Varangians from Lenin and the Bolshevists. As the story is developed, it brings to the front some of the most imposing figures which have trod the stage of history, and shows them playing their parts in strange and stirring scenes. It is full of interest, especially at present, but it is little known, for most books on Church History ignore the very existence of the Eastern Church, of which the section found in Russia is by far the largest. Therefore, if any reader is stimulated to cultivate a closer acquaintance with the great organisation which has sustained the spiritual life of the Russian people during the past millennium, the author will consider that his work has not been undertaken in vain.

H. Y. R.

CONTENTS

THE STORY OF
THE RUSSIAN CHURCH

CHAPTER I

RURIC, ASKOLD, AND DIR

BEFORE we begin our story it will be profitable to glance at the arena on which the fortunes of the Russian Church and State have been developed.

Speaking generally, Russia is an immense plain. In the centre towards the west there is a tableland about a thousand feet above the level of the sea. This glides down gently on all sides till it reaches the Arctic Ocean on the north, the Ural Mountains on the east, the Black Sea on the south, and the Carpathians on the west. In some districts the plain moves forward in gentle undulations. In others it is flat, and the eye travels without interruption to the horizon. Further, along the whole length of the western boundary from the White Sea and the Gulf of Finland, up the Niemen and down the Dnieper, the plain is wet and spongy, filled with marshes and swamps and boglands and lakes. These not only formed a line of defence which invading armies found it difficult to pierce, they formed an obstacle to trade and social intercourse so serious that for centuries they cut off Russia from the nations of Western Europe and from the political and religious movements which were developing among them.

The vast expanse of the Russian plain is divided by a line running diagonally from Kiev in the south-west to Kazan and beyond it in the north-east. The region on the northern side of this line is covered with forests of oak, elm, maple, birch, pine, larch, and fir, which thin

I

out into patches of low shrubs and then into sheets of moss on the shores of the Arctic Ocean. The region to the south of this line is practically without wood. It is covered with a deposit of black mould forming a belt many miles broad, stretching from the western frontier to the Ural Mountains, and forming an arable region which is unequalled on the globe. Its fertility is wonderful, and it only needs modern methods of agriculture to make it a granary which will put the world beyond the reach of famine. The belt of black mould passes into that of the fertile steppe, and that again into the saline barren steppe which goes eastward to the Caspian Sea. Farther south is a narrow strip along the shores of the Black Sea where the vine and olive and various fruit trees thrive, and there the ancient Greeks had many settlements.

The Russian plain is drained by a number of great rivers whose main streams and tributaries form a network which has been of immense service to travellers. Those who were afraid to plunge into the trackless forest and who were unwilling to risk their lives in the plain had no hesitation in sailing up and down the rivers as business might require. In this way regular trade routes were established, and the number of those who used them increased from year to year.

As far back as we can go we find various tribes moving over the plain. It is difficult to realise how few they were in number and how hard they had to fight for their existence. In the beginning of the seventh century the Slavs, whose headquarters were in the Middle Danube, broke up and scattered. Some of them pushed eastward till they reached the region between Novgorod and Kiev—a region wild, unexplored, and practically empty. There they settled and built solid wooden huts in clusters surrounded by a stockade. As they increased in size the villages became little towns with cultivated districts lying round them.

In the following century new faces began to appear. These were the Varangians,[1] men of Scandinavian stock, half traders and half marauders, who while their kindred

[1] Thomsen, p. 14.

sailed westward to carve out kingdoms with the sword in England and Northern France, pushed eastward to see what fortune had in store for them. As they came into contact with the Slavs they settled among them, sometimes starting business on their own account, and sometimes hiring themselves as mercenaries to defend the towns, and to escort the traders' caravans. After a time they assumed the rôle of military governors in the districts they protected, and claimed the payment they received for their services as tribute due from subjects to princes. Their claims were not always conceded, for the little towns were democratic communities little disposed to allow any one to assume lordship over them.

In the ancient chronicles [1] we are told that after the tributaries had driven out the Varangians, the towns and tribes began to quarrel among themselves, and that finally they invited the Varangians to come back and restore order. The chronicle says that three brothers accepted the invitation. Ruric, the eldest, settled in Novgorod; Sineus, the second, settled near Bielozero; and Trevor settled in Izborsk. From these and the Rus they brought with them the Russian land took its name. After two years, Sineus and Trevor died, and Ruric became sole ruler. It may be doubted, however, whether the three princes entered Russia on terms so complimentary. It is much more likely that they opened their way to their position by force, for Nestor says that after they landed on the shores of the Gulf of Bothnia they began to build fortifications and wage war everywhere. The Slavs probably received them as protectors and masters because they could not help doing so.

A short time after the first Varangian invasion a band of adventurers went farther south to see what could be done. Traders were accustomed to drift along the rivers, taking with them cargoes of amber, wax and honey, woodwork, furs and linen, and slaves, and to bring back with them not only silks and satins, wines and fruits, and enamelled and

[1] Quoted by Thomsen, p. 13.

jewelled ornaments, but also wonderful tales of the walls and gates, the temples and palaces, the bazaars and markets, the wealth and magnificence of the great city on the Bosphorus. Askold and Dir, two of Ruric's chieftains, therefore gathered their followers together and started down the Dnieper for Constantinople.

On their way they halted at Kiev. It was a flourishing town before they reached it, and they saw its strategic importance. It lay on the great trade route between the Black Sea and the Baltic just where the forest lands end and the belt of black mould begins. Boats on the river and caravans on the plain brought merchandise to it from every quarter, so, without losing sight of their original objective, Askold and Dir established themselves in Kiev in 862, made the place the headquarters of the Varangians in the south, and assumed the lordship of the surrounding district.

The Greek Emperor had already heard of their fame and was not a little alarmed by it. In order to propitiate them he sent them presents of gold and silver and costly silks. At the same time he sent them a monk with the rank of bishop to preach Christianity. It is said that two hundred Russians were baptized, and that Askold was one of the number. If he were, his conversion did not check his piratical ardour. In 865 he and his comrades reached Constantinople and attacked it. The chronicler says : " The defence of the city was not successful until the Patriarch Photius took the robe of the Virgin Mary, which was preserved in the Church of Blachern, and plunged it into the sea, whereupon a tempest arose and wrecked the vessels of the heathen. Overwhelmed with consternation, they believed in the God who had smitten them, and became the first-fruits of their people to the Lord." In a letter to the bishops of the East, written about 867, Photius says : " The Russians, so notorious for their cruelty, who had conquered their neighbours and who in their pride had dared to attack the Roman Empire, have now renounced their superstitions and professed the religion of Jesus Christ. Lately our most formidable enemies, they have become our most faithful friends. We have sent them a bishop and a priest, and they show the greatest enthusiasm for Christianity." In the following year the Emperor Basil, the Macedonian, sent another monk who extended the work of evangelisation, but both the Patriarch and the Emperor deceived themselves if they thought that the enthusiasm for Christian principles was widespread or deep.

Legend says that these were not the first missionaries who visited Kiev. Andrew, our Lord's disciple, the Apostle of Greece and Scythia, is said to have come up the Dnieper on his way to Rome, and to have planted a cross, and to have prophesied, " On these hills shall hereafter shine forth the grace of God. There shall be a great city here, and God shall cause many churches to rise in it." If the legend does nothing more, it gives us a reason for calling St. Andrew Russia's patron saint.

The efforts of the missionaries from Constantinople were probably preceded by those of unknown missionaries from the south and west. To the south, on the shores of the Black Sea, lay the kingdom of the Khozars. About the middle of the seventh century they embraced Judaism. In the following century they were converted to Christianity, and as they had commercial relations with their Russian neighbours, we may conjecture that the gospel entered the country along with their merchandise. In Bulgaria, Christianity was first preached by captives from the Byzantine Empire. There a princess who was being educated at Constantinople professed the Christian faith during her residence in that city, and on her return home set herself to convert her brother Bogoris, the reigning prince. She succeeded, and in 863 Photius dispatched some monks to evangelise the Bulgarian people. Unfortunately the monks were so dangerous to the public peace that Bogoris ejected them and sent a request for missionaries to Pope Nicolas I. The Pope joyfully responded. But his hope of including Bulgaria within Roman jurisdiction was shortlived, for Bulgaria had resolved to retain its independence. Similarly the kingdom of Greater Moravia was the scene of energetic propaganda. It had been conquered by Charlemagne, who introduced into it a number of Latin missionaries. Under Rastislav, however, it not only regained its independence, but ejected the Latins and asked the Byzantine Emperor Michael III. to send missionaries who were Greek. The most famous of these were the brothers Cyril and Methodius, who arrived in 863.

Cyril and Methodius were sons of a Greek of noble birth who lived at Thessalonica. The name of the former was originally Constantine. He assumed that of Cyril when he become a monk at Rome, shortly before his death. He was educated along with the young Prince Michael, but fearing the snares of a courtier's life he became a missionary among the tribes near the Black Sea.

Methodius was a soldier. For ten years he was charged with the defence of the Slavonian frontier, then he threw up his commission and entered a monastery on Mount Olympus, whence he proceeded to join his brother on his mission to the Khozars. He accompanied him also to Moravia and to Rome. After his brother's death, which occurred in 871, he returned to Moravia, and it is probable that he died there in 880.

Both the brothers were familiar with the Slavonic language, and preached in it with such success that in Greater Moravia a national Church came into being. The antagonism between East and West was at this time rapidly becoming acute, and the German clergy who were already in the country made loud complaint regarding the use of the Slavonic language in Divine worship. The brothers were therefore summoned to Rome, where, in the Pope's opinion, they succeeded in justifying themselves. Thereafter, in order to further the work of evangelisation, to provide copies of the Scriptures for the instruction of converts in the Christian faith, and to furnish the Church with a ritual which it could understand, Cyril reduced the Slavonic language to writing. Taking the Greek alphabet as a basis, he added to it fifteen new letters, most of them modifications of more cumbrous Glagolite characters already in existence.[1] He then proceeded to the work of translation. He certainly translated the Gospels, which is all that the oldest MSS. contain. He probably translated the Psalter and the Acts, as MSS. of an early date contained these also. It is just possible that he finished the translation of the whole of the New Testament, but the translation of the Old Testament was not undertaken till many years after his death.

His work in this connection did not receive the welcome it deserved. If the Western clergy were incensed and alarmed because the gospel was preached and services conducted in the Slavonic language, they were still more incensed and alarmed by the translation of the Scriptures, and by the appearance of Slavonic service-books. They saw plainly that if the use of Slavonic was permitted, the Church of Moravia would range itself along with other Churches which used that language and which looked to Constantinople, and in the long-run it would be lost to Rome. Therefore they denounced the translations to the Pope on the ground that it was unseemly that any nation should possess a peculiar alphabet except the Hebrews, Greeks, and Latins, whose languages had been inscribed on the Cross of our Lord.[2]

In response to their clamour in 879, Pope John VIII. issued a Bull interdicting the use of Slavonic in Church services. Methodius found it necessary to make a second journey to Rome. There can be little doubt that before he started he appealed for protection and support to Sviatopolk, King of Moravia, and that Sviatopolk made strong representations on his behalf. At any rate, in 880 the Pope sent another Bull to Sviatopolk in which he declared that He who created Hebrew, Greek, and Latin created other languages also for His own glory. He therefore ordained that sermons should be preached and the works of Christ our God should be made known in the Slavonic language, because the precept runs, " Praise the Lord all ye people, and laud Him all ye nations." This

---

[1] Krasinski, p. 23, note.   [2] Henderson, 75.

was not taken to mean that Latin was to be expelled from the Church ritual, or that the indiscriminate use of the translations into Slavonic was to be permitted. All it was held to signify was that after the Gospel had been read in Latin it should be read also in Slavonic for the benefit of those to whom Latin was an unknown tongue. The victory for the vernacular which Methodius won was therefore much less conclusive than it seemed.

It was not difficult for the Western clergy to read between the lines of this second Bull that the Pope was in secret sympathy with them, and they continued their clamour and denunciation in Moravia wherever they could get a hearing. Eventually, when the Moravian kingdom was overthrown, they persecuted the Slavonic clergy and people with such bitterness that some fled to Bulgaria, some to Poland, and some to Kiev. Wherever they went they took with them their alphabet, their MSS., their translations and service-books, and they succeeded in making Slavonic the official language of the Church. " It is," says Neale, " not only the Church language of all the Russias, but of Moldavia, Wallachia, Serbia, Bosnia, Montenegro, Slavonia proper, Dalmatia, and Bulgaria. This noble language is perhaps more completely a Church language than any other. Unlike its rivals in this respect —Greek and Latin—it had no previous literature. It was adapted to ecclesiastical purposes in its full freshness and vigour and not in its decay, and it has not, like Latin, served as the medium of works purely literary. The Church gave it its letters, and its letters, obsolete in other respects, now serve only for the use of the Church." [1]

As a spoken language, five great dialects were ultimately formed from it—the Russian, the Polish, the Tcheck, the Illyrian, and the Croatian. As a printed language it remains unaltered in Church books to the present day. It therefore keeps the sentiment of Pan-Slavism alive as nothing else has been able to do, and it forms a bond of union among the nations of Eastern Europe which has withstood many strains.

[1] Neale, *History of the Holy Eastern Church*, ii. 822.

Within Russia itself, and excluding Poland, the number of languages and dialects spoken is about 150,[1] but wherever the Orthodox Church is established it uses the Slavonic in all its books and services, and every churchman, even of the lowest grade, is familiar with it. It is nowhere the language of Russia any more than the language of Wiclif and Chaucer is the language of modern England, but its archaic forms and constructions are considered to lend dignity to the ritual in which it is used, and it is understood by practically all the worshippers. The Latin employed in the services of the Roman Church is a dead language known to few and spoken by none. It therefore makes no appeal to the understanding, the conscience, or the heart. The appeal of Slavonic, on the other hand, is all the more impressive because it suggests to the worshipper the continuity of his own service with that in which millions engaged in the centuries of the vanished past. He realises that his Church has behind it the unbroken tradition of a thousand years.

Politically the use of Slavonic in Church services has had the same unifying influence. When Russia was really a collection of independent cities and principalities always jealous of each other and often at war, the Church was the one and only institution that held them together as an organism whose parts were articulated and united to a common head ; and one of the instruments which it used most effectively in establishing its universal authority was this universal language, which took no account of political frontiers and formed the vehicle by which Russians in the most distant parts of the land, and even in the bitterest rivalry, laid their petitions at the feet of Divine mercy and formulated the doctrines of their common faith. Cyril's alphabet and his translations were meant simply to supply the needs of the people among whom he laboured, but they have had a far wider influence than he dreamed of. He has become unconsciously a more successful empire-builder than some of the Tsars.

[1] Alexinski, p. 33.

CHAPTER II

VLADIMIR

RURIC died in 879, leaving his young son Ivor to the care of his tutor Oleg. Three years afterward Oleg started for the south, caught Askold and Dir by treachery outside Kiev and slew them, made himself master of the city, and declared it to be the metropolis of his dominions. From this time the name Rus attached itself exclusively to the surrounding region, and from this centre it has spread over all the territory acquired by the Russian crown.

In 903 Oleg married Igor to Olga. Her origin is uncertain, but she proved herself an excellent wife, and after her husband's death a competent regent during her son's minority. Continuing his journey south, conquering and plundering as he went along, Oleg drew near Constantinople in 907. The Emperor, Leo the Philosopher, made haste to come to terms. Oleg fastened his shield in triumph on the Golden Gate and returned home laden with spoil and glory. The treaty drawn up on this occasion is said to be the first written agreement seen in Russia. Oleg died in 912 and was succeeded by Igor, Ruric's son. He made two expeditions against Constantinople. In the first, his ships were destroyed by Greek fire and his land forces were routed. In the second, he was more successful. The Emperor agreed to a treaty in which Igor's dominions are officially styled Russian Land, and the progress of Christianity therein is indicated by the fact that, when the treaty was confirmed at Kiev, Igor and his heathen companions laid their swords at the feet of Peroun, and swore by their idols to abide by the terms of their compact; while the Christians in the army met in the Church of

Elijah and took the oath on a copy of the Gospels. In
945 Igor was slain in an expedition against the Drevlians.
Olga, his widow, took a terrible revenge, and then settled
down at Kiev to act as regent for her son Sviatoslav.

Olga was a heathen to begin with, but heathenism
ceased to satisfy her, and she began to inquire into the
Christian faith. The chronicler says that she went to
Constantinople, that she was instructed by the Patriarch,
and that when she was baptized the Emperor Constantine
Porphyrogenitus acted as her godfather. On her return
to Russia she tried, without success, to convert her son ;
but he declared liberty of opinion within his dominions,
and he allowed his children to be instructed by his mother
and her priests. In 965, when she felt death approaching,
she forbade the heathen rites which were customary, and
commanded her funeral services to be conducted in accordance with the Christian practice. " The people, by whom
she was surnamed The Wise during her lifetime, began to
bless her as a saint after her death, when they came themselves to follow the example of this morning star which had
arisen and gone before to lead Russia into the way of
salvation." The chronicler says of her : " As the moon
shines at midnight, so she shone in the midst of a Pagan
people. She was like a pearl amid dirt, for the people
were still in the mire of their sins and were not yet purified
by baptism."

Just before his mother's death, Sviatoslav attacked
the Bulgarians on the Danube, captured their capital and
all their fortresses. In a transport of delight he proposed
to transfer his metropolis from Kiev to a town which
commanded the land route to Constantinople. John
Zimisces, the Emperor, saw the danger in which he would
be placed if Sviatoslav's intentions were carried out, and
asked him to evacuate the country in accordance with
the terms of the treaty made with his predecessor.
Sviatoslav refused. In the war which followed he was
forced to make peace. On his way home he found the
difficult passage of the cataracts of the Dnieper was stopped

by the Petchenegians. His attempt to force his way through failed. He and his followers were all slain, and his skull, bound with gold, became the drinking-cup of a Petchenegian chief.

Before his departure he divided his realm between his three sons—Oleg, Yaropalk, and Vladimir—giving them respectively Kiev, the Drevlian country, and Novgorod. In the civil war which instantly broke out, Oleg was trampled under foot by his own soldiers as they fled before Yaropalk. Yaropalk was inveigled into Kiev and assassinated there. Vladimir thus became sole ruler of Russia in 980.

He soon proved that he was a skilful warrior. He not only consolidated the territories he had received from his father, but extended them. He conquered Red Russia from the Poles, and made Livonia and Lithuania his tributaries.

Unfortunately his morals were much below his military abilities. He had four wives, and in addition to these he had 300 concubines at Vouchiegorod, 300 at Bielgorodok, and 200 at Berestov. " In this respect," says the chronicler, " he was a perfect Solomon."

Like his father and his ancestors he was at first a pagan, and at Novgorod and at Kiev he erected statues of Peroun, the god of thunder. It was in this connection that the first and only martyrs of the Christian faith perished in Russia. On his return from the conquest of a Finnish tribe, Vladimir resolved to hold a festival in honour of his gods. A human sacrifice was demanded, and the victim drawn by lot was a young man, a Christian, and the son of a Christian. Inspired by paternal love and by hatred of their cruel superstition, the father refused to surrender his son to the king's messengers and mocked at the idol, whereupon the populace fell upon the father and the son and murdered both of them. The Russian Church now counts them among its saints, giving them the names of Theodore and John.

At first sight nothing appears more improbable than

that this marauding and lustful idolater should become a humble Christian, yet this is what took place. Just as the life of St. Paul falls into sections, one before his conversion on the road to Damascus and one after it, so does the life of Vladimir. We know nothing about his mental processes, but he could not help seeing that the religion in which he was brought up was losing its hold everywhere.

If he was to make a change, his first choice was between Christianity and Mohammedanism. Western Europe was Christian, the great Byzantine Empire was Christian, Hungary, Poland, and Scandinavia were becoming Christian. But on the east and south lay the rising power of the Mohammedans, who were carrying the Crescent in triumph through Central Asia and along the shores of Africa. A struggle between the two and a fight for mastery was in the long-run inevitable. In the meantime Russia lay between them. It must cast in its lot with one or other, or be attacked by both. The moment was intensely critical, for, without doubt, if Russia ranged itself with Islam, the flood of invasion which was with such difficulty driven back from Central Europe in later days, would have submerged it entirely, and would have reduced Christianity to impotence for centuries. Fortunately for Europe, Vladimir resolved to become a Christian, and from his time onward Russia became the eastern bulwark of the Christian faith.

The next question he had to decide was which of the two competing forms of Christianity he was to accept— the Western or the Eastern. The Western Church, which looked to Rome as its metropolis, was supreme over Italy, Gaul, Germany, and Spain, and the claims of the Pope to be a universal spiritual ruler were endorsed by the Western Emperor. But the Eastern Empire was even more splendid than the Empire of the West, and the Eastern Emperor not only inherited the name and the traditions of the Cæsars, but added to them new glories of his own. The prestige of Rome was diminished by the fact that it was far away, that communication with it was difficult and infrequent, and that the Roman priests who had appeared in Russia had done little to commend themselves to the people. On the other hand, Constantinople was near, communication was easy, and the volume of trade flowing to and from it was increasing. It was monks from Constantinople who conducted the Christian propaganda and organised the congregations which they formed, and determined their ritual. Practically all the Christians with whom Vladimir came into contact belonged to the Eastern Church, and it was almost inevitable that when he became a Christian he should belong to it too.

The chronicler, however, tells the story much more dramatically, and glorifies Russia by suggesting that its favour was courted by surrounding monarchs. He says that in 986 ambassadors arrived from various countries. The first were the Bulgarians from the Volga, who set forth the advantages of Mohammedanism. Their description of the joys of paradise captivated Vladimir's imagination, but their insistence on abstinence from intoxicating drink was fatal. " Drinking," said he, " is the joy of the Russians, and we cannot do without it." The ambassadors of the Latin Church were dismissed with the curt order, " Go home ; it was not from the Pope that our fathers received their religion." Jews from the Khozars next came forward. When Vladimir learned that for their sins they had been driven from their own land, he cried angrily, " You are cursed by God in this fashion and you wish to teach us. Go. We have no desire to be without a fatherland like you." Then a philosopher from Greece appeared. He explained why Christ was crucified, outlined Church history to the Seventh Council, expounded the leading doctrines of the Christian faith, and finished with a picture of the Last Judgment. " Receive baptism," said he, " and blessedness will be your portion."

Vladimir called his boyars together, and on their suggestion sent commissioners to see where God was worshipped most worthily. When their arrival at Constantinople became known, orders were given for a service of great

splendour. They were therefore taken to the Church of St.
Sophia, which was then at the height of its magnificence.
None of them had seen anything to equal it, and the size
of the building, the multitude of the clergy, the gorgeous
sacerdotal vestments, the exquisite singing of the choirs,
the sweet odour of the incense, and the sight of the deacons
issuing from the vestry in long lines with lighted torches
in their hands filled them with astonishment. On their
return to Kiev they declared they scarcely knew whether
they had reached heaven or were still on earth, and they
ended by saying, " No one who has tasted sweet will afterward take that which is bitter, neither can we abide any
longer in heathenism." Vladimir was still undecided,
when one of his boyars said, " If the Greek religion were
not the true religion, would your grandmother Olga have
accepted it ? " Vladimir revealed his decision by asking,
" Where shall we be baptized ? " His boyars answered,
" Wherever it shall please you."

It is difficult to determine how much of this is fact and
how much is fact embroidered by fiction, but it is easy to
see that these early Russians were persuaded to accept
Christianity by the appeal of a gorgeous ritual to their
æsthetic sensibilities. So far as the account shows, they
had no sense of the futility of idol worship, and no intellectual relief springing from the conception of one living
God, Creator, Preserver, and Governor, who is supreme
in earth below and heaven above. They had no conviction of sin, from whose guilt and penalty they required
deliverance. They had no consciousness of weakness
needing the sanctifying energy of the Holy Spirit. The
impulse to conversion was given by the music, colour, and
impressiveness which they believed the worship of God
required. In this respect these early Russians are not
different from the generations which have followed them.

It is also evident that the Russian Church is the daughter
of the Church of Byzantium. As it took over the Byzantine
ritual, so it took over Byzantine theology. Russians, like
the rest of the Eastern Church, have seldom felt the need of

finding their own way to conclusions on Christian doctrine, and in all the years that the Russian Church has existed there has not arisen any one worthy to take his place beside the Greek or Latin Fathers of the early centuries or the Schoolmen of the Middle Ages, or the leaders of Reformation and post-Reformation times. The theology of the Russian Church was accepted ready-made, and whereas the history of thought in the West palpitates with life, there is no movement in Russian thought worth chronicling

Immediately after Vladimir had resolved to become a Christian he resolved to be baptized. But he also resolved to appear for baptism not in the guise of a humble penitent, but as became his rank in that of a conqueror. He therefore marched an army along the coast of the Black Sea to Kherson, an outpost city of the Eastern Empire, and besieged it. After entering it in triumph, he informed the Emperor, Basil II., that he wanted Basil's sister Anne for his wife, that he also wanted relics of saints for his churches, and priests to baptize his people. If these demands were refused, he would attack Constantinople at once. Basil, who was in great trouble in other parts of the Empire, could not risk war with Russia at that moment, and he yielded on condition that Vladimir sent auxiliaries to help the Imperial troops. Anne shuddered at the prospect before her, but the will of her brothers and the interests of the Empire prevailed. Vladimir got rid of his wives and concubines by distributing them among his vassals. When this distribution was finished he received baptism in Kherson, and the marriage with Anne followed immediately. After building a church in Kherson and dedicating it to St. Basil, he returned to Kiev with his bride, a number of monks, and a miscellaneous collection of relics.

One of these monks was a Syrian named Michael, and his name stands first on the list of the Russian Metropolitans.

After reaching Kiev, Vladimir set himself to convert his subjects. They were not entirely ignorant of Christian truth, but they were quite unprepared for the forcible and wholesale measures which he took to identify them with Christianity.

First he caused his sons to be baptized. Then he proceeded to destroy the idols and to root out their worship. This was not difficult, for there was no organised opposition to overcome, and Vladimir made it perfectly plain that he would tolerate no disobedience to his revealed will. On the hill above the Dnieper stood images of Peroun, the god of thunder, with his trunk of wood, his head of silver, and his moustaches of gold, of Dazhbog, the god of the sun, of Atribog, the god of the wind, and others. In the year 988, on the appointed day, in presence of the assembled citizens, some of these were cut to pieces, others were burned, others were overthrown. While the image of Peroun was lying on the ground it was scourged with switches, then tied to the tails of horses and dragged to the Dnieper, where it was tumbled in. The people followed it as it was borne down the stream until it disappeared in the rapids. Next day proclamation was made that all Russians, rich and poor, young and old, masters and slaves, must come to the river and receive baptism or be counted as the king's enemies. At a given signal the multitude plunged into the water, some of them standing in it up to their necks, others up to their breasts, holding their young children in their arms, while the priests on the banks recited the baptismal formula. Vladimir was overjoyed at his success in bringing his people to salvation, and in token of his gratitude for the mercies which he and they had received he built a church to St. Basil on the site which had formerly been sacred to Peroun.

In Novgorod many of the citizens had to be killed before the survivors submitted to the Christian rite. Some endeavoured to escape by saying they were already Christians, and when their deceit was exposed all were commanded to hang a cross round their necks in token of their conversion to the new faith.

Thus Russia was Christianised in name, but in name only. We are told in the Scriptures that devils came out

2

of the possessed at the command of the Lord Jesus, but the heathen customs and superstitions did not lose their hold on the people's life at the command of Vladimir. Some of the old gods, like their worshippers, received new names, but they kept their old characters and attributes. Thus Peroun, the god of thunder, reappeared as Elijah ; Voloss, the guardian of the flocks, became St. Blaise ; Kouzma, the protector of blacksmiths, became St. Kosmas ; and Didlado became the Virgin Mary. For centuries the Christianity of Russia was a mere veneer on the surface of a solid mass of heathen superstition and ignorance, and even to-day, although Christian dogma and Christian idealism have been taking a firmer hold on Russian thought and life, Christian ethics are challenged in all directions by practices which survive from heathen times.

Happily for Russia, Vladimir was conscious that more than wholesale baptism was required to lift his people to the Christian level. He therefore sent to Bulgaria for priests to instruct the people in the faith to which they had sworn allegiance. These priests brought with them the translation of the Scriptures made by Cyril and Methodius, and with these as their text-books they went among the people preaching everywhere and organising their converts into little Christian communities. Vladimir greatly assisted them by building churches in the towns and villages. In Kiev, in addition to the church of St. Basil, he erected a church to the Virgin Mary on the place where the Varangian father and son suffered martyrdom, and he endowed it with the tithes of corn and of cattle and of the profits of trade for the support of the clergy and the benefit of the poor. Hence it was called the Church of the Tithes.

Under his auspices the Church was formally organised on the Byzantine model. Leontius, who succeeded Michael in the office of Metropolitan, marked out the dioceses of Novgorod, Rostov, Chernigov, Vladimir, and Bolgorod, and appointed bishops to them. Each bishop was recognised as supreme in his own diocese, as possessing the right of appointing the priests, the deacons, and the other officials of the parishes, as well as of appointing the abbots and abbesses of the religious houses in the area allotted to him. The first two bishops of Rostov, however, were driven out by the tribes who inhabited that region, and many years of labour and suffering had to elapse before their successors persuaded the fierce heathen to receive the gospel.

With a view to extending the benefits of education, Vladimir established several schools and compelled his courtiers to send their children for instruction. But the ignorant parents thought that letters were an invention of the devil, and they resisted his royal order as they would have resisted an order for their children's execution.

Alongside these efforts for the benefit of his subjects, Vladimir made a strenuous effort to put at least one section of the law on a definitely Christian basis. He recognised that Christianity introduced into the life of the State a set of principles which were not found in pagan law and custom. In addition to that, he says that on reading the Nomocanon he discovered there were certain matters which it does not belong to the prince to take cognisance of, inasmuch as they belong to religion. He therefore resolved to commit the administration of justice in certain fixed cases and among a certain class of his subjects to the Metropolitan and the bishops. The matters assigned to them were—divorce and offences against the law of chastity, sacrilege in all its forms, disputes regarding the property of a person deceased, and the supervision of weights and measures used in the markets. The persons under their jurisdiction were—all the clergy with their wives and families, all the servants of the Church whatever their employment, and all who came under the care of the Church, such as the sick in the hospitals, the blind, the lame, and the poor.

After his baptism Vladimir's personal life underwent a change even greater than that which he imposed on his people. He did not succeed in throwing off all the effects of his heathen days, but he endeavoured to develop the virtues of a truly Christian character. He was faithful to his Greek wife Anne; he cultivated the spirit of meekness; he visited the sick and gave gifts to the poor. He shrank from bloodshed to such an extent that he refused to pass sentence of death on murderers, with the result that crimes of violence became common, and the clergy had to beg him to remember that God expected him not to bear the sword in vain. He allowed surrounding nations to lay waste his frontiers with impunity until his boyars insisted that he must protect his subjects.

In the propaganda of the Christian faith he himself laboured diligently, so that in his reign Christian faith was preached and converts were made in Murom, Polotsk, Smolensk, Pskov, Lutsk, Tmutarakan, and many other places.

Up to the measure of his ability, Vladimir endeavoured to walk worthy of his high calling in Christ Jesus, and to bring his subjects into contact with the saving grace to which he himself owed so much. The sins and shortcomings of his heathen days are all too evident, but the change in his personal character and the change he wrought among his people are equally unmistakable. He died in the summer of 1015 in an expedition on the Steppes. His body was brought to Kiev and placed in a marble coffin beside that of his Greek wife Anne, who had predeceased him, and his memory was soon surrounded with a halo in which he appeared to Russian piety as equal to the Apostles, and as one of the patron saints of his native land.

CHAPTER III

YAROSLAV

VLADIMIR divided his dominions between his twelve sons, and his ill-advised action led to bloody feuds. Immediately after his death Sviatopolk seized Kiev and began a career which earned for him the name of The Accursed. His soldiers surprised his brother Boris and slew him in the act of prayer. They also waylaid and murdered Glieb. Sviatoslav fled towards Hungary, but was overtaken near the Carpathians and done to death. Yaroslav, however, gathered the men of Novgorod, marched south and drove Sviatopolk out of the country.

Yaroslav thus became master both of Novgorod and Kiev, but his troubles were not over. His brother Mstislav attacked him and compelled him to surrender some land on the Dnieper. He was also attacked by the fierce Petchenegians, who came right up to the walls of Kiev. After a bloody battle he routed them with great slaughter. To commemorate his victory he extended the boundaries of Kiev to take in the battlefield, and he surrounded the city with a brick wall. He also built and adorned the Cathedral of St. Sophia.

Under Yaroslav Kiev reached the height of its glory. Traders came to it from far and near. Definite sections of it were set apart for the members of the German, Dutch, and Scandinavian nations. Churches were built, monthly markets and annual fairs were established. The system of bartering goods for skins and pelts began to be superseded by the use of leather tokens cut from the skins and used as a medium of exchange. As silver became common, leather tokens were in their turn superseded by coins of the precious metal bearing a rude impression of the features of the prince.

It was under Yaroslav that the last expedition against Constantinople took place. It was disastrously repulsed, and with this repulse there vanished for centuries the hope of fulfilling a prophecy written by an unknown hand on the pedestal of the statue of Bellerophon, to the effect that Russia would one day occupy the capital of the Eastern Empire.

Yaroslav, however, extended his connection with other countries by means of marriage. His own wife was a daughter of the King of Sweden ; his sister married Kasimir, King of Poland ; his daughter, Elisabeth, married Harold Hardrada, came with him to England, and after his defeat at Stamford Bridge in September 1066, accompanied him to the Western Isles, from which she returned to Norway after his death. His second daughter, Anne, married Henry I., King of France. His third daughter, Anastasia, became the wife of Andrew I., King of Hungary. If Yaroslav's successors had established similar relations with foreign countries, Russia would have been brought into the stream of Western European life, and its development, both political and social, might have been profoundly modified. Unfortunately this did not take place.

Yaroslav was a lover of letters. He not only studied the Scriptures himself, but translated portions of them into the language of his people, and placed his translations in the Church of St. Sophia for the benefit of all who could read. By his orders also the Nomocanon was translated from the Greek that the Russian clergy might guide themselves by its rules. In Novgorod he established a public school, and in many of the towns of Russia he planted monks, provided their salaries, and sent them out to evangelise the surrounding regions. Further, in order to make Kiev equal in splendour to Constantinople, he engaged Greek artists who adorned the churches with paintings and mosaic work, and by the help of three Greek musicians he introduced the practice of singing in eight parts or tones. He also founded two monasteries at Kiev—that of St. George for men, and that of St. Irene for women.

It is noteworthy, however, that the most famous of all the monasteries at Kiev, the Petcherski Lavra, owes its beginning to a simple monk, a man from Lubetsch, who visited Mount Athos, received the tonsure there, took the name of Anthony, and proposed to remain with the brethren for the rest of his life. His superiors, however, sent him back to Russia, assuring him that blessing would attend his labours in his native land.

While visiting Kiev he perceived on the cliffs above the Dnieper a shallow cave which the monk Hilarion had dug out. Anthony established himself in this cave, and the fame of his sanctity spread abroad. Disciples joined him and constructed a subterranean church and cells. Their number increased, and the Grand Prince gave them the mountain in which they had taken up their abode. There they built a large church and cloisters. In the meantime Anthony, disliking so many people about him, retired into the forest. On his refusal to become head of the monastery, the monks chose Barlaam. Theodosius, Barlaam's successor, gathered a hundred monks and imposed on them the strict rule of the Studium Monastery at Constantinople. He also procured architects from Greece and founded the stone Church of the Assumption, but he did not live to complete it.

During the reign of Yaroslav the religious houses which were multiplying were quiet retreats in which men could save their souls, as they believed, by meditation, prayer, and austerity. They were centres of such learning as was to be found, they were schools in which pupils received some rudiments of education, they were hospitals in which the poor and sick were cared for, they were in many cases the outposts from which missionaries carried the light of Christian truth into regions lying in heathen darkness. Little by little they leavened the life of the people and prepared the way for better days to come.

The Church of Russia was undoubtedly the daughter of the Church of Constantinople, but its subjection to the Mother Church was of the smallest. It amounted to little more than this : that the Patriarch of Constantinople selected and consecrated the Russian Metropolitan, that he was prayed for by name in the Russian services, and that contributions were sent to Constantinople when these were required. Further, certain monasteries, which were called Stauropegia, were under the direct control of the Patriarch and did not recognise the authority of the Metropolitan. In fact, the influence of the Grand Prince was often more powerful than that of the Patriarch. In the reign of Vladimir, the Metropolitan Michael fixed his headquarters at Pereyaslavl, but Yaroslav transferred them to Kiev on his own initiative and seized the first opportunity of asserting his independence of external control. When Theopemptus, Metropolitan of Kiev, died in 1051, Yaroslav compelled the bishops, without reference to Constantinople, to elect Hilarion, one of their own number, to the vacant office. Hilarion, however, was not easy in his mind about this infraction of ecclesiastical order, and in order to put himself right he requested and obtained a letter from the Patriarch Michael Cerularius confirming his appointment.

Yaroslav's greatest achievement was his codification of Russian law. The work was not finished till after his death, but as it was begun under his auspices, it is justly associated with his name.[1] The need for it arose from two sources : First, there was a great accumulation of undigested legal material. This included the original tribal customs, with their modifications under Slavonic and Varangian influences, the legislative enactments of local Russian princes, the regulations framed by the Church, as well as the Nomocanon and other Church works with their interpretations by Byzantine lawyers. Second, the judges in the ecclesiastical courts were usually Greek monks from Constantinople who were ignorant of Russian traditions, and some way had to be found to harmonise their principles as Christians with the laws which they were charged to administer. The point of difficulty arose, not in connection with purely political matters—these were attended to by the secular courts—nor in connection with

[1] Kluchevski, i. 142.

purely ecclesiastical affairs which were attended to by the
courts of the Church, but in connection with matters which
were partly political and partly religious or ecclesiastical,
and in connection with persons over whom both Church
and State had some control.

Two sections of Yaroslav's work are distinguishable.
First, there is the digest of civil and criminal law, applying
to members of the ecclesiastical community and dealing
with offences ascribed to them. This is called the Pravda.[1]
Second, there is the digest of ecclesiastical law, called the
Ordinances, applying to all Russians who were Christians,
whether inside or outside the ecclesiastical community.
This dealt with acts of sin as distinct from acts of crime,
and also with acts in which sin and crime are mingled.
The code distinguished between injury done to the person
and injury to property. It regards injury done to the
person as a diminution of his value to the State, and the
penalties it imposes are in every case a fine equal to the
industrial loss caused by the offence. It did not provide
for torture or for death. Yaroslav's lawyers were guided
not only by general considerations of humanity, but by
definitely Christian principles. They held that man is
made in the image of God, and is therefore to be treated
with respect. Yaroslav's successor, Monomachus, en-
joined his sons never to kill a man, bad or good, whatever
might be the provocation. In this respect Yaroslav's
code is a remarkable tribute to the power with which
Christian teaching had already laid hold on the Russian
life.

The offences dealt with under the Pravda were such
as murder, assault, and damage to property. Under the
Ordinances the courts dealt with such things as rape,
adultery, desertion, and divorce, marriage within prohibited degrees, necromancy, and witchcraft. The code
largely increased the number of offences liable to be dealt
with. Among the heathen, for example, offences against
women were not looked on as serious, and the fact that

[1] Mouravieff, 357 ; Kluchevski, i. 144.

they were singled out for punishment is a symptom of the moral enlightenment which was permeating the nation through the influence of the Church.

One great service rendered by Yaroslav's code was the introduction of the Christian conception of the family. Among the heathen the unit was the family, not the family as consisting of husband and wife and their children, but the family group, consisting of the husband, his wives and concubines, his sons and daughters, his sons-in-law and daughters-in-law, with their children, and all others who were willing to live and work with them. The property of the group was held in common, but the head of it was an irresponsible despot with rights over his dependants which reduced them to practical bondage, and that often led to immoral relations with his sons' wives. Among the heathen, wives were secured by capture or purchase or by dowry, and the consent of the bride-to-be was not considered necessary. In order to protect the freedom of marriageable girls, a fine was imposed on the parents of a daughter who, after a marriage entered into against her will, committed suicide. It was also enacted that those who entered into marriage unions without the blessing of the Church were nevertheless bound to consider these unions permanent. Forcible separation or repudiation or divorce, unless with the consent of the Church, were forbidden, and provision was made that the goods of the wife should not be held liable for the misdemeanours of the husband. In other words, the Church made an endeavour to assert that the rights and responsibilities of women are equal to those of men, and that a true marriage is the voluntary union of one man and one woman in a solemn covenant that lasts for life.

The ideal aimed at by the code was one to which the Russian people were slow to respond.

CHAPTER IV

MONOMACHUS

THE period which followed the death of Yaroslav brought ruin to Kiev as a political centre, but was not entirely disadvantageous to the interests of the Church. The strife was largely due to the practice governing the succession of princes to place and power. They all held that Ruric had come into Russia as a military governor, and that as Ruric's descendants they were a dynasty among whose members the government of Russia was to be divided. On this basis they constructed a system of transference which created the maximum of heartburning. The princes were arranged in order of seniority, with the Grand Prince of Kiev at their head. The principalities were also arranged in order of importance, with Kiev as their head. The rule was that the senior prince should take the most important principality, the next in order of seniority was to take the next in order of importance, and so on. But what was meant by seniority? Is the senior prince the oldest surviving brother of any given ruler, or is he the oldest surviving son? At first it was easy to answer the question, but when the original stock had split into branches, and when these produced princes, all of them nearly equal in age and all claiming a share of the dynastic inheritance, a satisfactory adjustment of claims became impossible. Besides, the number of princes never corresponded with that of principalities. At one time there were 293 princes and only 64 principalities, and no prince would consent to be thrown out. Further, it did not always happen that the prince who was first on the list was fitted to govern those who came behind him. A junior prince was often a strong man who was resolved not to remain in obscurity if he could force his way into the sunlight.

Yaroslav divided his dominions among his sons, appointing Isaiaslav to Kiev. For a short time there was a gleam of goodwill between him and his brothers, but it did not last long. Isaiaslav was driven from Kiev, and fled for his life to Germany, where he asked the Emperor to help him to regain his dominions. The Emperor answered him coldly, whereupon Isaiaslav sent his son to Rome to implore the assistance of the Pope. Gregory III. joyfully seized this opportunity of interference, and on the assumption that he was the Vicegerent of God with power to dispose of earthly kingdoms, wrote a letter in which he assigned Russia to Isaiaslav, and intimated that he was sending ambassadors to explain what had been written, and to mention what had been omitted.[1] The letter is dated 15th May 1075. At the same time he wrote Boleslas, King of Poland, commanding him to restore to Isaiaslav what Poland had seized. " For," said he, " thieves shall not enter the kingdom of heaven."

It happened, however, that Isaiaslav regained his throne without foreign assistance, and having done so, he turned his back on the Church of the West, which had only given him fair words in his time of need. He died in battle in December 1078.

Early in his reign Hilarion, Metropolitan of Kiev, died, and the Patriarch of Constantinople appointed a Greek named George to the vacant office, and sent him to Kiev without previously acquainting the Grand Prince with what he meant to do. The Grand Prince, however, was resolved to be master, not of the State only, but also of the Church, and he made George so uncomfortable that, after eight years, he returned to Constantinople, where, if he had less eminence, he had more peace. George was succeeded by John II., a Greek by birth, learned and renowned for his Christian virtues and the friend of all who were in need. " Never have we had, and never can we have, his equal," says the annalist. John wrote a book called *The Ecclesiastical Canons*, in which he sharply reproved the

[1] Mouravieff, 362.

Russian princes for giving their daughters in marriage to
princes professing the Roman form of religion, denounced
Russian merchants who sold Christians as slaves to the
heathen (a very common practice in these days), and
launched his anathema against those who married within
forbidden degrees, or without the ceremonies prescribed by
the Church.   He also forbade the clergy to bless those who
entered the wedded state for the third time, and he imposed
penance on those who broke the law of chastity.   His
whole influence was on the side of morality and the fear
of God, and he raised the Church to a commanding position
which it had never reached before.

Although there was a strong feeling against the Western
Church, an incident which happened at this time shows that
the feeling was not so bitter as it became at a later date.
A feast was held in honour of the translation of the relics of
St. Nicholas from Lycia, in Asia Minor, to Bari, in Italy, and
it may have been in consequence of this that Pope Urban II.
sent an embassy to Kiev in 1091 in the hope of reviving
the pretext for interference, for which Isaiaslav had given
Gregory an opening.   The Pontiff, however, was baffled.

After the death of Ysevolod, his son, Vladimir Monomachus, might have seated himself on the throne without
much opposition, but he waived his claim in favour of his
uncle, Sviatopolk, on the ground that Sviatopolk was his
senior.   Unfortunately, Sviatopolk was totally lacking in
wisdom, and the twenty years of his reign—1093–1113—
brought his people nothing but calamity.   The misery of
incessant civil war was increased by the misery of invasion.
The Polovtsi swept over the country, burned the villages
and massacred or enslaved the inhabitants.   " The towns
are deserted," says the annalist ; " one sees everywhere
villages on fire, churches, houses, farms reduced to heaps
of ashes, and the unfortunate citizens expiring under the
swords of their enemies or waiting death with terror. . . .
In the meadows there are neither horses nor cattle, the
fields are covered with weeds, and wild beasts make their
lairs in places which were once the dwellings of Christians."

After Sviatopolk's death, the people of Kiev and the appanaged princes pressed Monomachus to accept the heavy burden of responsibility as Grand Prince,[1] and for twelve years (1113–25) he gave Russia the benefit of wise and firm administration which was like a gleam of sunshine in the midst of a storm.   He came to close quarters with the Polovtsi no fewer than nineteen times.   Sometimes he fought them off, sometimes he bought them off, and on the whole delivered his territory from their attacks. He also sent an army into Thrace, whose appearance terrified the Emperor Alexis Commenius to such an extent that he quickly asked for peace.   From the Emperor he received precious gifts—a crucifix made of the wood of the true Cross, a cornelian cup which had belonged to the Emperor Augustus, and the crown, the golden chain, and the necklace which belonged to the Emperor Constantine Monomachus.   Neophytus, the Metropolitan of Ephesus, brought these regalia from Constantinople and performed the ceremony of coronation for the first time in Russian history in the Cathedral of St. Sophia.   The cap used on this occasion has been used at the coronation of all the Tsars of Russia, and the ritual is the model to which all subsequent coronation services have conformed.

Just at this point Nestor, the father of Russian history, died, and the annals with which his name is associated were continued by more obscure successors.

Monomachus' success in dealing with foreign foes was equalled by his skill in repressing internal disorder, but his reign was too short to let him make any substantial improvement in the social condition of the people, even if he thought such an improvement was necessary.

The constitution of Russian society in those days was not unlike that of Athens or Rome.   The upper classes enjoyed all the luxuries of life.   The lower classes enjoyed none of them.   These upper classes were mainly three in number—the princes and their families, the boyars, and the clergy.   These were a small fraction of the whole

[1] Kluchevski, i. 191.

population, and they lived for the most part in the towns
and cities. The lower classes were scattered over the
plains and forests. The upper classes dwelt in solidly
built mansions, artistically furnished, and provided with
every known convenience and comfort. They dressed
well and fared sumptuously every day. The lower classes
lived in rough huts, wore rough clothing, and had nothing
but the plainest food.

Some of them were free men, who with their own stock
and implements or with those which they hired, farmed
land which they leased from the State, or from a boyar,
or from a monastery. When their lease was ended they
might come and go as they chose, but many of those who
laboured on the land were slaves, captives taken in war,
or the children of captives. Bought and sold like cattle,
they had no more chance of becoming free than if they had
toiled in the brickfields of Egypt before the time of Moses.
In the general shuffle and change of places which followed
the death of a Grand Prince, the civil wars that broke out
only aggravated their misery. Masters might come and
go ; they remained in a hopeless servitude, and neither
Monomachus nor the clergy saw any reason for relieving
them.

At the same time, although Monomachus did not apply
the ethical teachings of Christianity to the life of the State,
he tried to apply them to the life of the individual, and,
considering the times in which he lived, and the disadvantages under which he laboured, he might be called an
eminent Christian. He has left a paper which shows his
real goodness, and, along with interesting biographical
details, it sets forth his accurate if limited conception of
the duty of those who profess the Christian faith. He
says :

" O, my children, praise God and love men. It is not
fasting, nor solitude, nor the monastic life that will procure
your eternal blessedness, but only doing good. Forget not
the poor, nourish them. Remember that riches come from
God and are given only for a short time. Do not bury

your wealth in the ground, for this is against the precept of the gospel. Be fathers to orphans, judge the widows, and do not let the powerful oppress the weak. Put to death neither innocent nor guilty, for nothing is so sacred as the life and soul of a Christian. Never take the name of God in vain, and never break the oath you have made in kissing the crucifix. My brethren said to me, ' Help us to drive out the sons of Rostislav or else give up our alliance.' But I said, ' I cannot forget that I have kissed the cross.' I opened the Book of Psalms and there I read with deep emotion, ' Why art thou vexed, O my soul, and why art thou so disquieted within me ? Put thy trust in God.' Be not envious at the triumph of the wicked and the success of treachery. Fear the lot of the impious. Do not desert the sick. . . . Receive with joy the blessing of the clergy. Do not keep yourself aloof from them. Do them good that they may pray to God for you. Drive out from your heart all suggestions of pride, and remember that we are all mortal—to-day full of hope, to-morrow in the coffin. Abhor lying, drunkenness, and debauchery. Love your wives, but do not let them have any power over you. Endeavour constantly to obtain knowledge. Without having quitted his palace my father spoke five languages." Thereafter he gives them instructions about their conduct in war, on the journey, in times of sickness, and advises them to be able to do anything they order their servants to do. In conclusion he says : " O my children, fear neither death nor wild beasts. Trust in God far surpasses all human precautions."

When he felt his end approaching, Monomachus caused himself to be carried to the banks of the Alta, where Boris was murdered, and there he breathed his last on 9th May 1125, in the seventy-third year of his age. His body was laid to rest in the Cathedral of the Assumption at Kiev.

His first wife was Gyda, daughter of Harold, King of England. By his second wife he had seven sons, and as he divided his realm between them on the accepted principle, he prepared for it and for them a long series of troubles.

CHAPTER V

DECLINE OF KIEV AND RISE OF VLADIMIR

IN 1124, the year before the death of Monomachus, Russia suffered from a series of calamities. In the south there were two earthquakes, in the north there was a terrible hurricane, in Kiev fire destroyed the greater part of the city. In 1126, the year after his death, prolonged drought resulted in a scanty harvest, and there was famine in the western provinces. The following winter was exceptionally cold. The starving people fell dead in such numbers that graves could not be dug for them. To these things were added the horrors of invasion and civil war.

Monomachus was followed by his son Mstislav, who reigned until 1132. He in his turn was followed by his son Isaiaslav. He was promptly expelled from his throne by his uncle Yuri Dolgorouki. He regained it in 1150, was again expelled in 1152, reascended in 1155, and died in the same year. During his reign the Metropolitan, a Greek named Michael, died, and as the patriarchal throne of Constantinople was vacant, Isaiaslav called together the bishops of Tchernigov, Bielgorod, Pereslavl, Yurief, Vladimir, and Smolensk, and ordered them to appoint one of their own number, or at least some one who was not a Greek, to the vacant post, and to do so without waiting for permission from the Patriarch. Niphont, Bishop of Novgorod, denounced this as an infraction of order; but the other bishops, overborne by the vehemence of the Grand Prince, yielded and selected Clement, a monk of Smolensk. The difficulty of a valid consecration was got over by Onuphrius of Tchernigov, who laid on Clement's head the dead hand of St. Clement of Rome, which had been brought to Kherson

3

by the great Vladimir as a holy relic. Niphont still protested. He was therefore imprisoned.

Soon afterwards Yuri Dolgorouki captured Kiev and, finding Niphont immured in the Petcherski Lavra, released him and drove out Clement. The Patriarch Cosmos II., who had just been enthroned at Constantinople, also sent Niphont a letter thanking him for his noble defence of ecclesiastical law and order, and declaring him to be one of the Fathers of the Church. Further, on the request of the Grand Prince Yuri, that the Patriarch would send him a Metropolitan with a valid consecration, Constantine was dispatched and Yuri received him with honour. The bishops were then compelled to call a Council at which they cursed the name of Isaiaslav, and cancelled all the orders issued by Clement. In this way the dependence of the Russian Church on Constantinople was formally recognised.

At the same time, although Yuri for his own purposes recognised the supreme authority of the Patriarch in matters pertaining to the Church, he fretted under the political restrictions which his subjects laid upon him. In those days the towns were practically self-governing republics,[1] and although they were presided over by a prince, they never forgot that he was an official whom they had appointed by a popular vote. They laid down the limits within which his authority was to be exercised, and they admitted him to his post only after he had subscribed a sort of contract binding himself not to intrude upon their rights and liberties. All this was anathema to Yuri. He wanted a realm in which he governed uncontrolled, and he created one.

It happened that when Monomachus had occasion to visit the district of Suzdal, he built a small settlement for his convenience on the banks of the river Kliasma, and called it by his own name Vladimir. Yuri transferred himself to it and built other villages in the neighbourhood. One of these villages was Moscow. It is not certain whether Yuri called it into being, or found it already in existence,

[1] Kovalevski, 132.

and the origin and derivation of the name Moscow is unknown. It appears for the first time in a letter which Yuri wrote in 1147 to Sviatoslav Olgovitch in which he says: "Come to me, brother, to Moscow." In it he placed a garrison, and practically laid the foundation-stone of Russia's most famous capital.

Andrei Bogolubski, Yuri's son, shared his father's determination to be an independent ruler, and although he did not set foot in Kiev once in thirty years, he found a pretext for charging the city with rebellion and sent his son to attack it. Ten other princes joined the expedition, and on 18th March 1169 they took Kiev by storm. For three days the city was given over to the soldiers. Palaces, monasteries, churches, and private houses went up in flames. Holy ikons, illuminated missals, crosses, sacerdotal robes, and church furniture were carried in derision along the streets. Then when the city was a ruin, Andrei instructed his victorious son to hand it over to Gleb, Andrei's younger brother. In this way he removed the only rival that the new city of Vladimir had to fear.

In the following year he found a pretext for dealing with Novgorod, but while his soldiers were attacking the city they were seized with panic. The legend is that the bishop and the clergy were going in procession round the city walls to encourage the defenders when an ikon of the Virgin which they were carrying was struck in the face by a hostile arrow. The Virgin's eyes thereupon streamed with tears, and the portent shook the nerves of Andrei's men so thoroughly that they allowed themselves to be taken prisoners. But the clergy and the citizens were too wise to suppose that Andrei would consider himself defeated, and they accepted as governor the prince whom he nominated.

As Kiev was now destroyed, and as Novgorod was lying subject at his feet, Andrei resolved to give Russia a new political centre. As the older cities already possessed the recognised rights of self-government, he fixed on Vladimir, which was not subject to any of these disadvantages;

and in Vladimir he built the Cathedral of the Assumption. In this he set up the famous Golden Gates. Unfortunately the work of erection was hurried, the mortar did not set firmly, and when the gates were being opened with great pomp and solemnity they fell upon twelve bystanders. Andrei prostrated himself before the ikon of the Virgin which had been brought from Constantinople, and which was reported to be the work of St. Luke, and prayed, " Save these people, or I shall be guilty of their death." When the gates were lifted the twelve arose unhurt.

He had now a city, a cathedral, and a miracle-working ikon, but he had no Metropolitan, and he desired one. Taking occasion from the strife then raging between the claimants for the Metropolitan throne of Kiev he asked the Patriarch to consecrate a separate Metropolitan for Vladimir. The Patriarch was unwilling to break the unity of the Russian Church, and the utmost he would sanction was that the Bishop of Rostov should reside at Vladimir. At the same time, as a sop to Andrei's vanity, he appointed a feast to be held annually on the 1st August to commemorate Andrei's victory over the Bulgarians. It was the day on which the Emperor Manuel commemorated his victory over the Saracens.

In those days there appeared the first of a long series of dissenters from orthodoxy in the person of Nestor, Bishop of Rostov. He was charged with breaking the law of the Church by compelling men to fast on the festivals of the Nativity and the Epiphany if they fell on a Wednesday or a Friday. In 1162 he was summoned to Constantinople to justify himself. Leon, a bishop who had assumed charge of the diocese in his absence, repeated Nestor's offence, and Andrei sent him away for trial. The Patriarch acquitted Nestor but condemned Leon. In the meantime Theodore, a monk of the Petcherski Lavra, advocated the same practices. Andrei put him to death. Unwarned by his fate, Constantine II., who was acting as a Metropolitan of Kiev, convened a Synod and used it to give Nestor's doctrines currency; but the siege and sack of the city were interpreted as a proof of Heaven's anger against those who introduced innovations, and the new views died away.

About this time also the practice of confining the office of bishop to monks became definitely established. For long that office was open to secular priests, but the tide of feeling against them became too strong to be resisted. They had many worldly entanglements, whereas the monk was supposed to devote his whole attention to prayer and meditation, to self-mortification, and to works of charity. The people thought that their religious interests would be safer in his hands, and they gave him a veneration which the priest did not share. Besides, the work of a secular priest was confined within a narrow sphere and presented no prospects of rising to eminence, whereas a monk, even if he were of the humblest ancestry, might become a bishop, standing on a level with princes. He might even become Metropolitan, standing on a level with the Grand Prince. Ambitious men invariably became monks, and their abilities naturally gathered the reins of powers into their hands.

The Russian Church cheerfully acknowledged its dependence on Constantinople, but it had no hesitation in asserting itself against Rome. On the death of the Metropolitan Constantine in 1164 the Patriarch sent John IV. to succeed him. His administration lasted for two years, and is notable for the answer he sent to the demand of Pope Alexander that he and his clergy should acknowledge the supremacy of the Roman See.[1] John says that the Orthodox Church objects to the doctrine of the procession of the Spirit from the Son, not only because of the manner in which the doctrine crept into the Church, but still more because of the doctrine itself. " It is," says he, " a fundamental heresy "; and this is the opinion of the Orthodox Church down to the present day. It forms an unsurmountable barrier to union with the Churches of the West.

[1] Mouravieff, 369.

Andrei was assassinated in 1174, and the disorder which his strong hand had kept in check burst out in all directions. In the confused strife Kiev was once more put to fire and sword. Droves of the fierce Polovtsi swept over the country and settled like locusts on a harvest-field. They stripped the churches of their gold and silver ornaments, they gutted the monasteries, they killed the priests and their wives, the monks and the nuns, the aged and the infirm, and sold the remainder of the people as slaves. Kiev was reduced so low that in 1212, when Ysevolod's sons were arranging the distribution of his dominions, none of them would take the city even as a gift.

While Russia was being desolated by internal strife, enemies were threatening it without. The Crusaders, who had captured Constantinople, compelled the Emperor and the Patriarch to fly, and their success stirred the Roman Pontiff to establish an archbishopric in Galicia and to start a propaganda in the surrounding regions. At the same time the Order of the Brethren of the Sword gathered strength on the shores of the Baltic, overran Lithuania, and came within striking distance of Russian territory. On the east the Tartars appeared. Starting from the centre of Asia, where Genghis Khan had raised his standard, a section of them surged through the Caucasus and attacked the Polovtsi who, in terror, besought assistance from the princes of Kiev and Galicia. The Tartars assured the Russians they had nothing to fear if they refrained from helping the Polovtsi, but in a moment of madness they put the Tartar ambassadors to death, and then, in terror, waited for the coming storm. On 31st May 1224, on the banks of the river Kalka, near its entrance to the Sea of Azov, eighty thousand men opposed the march of the invaders and were completely defeated. Then the Tartars retired and the Russians resumed their civil war.

Thirteen years later another section, led by Batu, passed through Kazan and swept like a destroying flood over the centre of Russia, submerging Riazan, Kolomna, Moscow, Vladimir, and Susdal. In February 1238 the

Grand Prince Yuri met them on the banks of the river Sit. His army was cut to pieces, and his headless corpse was afterwards found and buried by the Bishop of Rostov. The Tartars then turned towards Novgorod; but seeing the dense forests, the swollen rivers, and the far-reaching swamps surrounding it, they directed their march southwards. Kozelsk gave them so much trouble that they called it the wicked city. When at last they took it by storm they massacred all its inhabitants, and its prince, although only a child, was literally drowned in blood.

Mangou, grandson of Genghis Khan, next led an army through Southern Russia to Kiev. In spite of its terrible experiences, the city still retained relics of its former splendour, and when Mangou saw its white walls and towers and the cupolas of the churches gleaming with gold and silver, he promised to spare it if it surrendered. The Kievans, however, killed his ambassadors, and Batu, with an enormous army, came to Mangou's assistance. After a fierce assault in 1240 the gates were burst open and the Tartars rushed into the city. Old and young were indiscriminately put to death. All the buildings were set on fire. The Cathedral of St. Sophia was completely plundered. The Petcherski Lavra was levelled with the ground. The massive golden cross which adorned its dome was carried off with other spoil, and somewhere in the wild confusion Joseph, the Metropolitan, perished. The sun of Kievan glory had set, and the first period of Russian history was closed. With the exception of Novgorod all Russia now lay under the Tartar yoke. The princes were dead or in exile, the nobles were decimated and reduced to poverty, and their wives and daughters became the slaves of barbarians. Hundreds of thousands of the common people were carried into captivity and sold like cattle in the market, and in many a district a whole day's journey did not reveal a house standing or a human being left alive.

CHAPTER VI

ALEXANDER NEVSKI

AFTER the Tartars had finished with Kiev they passed into Volhynia and Galicia. Thereafter, one section went through Silesia and Moravia into Hungary, where the battle of Mogi laid the country at their feet. The other section went into Poland and defeated the Polish forces with such slaughter that nine sacks full of human ears were sent to the Great Khan as an indication of their victory. Serbia and Dalmatia were next ravaged, and there seemed nothing to prevent their entrance into Germany and Italy. But their lines of communication were now very long. The country was more and more unsuitable for the operations of their light cavalry, and a crisis occurred at the Tartar headquarters. Batu therefore retired and established himself in the vast prairie round the lower Volga, in an encampment which developed into the important town of Serai.

From Serai, the Golden Horde, as it was called, dominated Russia. Differences of race, language, and religion made fusion between the conquerors and the conquered on a large scale impossible. Besides, the Tartars had no desire for fusion. So long as their subjects gave them no trouble, they were content. At the same time they made the Russians feel the burden of the yoke. Every Russian prince on his appointment to office had to travel to Serai, and sometimes even across Asia to the residence of the Great Khan on the Amur, and wait humbly for recognition. The journey was difficult and dangerous, and often took more than a year. On pain of exposing his people to the Khan's wrath he had to get permission for any military operations he desired to undertake, and when Tartar commissioners brought a letter from the Great Khan he had to go out of his city gates on foot to meet them, had to provide a carpet of expensive furs for the commissioners to stand on, and had to kneel while the letter was being read. Every Russian, great and small, had to pay a capitation tax, and there were other taxes which pressed on them with severity. Only the clergy'were'exempt. All others who could not pay were sold into slavery.

It is difficult to say how far the Tartar influence affected Russian life. It is sometimes maintained that the habit of wearing turbans and flowing robes, and of shutting up the women in their own apartments, was one result of it. This may have been so, but the influence of Constantinople on these points cannot be excluded. We find the consequence of the Tartar domination not so much in external things as in a lowering of the moral tone which manifested itself sometimes in brutality and sometimes in chicanery. In the legal code of Russia up to this time there was no provision for torture, but the Tartars used it freely and taught the Russians to use it as they did themselves. Up to this time the Russian princes settled their disputes for the most part by force of arms, but arms were worse than useless against the myriads which the Tartars set in motion, and the princes had to reach their ends by flattery and fawning, by craft and duplicity, which in the eyes of their ancestors would have been despised as cowardice. Those who reigned in Kiev were as different from those who afterwards reigned in Moscow as the reckless Esau was from his scheming brother Jacob.

One immediate and visible result of the Tartar domination was a great increase in the number of Russian Churchmen. The reason is not far to seek. The Tartars were heathen to begin with. Subsequently they became Mohammedans, but at no time were they fanatics, and they allowed their subjects to worship God as they chose. In Batu's time there were many Christians even in Serai. In 1261 they had a bishop named Metrophanes, and a century afterwards, in addition to many Orthodox establishments, there were no less than ten Latin convents. Uzbeg, who followed Batu as Khan, gave his sister, Kontchack, in marriage to Yuri of Moscow, and allowed her to receive Christian baptism.   Uzbeg himself married, as one of several wives, a Christian named Taidula, whose name is preserved in that of the famous iron capital of Russia—Tula.[1]   He also allowed Pope Benedict XII. to send Latin missionaries to the countries round the Black Sea.

This policy of toleration was probably strengthened by the knowledge that the Church's goodwill would go far to secure the goodwill of those to whom the Church ministered. To secure this, in 1313 Uzbeg Khan gave the Metropolitan Peter a diploma making the Church lands practically inviolable, exempting Churchmen from taxes, and confirming their right to exercise religious discipline.   This diploma was endorsed by Uzbeg's successors.   It was therefore an advantage to be enrolled among the clergy. Exemption from taxation and from violence were things to be greatly desired, and people of all classes flocked into the Church as into an ark of refuge.

After the fall of Kiev, the only town in Russia that could be said to retain its independence was Novgorod, and the centre of interest shifts to it and the regions round it.   As it had no princes of its own, its citizens invited princes from other parts of Russia to rule over them, always reserving to themselves the right of ejecting the prince if he displeased them, a right which they exercised frequently and on small provocation.   These princes generally belonged to the line of Monomachus, and from 1240 to 1263 the ruler of Novgorod was Alexander, son of Yaroslav, third brother of Ysevolod of Suzdal.   He was a young man, and proved himself a wise counsellor, a successful administrator, and an able general.

When he was called to office Novgorod was threatened by foreign enemies.   The first he had to deal with were the Swedes.   They were Catholics, and they resolved to force Catholicism on Novgorod.   Pope Gregory IX. gave them his blessing and proclaimed a crusade.   Accordingly, Birgin, Prince of Sweden, with a large army, landed at the mouth of the Ijhora, and sent Alexander an insolent message

[1] Howorth, 154–5, 179 ; Karamsin, iii. 19, 426.

bidding him defend his territories if he could. There was no time to seek assistance. Alexander therefore collected his men-at-arms, called on God in the Cathedral of St. Sophia, received the blessing of the Archbishop Spiridon, and set out to meet the foe. Legend says that on the banks of the Neva an Ingrian chief saw in a boat propelled by shadowy rowers the shining forms of the martyrs Boris and Gleb hastening to the rescue of their kinsmen. Alexander's troops were greatly encouraged by the story and attacked the Swedes on 15th July 1240. His victory was complete. Only nightfall prevented him from completely destroying the Swedish forces. From this time he was called Alexander Nevski, and in this battle the first attack of Catholicism on Orthodoxy failed.

The next attack came from farther south. German traders had penetrated into Livonia. Missionaries followed them and built clusters of houses. Soldiers turned these into so many forts by surrounding them with palisades. The missionaries endeavoured to convert the heathen by preaching. The soldiers were so brutal that the work was a complete failure. Those of the Livonians who had accepted Christianity renounced it, plunged into the nearest river to wash off the effects of their baptism, and returned to the worship of the old gods. Pope Innocent III. preached a crusade against them, and Albert of Buxhoeweden entered the Dwina, built the town of Riga in 1200, and made it his capital. Then he created the Brotherhood of the Soldiers of Christ, to whom the Pope gave the statutes of the Templars. They wore a white mantle with a red cross on the shoulder, overran the whole country, and murdered all who refused obedience and baptism. In 1225 the Order of the Teutonic Knights was established. They wore a black cross, but their methods were equally brutal. In 1237 the two orders were united, and in 1241 they advanced against Novgorod. Alexander, who had been ejected from the city after a dispute with the citizens, was implored to come to their rescue, and in April 1242 he led their forces against the enemy at Lake Peipus. The battle fought on its frozen surface is known as the Battle of the Ice, and it ended in complete victory for the Russians. The attempt to impose Catholicism by force of arms was foiled so thoroughly that neither Germans nor Swedes repeated it.

Another attempt was made by diplomacy. When the Tartars were sweeping over the feeble barriers opposed to them, Pope Innocent IV. concluded that Russia's extremity was Rome's opportunity. He therefore sent the cardinals Haldus and Gemon to assure Alexander that if Russia would accept Roman teaching and recognise Roman supremacy, all the princes of Europe would come to his help. In a letter dated Lyons, 10th February 1248, he said that Alexander's father had promised to embrace the Roman religion, and declared he would have done so if death had not intervened.

Alexander found that his councillors preferred submission to the Tartars to submission to the Pope, and he replied that Novgorod did not see the need for Western teachers. They could tell Russia nothing from the time of Adam onwards which Russia did not already know, and as Russia had accepted the Orthodox doctrine formulated by the seven Great Councils it had no intention of sitting at the Pope's feet or of bowing to his authority.

These attacks created a general conviction that everything Western was hostile to Russia. They also persuaded the people that the Latin Church was their deadly foe, and drove them to conclude that love for Russia and zeal for Orthodoxy were sides of one and the same thing.

While Alexander was defending Russia on the west, he was also dealing with the Tartars on the east. They had assigned to him the whole of Southern Russia, including Kiev, and had placed his brother Andrei in Vladimir. In two years' time, however, Andrei's insubordination roused the Tartar anger to such a height that he had to fly for his life, while Alexander's more astute loyalty was rewarded by the gift of his brother's territory.

After the same fashion he acquired Galicia. Its prince, Daniel, was slow to acknowledge the Tartar supremacy, and even after he had done so he looked about for assistance to throw it off. In 1245 he sent word to Pope Innocent IV. that he was minded to unite with the Latin Church if the Pope would rouse the Western Christians to join him against the Tartars. Innocent promptly consecrated and dispatched a contingent of bishops, and promised Daniel a royal crown. Daniel replied it was not bishops he wanted, it was soldiers, and as the soldiers delayed their coming, he delayed his decision to enter the Papal fold. In 1249 the Papal legate left the country in anger. Four years later the Pope made a second effort. Before accepting it, Daniel stipulated that the Pope should not condemn the dogmas of the Greek Church until they had been discussed by a General Council, and that he should take effectual measures to unite Christendom against the Tartars. The stipulations were agreed to, and the Abbot of Messina placed a crown on Daniel's head. The Pope also sent letters to the princes of Bohemia and Poland asking them to go to Daniel's aid. The princes were preoccupied with the conflict between the Pope and the Hohenstauffen Emperors. Time passed to no purpose, and Daniel broke off negotiations for the second time. In 1257 Pope Alexander IV. sent him an angry letter, threatening him with the curse of the Church and with punishment by the secular arm if he did not give the Papal See the reverence which was its due. Daniel paid no attention to it. In fact, he did much to restore the prestige of Orthodoxy.

In these unhappy times of war and terror, and in spite of the privileges which the Tartars accorded to them, the Church had been suffering severely. For ten years there was no Metropolitan. The Episcopal Sees were reduced in number from three to five. Office was secured by simony. The parish priests were shamefully ignorant, and gross abuses prevailed in all directions. In 1251, however, Daniel selected a monk named Cyril and sent him to the Patriarch Manuel II. for consecration as Metropolitan of Kiev. Never did a pastor more fully justify the confidence reposed in him. During the thirty years of his official life, he travelled over Russia incessantly, appointing bishops, organising their dioceses, restoring discipline, and spreading enlightenment. In 1274 he convened a Reforming Synod which examined the life of all inferior clerks and laymen before their appointment to ecclesiastical office. It also rooted out simony and revised the ritual of the Sacraments, forbidding the practice of affusion in place of threefold immersion in baptism, a practice which had crept in from the West. But Cyril's ecclesiastical efficiency was no protection to his prince. Daniel was intriguing against the Tartars. The Tartars heard of it and Daniel had to fly for his life. Galicia was then transferred to Alexander.

Alexander was now the most representative of all the Russian princes, and by his adroitness and favour with the Tartars, he frequently averted much misery. The people were exasperated by the burdens laid on them, and revolts often occurred. These were crushed with pitiless severity. In Novgorod, however, Alexander's vigorous arguments, coupled with the fact that a Tartar army was on the march, prevailed on the people to lay down their arms, to open the gates, to admit the Tartar officials, and to permit them to go from house to house exacting tribute.

On the last of his journeys to Serai, Alexander had to go for his own sake, for he had failed to supply a levy of troops demanded of him. Fortunately, Berak the successor of Batu was a man of easy temper, and Alexander's excuses were accepted. But he was detained many months at the Khan's court, and when at last he was released, worn out with fatigue and anxiety, he died on the homeward journey at Goroditz on 14th November 1263. When the news reached Vladimir, Cyril was presiding at a meeting of the clergy. Interrupting the proceedings, he cried with a loud voice, " The sun of our country is set." Then he said mournfully, " Alexander is dead." The public grief was expressed in one sentence, " We are lost." Alexander's body was conveyed to Vladimir, where it lay in the Church of the Virgin till Peter the Great transferred it to what became the great Lavra on the banks of the Neva.

CHAPTER VII

IVAN I.

AFTER Alexander's death a new stage in Russian history begins. The political centre, which had shifted from Kiev to Novgorod, now shifts to Great Russia, in which Vladimir, for a short time, and afterwards, permanently, Moscow was the capital.

It seemed unlikely that any one of the scattered and lonely hamlets of Great Russia would rise to commanding eminence, but Moscow did this. Various causes combined to give it importance. For a long time the aggregate of large and small principalities which formed Great Russia was enclosed by its enemies in a ring-fence, from which the only exit led to the north, and to Siberia. The inhabitants could wander at will within this fence, and as Moscow was situated just where three great land roads crossed each other, it was natural that travellers from all parts should drift backwards and forwards through Moscow, and that some of them should settle there. Further, in these troublous times Moscow was a desirable place to live in. On all sides buffer principalities lay between it and foreign enemies. These not only absorbed the first shock of invasion, they frequently repelled it, so that while towns nearer the frontiers were being stormed and sacked, Moscow remained unhurt. Between 1238 and 1369 Moscow was possibly the only city in Russia which suffered no injury at the hands of an enemy. It thus became a refuge to which the harassed inhabitants of outlying districts betook themselves, and many pioneers who had pushed out into the wilds were glad to return to the shelter of its walls. There was another cause of even greater importance. This was the character of the Muscovite princes.

As they belonged to a junior line, they had no hope of
attaining supreme dignity by the ordinary law of succession.
Therefore, they resolved to rise by their own exertions,
and of all rival princes they became the sworn foes.   They
were all men of one type, and that type was not the warrior.
" In their passionless faces," says Soloviev, " it is difficult
for the historian to discern each one's characteristic traits.
They are all imbued with one idea, they all walk in one
path, slowly, cautiously, but uninterruptedly, inflexibly.
Each one takes a step in advance of his predecessor, each
one renders it possible for his successor to advance a step
beyond him." [1]   Kluchevski says, " They are as like as
peas in a row."   They were first-class business men, quick
to discern an opportunity of advancing their own interests,
and completely unscrupulous in the way they used it.
For the age they lived in, they were wonderfully abstemious.
In strange contrast to the rest of their countrymen, they
never got drunk after dinner.   In this and in other ways
they kept their wits about them and profited by other
men's folly.   To a large extent their success depended on
their management of the Golden Horde, and in that they
became experts.   So long as the Horde was united, the
Muscovite princes displayed themselves as its humble
servants.   When the Horde was split by internal disputes,
they played off one section against the other.   When
they had a chance of throwing off its yoke altogether,
they gathered their armies and fought.   When at last
they shattered it, they held a position of leadership which
no one in Russia could dispute.

One result of the long civil wars was that only two
rival princes were left to struggle for supremacy over all
the rest.   These were the Prince of Tver and the Prince of
Moscow.   On the death of Grand Prince Andrei in 1304
the vacant throne was claimed by Michael of Tver, Andrei's
cousin, and by Yuri of Moscow, Andrei's nephew.   Batu
decided in favour of Michael.   On his death in 1313 Uzbeg,
his successor, deposed Michael and installed Yuri.   In the

[1] Quoted by Ralston, 125.

war which followed, Yuri was defeated and his Tartar wife Kontchak, Uzbeg's sister, was captured. She died in captivity, and Yuri persuaded Uzbeg that Michael had poisoned her. He was therefore summoned to Serai, where he was executed on 22nd November 1319. Yuri was now beyond dispute Grand Prince, but in 1325, on another visit to Serai, he was stabbed to death in Uzbeg's presence by Michael's son Dimitri.

Yuri was succeeded at Moscow by his brother Ivan, while Michael's son Alexander became Prince of Tver. In 1328 Alexander allowed himself to be hurried into open rebellion by murdering some Tartar envoys. Ivan instantly profited by this act of folly. He repaired to Serai and wrought up the Khan's passion to such an extent that he was furnished with fifty thousand men and commanded to punish Tver to the uttermost. Armed with this authority, he compelled the appanaged princes to join him, and together they marched to the doomed city. When they had finished their work, it and the region round it were a desolation.

Ivan's hold over the other princes was strengthened by financial arrangements which made them practically helpless. He got himself appointed Collector-General of Tartar tribute. From the Tartar point of view he was an ideal collector, for the sums he contracted to transmit were always forthcoming. From the princes' point of view he was the reverse. He was not only rapacious—he levied blackmail. If a city or a prince refused to comply with his demands, he depicted them to the Golden Horde as rebels against Tartar authority, and the fear of vengeance invariably made them capitulate.

By proceedings such as these he became able to purchase for himself immense estates in the governments of Novgorod, Vladimir, Kostromo, Rostov, and elsewhere. At the same time, by concentrating the processes of taxation, he gave Russia the beginning of a unified financial system, of which Moscow was the centre.

His personal position was now one of great importance, but he was not content with the importance of his capital,

4

and he set himself to enhance it. He rebuilt the fortifications of the Kremlin, he erected several churches, and
he established great fairs, in which were displayed the
products of Italy and Greece and the East. To these he
attracted merchants from Germany and from Persia and
from all the countries between. In this way he added
much to the wealth of his subjects, but he added more to
his own, for he took into his private custody all the sums
derived from taxes and tolls and customs. It was not
for nothing that he wore a purse at his girdle and that he
was dubbed " Kalita " (money-bag). The sums he doled
out in relief of the poor were as nothing compared with the
sums which he collected for his own benefit.

All this concentration of power and wealth soon made
those who worshipped the rising sun turn their steps
towards him. He welcomed them, and although his right
to act as their superior was not formally acknowledged he
assumed authority to arbitrate in their disputes, to distribute rewards and preferments, and to decide the possession
of lands and heritages. Those who supported and obeyed
him found their advantage in doing so. Those who resented his interference were kept in fear of Tartar vengeance.
Within his own dominions he ruled with a firm hand,
and for forty years gave them the benefit of peace. Out-
siders looked with envy on the Muscovites, and agreed that
Ivan was the Builder of the Russian Land.

His most astute proceeding was the transference of
the Metropolitan throne from Vladimir to his own capital
of Moscow. He made no violent attempt to effect this,
and he accomplished his end apparently by force of circumstances. Kiev was even yet the nominal seat of the
Metropolitan, but Kiev was in ruins. Residence there was
impossible, and it was abundantly evident that some other
city must be chosen as the ecclesiastical centre. In 1299
Maximus the Metropolitan, with the approval of a Synod
of Bishops, removed his episcopal throne to Vladimir,
still keeping his title of Metropolitan of Kiev and of all
Russia. Nine years afterwards he died. Peter, who
succeeded him, continued his official headquarters in

Vladimir, but in the twenty years in which he held office he spent little time there. Residence in Moscow was more convenient from every point of view. On one of his visits to the city he made Ivan's acquaintance, and a warm attachment sprang up between them. Both had an instinct for government. Each felt the advantage of the other's support, and co-operation between them became easy.

It should not be forgotten that at this time the principalities of Russia were separate and independent entities. There was a precedence of honour among them, nothing more. Each had its own prince, its own civil officials, its own manners and customs, and though they might combine against a common foe, they fell apart and resumed their quarrels when the common danger had disappeared. All this was repugnant to Ivan, who had set his heart on consolidating them into an organism, of which he and his heirs would be the head.

In this design he was greatly helped by the Church. It had all the articulation and subordination of parts which the principalities lacked. It made no difference in what part of Russia or in what principality a diocese was situated. It was part of one great organisation which covered the country. Its clergy were under the control of one and the same hierarchy, and the Metropolitan to whose authority all of them bowed, took no account of political frontiers or of political animosities. He claimed all the princes and their subjects as his spiritual children, and however bitterly they quarrelled among themselves they did not think of disputing his paternal authority. The Church, therefore, presented Ivan with an ideal which he resolved to turn into a concrete reality. He probably saw that he could not achieve his purpose in his own lifetime, but he could start the process and leave his successors to bring it to its culmination. He therefore did all in his power to create in men's minds the conviction that the centre of government both in Church and in State was one.

In pursuance of his policy he lodged the Metropolitan in the royal palace. Thereafter he secured accommodation for him in a hospice. Then he assisted in the erection of

the great Cathedral of the Assumption of the Virgin, in the wall of which Peter prepared for himself a cell which became his tomb on his death in 1338. One biographer says he died in Ivan's absence. Another says he died in Ivan's arms after giving him a charge to see that the Cathedral was completed, and promising that obedience would secure Ivan's name and fame in perpetuity. During his lifetime Peter worked hand in hand with Ivan, and did all in his power to strengthen the centralising tendency in political affairs which had already come to fruition in the Church.

In one of his visits to the Horde, Peter won for himself the respect of Uzbeg to such an extent that the Khan gave him a valuable proof of his goodwill : " Let no one injure the Church, the Metropolitan Peter, the archimandrites, or the popes in Russia. Let their lands be free from all tax and tribute. . . . Let them be under the sole jurisdiction of the Metropolitan Peter agreeably to their ancient laws. . . . Whosoever shall take anything from any of the clergy must restore it threefold. Whosoever shall dare to speak evil of the Russian faith or to injure any church, monastery, or chapel, let him be put to death." [1]   When Khanibec, the son of Uzbeg, endeavoured to free himself from the restraint imposed by these letters of privilege, and to exact the tribute from the clergy, Peter's successor, Theognostes, boldly stood up to him and not only saved himself from the wrath of the Khan, but preserved the imperilled immunities and liberties of his Church.

Ivan died in 1340, leaving behind him a great Empire in which the sentiment of unity and common nationality, and obedience to a central government both in Church and State, was beginning to find a place.

[1] Mouravieff, 53.

CHAPTER VIII

DIMITRI DONSKOI

AFTER the death of Ivan, the Tartars appointed his son Simeon to succeed him. He was crowned in the Cathedral of Vladimir by Theognostes and swore to live at peace with his brothers. He kept his word so far as they were concerned, but he bore himself with such arrogance both to them and to others that he earned for himself the title, Simeon the Proud. He also assumed another title, for which the facts of the case afforded less justification. Ignoring the detail that the Lithuanians were occupying a considerable portion of Russian territory, he described himself as Grand Prince of All the Russias. With a sure instinct he entrenched himself in Moscow and intrigued against his rivals, or if necessary fought them. In 1353 the Black Death swept over the country. It carried off Simeon and most of his family, his brother Andrei, the Metropolitan Theognostes, and multitudes more. Simeon was succeeded by his third son, Ivan II., and on Ivan's death in 1358 the heir to the throne was his son, Dimitri, a boy of ten.

Once again the fortunes of the country were saved by the Church. Before Theognostes died, he asked the Patriarch to nominate as his successor Alexis, and he was consecrated in Constantinople. Strangely enough, a short time afterwards the Patriarch consecrated another Metropolitan, by name Romanus, but as no diocese in Russia received Romanus, Alexis reigned alone. The fame of his sanctity had preceded him, and it reached even to the headquarters of the Golden Horde, so that in 1357 he was summoned to the bedside of Taidula, wife of Janibeg Khan, who was persuaded that he could cure her of a dangerous disease. Thanks to his ministrations she recovered, and in token of her gratitude obtained for him new letters of exemption and privileges for the Russian clergy. He had, however, scarcely returned to Moscow when a Tartar messenger appeared with tidings that filled the people with terror. Alexis went back to Serai, and, with the help of Taidula, secured peace for the State.

He performed an even greater service by terminating the absurd system under which the office of Grand Prince was passed from one brother to another, and from one branch of a family to another. At his instigation Dimitri, son of Ivan, claimed the dignity of Grand Prince as against his namesake of Suzdal, and appealed to the Khan Morad at Serai to pronounce in his favour. Morad did so. But the Tartars were no longer a unity, and Dimitri of Suzdal was nominated by another section of the Horde. Neither would yield to the other. After a stern battle, Dimitri of Suzdal fled, whereupon Dimitri of Moscow entered Vladimir in triumph and was crowned in 1363. Other foes were handled with equal success, and after a bloody struggle in which Moscow was besieged twice—in 1369 and 1370—by the united forces of Tver and Lithuania, Michael of Tver, in 1375, renounced his right to anything outside his own appanage, and formally recognised the youthful Prince of Moscow as his elder brother. The crown was therefore transmitted from father to son, and there can be no doubt that it was not the youthful prince, but the clear-sighted Metropolitan, who brought about this result by throwing the whole influence of the Church in the scale.

During this time the Church was alarmed by the appearance of the Strigolniki. The sect so called was founded about 1371 by a sheep-shearer named Carp in alliance with a deacon named Nikita. These men were disgusted by the ignorance and covetousness of the clergy, and first at Pskov and afterwards at Novgorod, they preached that priests and monks did not receive the Holy Spirit at the moment of ordination, that they did not confer grace upon those to whom they dispensed the sacraments, and that they had no authority to pronounce absolution. They asserted that the hierarchy is a human invention, that any Christian is at liberty to preach the gospel, and that the choice of a

Christian congregation, not the imposition of a bishop's hands, qualifies any man to exercise the office of priest. They also said that the sacraments can be validly administered by believers to each other, even though none of the ordained clergy take part in the service. They denounced prayers for the dead, and said the practice of giving alms to priests for offering these was begotten by greed out of ignorance.

Of course they were furiously attacked, and although Carp and Nikita had many sympathisers they had no friends strong enough to save them from their enemies. Nikita was degraded and deposed. Carp was drowned in the river Volkhov. Their disciples were excommunicated and the propagation of their tenets was suppressed. As a sect they were wiped out.

After Dimitri's coronation there was a cessation of civil strife, but a rumour was spread abroad that the Tartars were coming to exterminate Christianity. The clergy therefore went everywhere preaching a Holy War. Mamai, the Khan, was, in fact, organising an advance into Russia, and Dimitri, at the head of the combined Russian princes, and with an army of two hundred thousand men, took up a position of resistance on the river Don.

Some time before this a boyar of Rostov who had lost his fortune sought peace in monastic poverty. His two sons followed his example. Near Radonej they built cells and erected a church, which they dedicated to the Holy Trinity. Stephen thereafter became an ordinary monk at Moscow, Bartholomew remained where he was and took the name Sergius. There in the depths of the forest, where he is said to have had no company except that of a bear, he gave himself up to meditation, prayer, and austerity. Disciples gathered round him. On the advice of the Patriarch communal life was introduced, and in 1354 he became their abbot. Sergius himself preferred solitude, and his rule was of the strictest, but Dimitri drew him into the stream of public life. He died in September 1392, leaving behind him not only a great name, but also a great institution, which did valuable work in his own and succeeding generations. In the fourteenth century the Troitska Lavra became the parent of thirteen desert monasteries similar to itself, and in the fifteenth to other two. These all gave birth to others, so that at the beginning of the sixteenth century the original foundation and its offshoots numbered twenty-seven desert and seven urban monasteries that twinkled like stars in the darkness from Moscow along the rivers to the White Sea.

Knowing the support that Sergius could give him, Dimitri went to the Troitska and besought the abbot's blessing. Sergius gave it, predicted victory, and ordered two of his most stalwart monks to accompany the prince to his army. When Dimitri returned to his troops he found the situation dangerous enough. Through the mediation of Oleg of Riazan, an arrangement had been made by which Jagiello of Lithuania agreed to attack the Muscovite forces on one side, while the Tartars attacked them on the other. A council of war was held to determine whether the Russians should cross the river or should delay. While the council was sitting, a letter arrived from Sergius urging Dimitri to cross at once and go forward, for the Lord would deliver his enemies into his hand. On the 8th September 1380 he transported his troops across the river and turned his boats adrift to make sure the fight would be a fight to the finish. All day long the armies swayed to and fro till the issue was decided by a flank attack made by a body of Russian troops which had been placed in ambush. A hundred thousand Tartars perished, and an immense booty became the property of the conquerors. Dimitri was acclaimed a popular hero with the title of Donskoi, and Russia thrilled with delight to discover that the legend of Tartar invincibility was unfounded.

Although this victory did not finally shatter the Tartar power, its importance should not be ignored. It was more than the repulse of an invasion, or the victory of Russians over the Horde ; it was the victory of Christianity over Mohammedanism. So far as Europe was concerned, it set a limit to the advance of the Crescent. It said in accents that were unmistakable, " Thus far and no farther." It is true that in after years waves of Tartar invasion rolled over the Russian land more than once, but they ebbed farther than they flowed, and at length they ceased.

CHAPTER IX

VASSILI I.

WHILE these events were taking place in Russia a new power was rising on the west. This was Lithuania. The Lithuanians were a race distinct both from the Teutons and from the Slavs. They dwelt originally on the shores of the Baltic between the Vistula and the Narva. One section was overpowered, robbed of its property, and nominally converted to Christianity by the swords of the Knights Hospitallers. Another section was similarly robbed and converted by the Knights of the Teutonic Order. The remaining section retired southward to maintain its national independence and its national heathenism. When civil war reduced the military power of Russia to a negligible quantity the Lithuanians filched away portions of their neighbours' territory. In this way under Mindovg they seized Vitebsk, Polotsk, and Smolensk; but the pressure of the military monks became dangerous, and to leave them without a pretext for attacking him, Mindovg professed himself a Christian.

After his death a period of confusion was terminated by the rise of Guedimin to supreme power. He not only reduced all his rivals in Lithuania to subjection, but occupied so much of Russian soil that he took the title, Grand Prince of Lithuania and Russia. Indeed, from this time forward the whole of Little Russia was lost to Russia for centuries.

Guedimin, was, however, in a difficult position. His country lay between Orthodoxy on the east and Catholicism on the west. Personally he was a heathen; but being anxious to conciliate his Orthodox subjects, he accepted Orthodox baptism himself, and allowed his sons to be trained in the Orthodox faith. He also respected the Orthodox clergy, and permitted Orthodox congregations to worship God after their own fashion. At the same time, he wrote to Pope John XXII. stating that he was willing to recognise the ecclesiastical supremacy of the Roman See.   The Pope sent two ambassadors to receive his submission, but before they arrived the Teutonic knights had plundered Vilna, whereupon Guedimin renounced Christianity in all its forms and returned to the faith of his fathers.   He died at Vilna in 1340 and was buried with heathen rites, his body being burned with those of his war horse and his favourite groom.

Olgerd, his son (1345–77), greatly extended the area of Lithuania.   His authority stretched from the Baltic to the Black Sea, and it was only the difficulties created by the Teutonic Knights and the war with Poland that prevented him from opening Russia to Western Europe.

After his death his dominions were divided between his brother Kestout and his sons, of whom Jagiello was one. By murdering his uncle, Kestout, and forcing his brothers to fly for their lives, Jagiello restored the unity which his father's will had broken up, and when an opportunity of extending his authority still further was offered by a marriage alliance, he seized it.   The last remaining representative of the Angevin dynasty in Poland was Hedwiga, daughter of Louis of Hungary.   Poland was distracted with war, and Hedwiga obtained her throne only after promising to allow the nobles and the higher clergy to choose her husband.   In all the history of Poland this is perhaps the only act of statesmanship which can be placed to its rulers' credit.   The political advantages of the union were obvious.   It ended the war with Lithuania, and enabled the two countries to present a united front to their common foes.   It formed a power that had to be reckoned with in European politics till the end of the seventeenth century.   It checked the advance of the Turks beyond Hungary and Transylvania, it kept the Great Russians from passing westward till the time of Peter the Great, and it destroyed the reason for the existence of the Teutonic Knights by removing any justification for their piratical crusades.   Of course, it was only the immediate issues that were apparent, but they were so alluring that, although Hedwiga loathed the barbarian bridegroom offered her, she sacrificed herself on the altar of her people's welfare, and married him in 1386.

Poland was by this time a Catholic country with a Catholic hierarchy, many Catholic monasteries and churches, and numerous adherents of the Catholic faith. As a condition of his marriage with Hedwiga, Jagiello had to accept Catholicism. He therefore abjured the Orthodoxy in which he had been brought up by his mother Juliana of Tver, and was baptized, receiving the name Vladislav II. Thereafter he signed a treaty which provided that all the possessions of Lithuania should be united to those of Poland, and that the people of Lithuania should be gathered into the Catholic fold. In order to make conversion easy he granted special privileges to the nobles, but he took other measures with the common people. On a given day they were assembled and divided into groups, which the priests sprinkled with holy water. Those in one group received the name John, those in another were called Paul, and so on until all were baptized. In this way their conversion from the one faith to the other was effected with ease and speed. Whether the result was satisfactory is another matter.

Jagiello's seat on the throne was not an easy one. When he moved his capital from Vilna to Kracow, Lithuania was filled with fear that it was to be absorbed by Poland, and the orders for wholesale baptism by Catholic priests were taken as proof that Orthodoxy was to be suppressed in favour of Catholicism. The fear was not baseless. In spite of Jagiello's orders there were many in Lithuania who clung to Orthodoxy. They were therefore subjected to pressure. Orthodox clergy were treated with violence, Orthodox churches were turned into Catholic chapels, Orthodox services were interrupted and broken up, riots ensued, and Jagiello found his position so difficult that, at last, in 1401 at Radom, he surrendered Lithuania to his cousin Vitoft on the understanding that the two States, although separated administratively, should have a common policy, and that in them both Jagiello should be recognised as overlord.

Vitoft, however, aspired not only to be an independent

Grand Prince, but to bring into subjection to himself the whole region over which the Kievan princes had formerly ruled.   He had designs even on Moscow.   In the hope of obtaining a foothold there he married his daughter Sophia to the Grand Prince Vassili on the 9th January 1391, and he used his position as father-in-law to meddle in the domestic affairs of the Russian Court and to make trouble in the Russian State.   As a proof that he was an independent prince he thought it important to secure for the Orthodox Church in his dominion the services of a special Metropolitan, and he found the man he wanted in Cyprian, who had fled to Kiev from Dimitri Donskoi's wrath at his abandonment of Moscow to the Tartars.   He was undoubtedly Metropolitan of Kiev and Russia, and his residence in Kiev might justly be considered to make it the ecclesiastical capital of the whole of the Russian land.   However, he returned to Moscow and the prestige of Kiev departed with him.   Vitoft resented this, and after Cyprian's death in 1407 he sent Theodosius to Constantinople for consecration.   The Patriarch refused to give it, and for three years there was no Metropolitan either in Kiev or Moscow.   Vitoft then determined to make the ecclesiastical breach with Russia complete.   In November 1415 he compelled his bishops to declare the Orthodox Church in Lithuania independent of the Church in Russia.   He also forced them to select a Bulgarian named Gregory Simblak as their Metropolitan.   He then sent Gregory to Constantinople to lodge a complaint against Photius, who had in the meantime been appointed Metropolitan of Moscow, and to demand consecration for himself.   His demand was refused.   On his return to Lithuania, Vitoft therefore compelled the bishops to ordain him, and he exercised the functions of a Metropolitan.   In 1418 Vitoft sent him to the Council of Constance to offer the Pope the submission of the Lithuanian Church on condition that it was allowed to retain the Byzantine ritual and the use of the Slavonic language in public worship.   This also was refused, and after Gregory's death the hierarchy in Lithuania remained headless until Photius came to Kiev, along with the Grand

Princess Sophia who was paying a visit to her father, and succeeded in patching up an ecclesiastical peace which lasted till Vitoft's death in 1480.

Vitoft's ambition was a distinct menace to Russia, but fortunately for that country it spurred him to enterprises which proved disastrous. War broke out between him and Jagiello. While it was going on he could do nothing against Vassili, and Russia was left in peace. Further, he began to think of attacking the Golden Horde and of seizing the lands over which it ruled. With a large army he met the Tartars under Timur at Poltava on 5th August 1339, and suffered utter defeat. Moscow, which had kept clear of entanglement with either of the combatants, was well pleased to see them destroy each other, and its princes made profit out of their calamities. Later, in connection with the Teutonic Knights, Vitoft again became Russia's saviour. A dispute regarding the province of Samogitia furnished a pretext for recourse to arms, but the real issue was the control of the Baltic Basin and the domination of Eastern Europe by the Teuton or the Slav. The battle of Tannenberg followed on 15th July 1410. After a terrific struggle, in which practically all the principal knights and forty thousand of their men were slain, Vitoft was victorious. The peace of Thorn in 1411 gave a respite to the vanquished, and from that time the power of the knights declined.

There remained the Tartars to be reckoned with. Vassili lived on good terms with them as a rule, but did not succeed in keeping his land free from invasion. In 1395 Timurlane found it necessary to attack Toktamish. After defeating him and reducing Serai to ruins he marched westward to attack Vassili, who had befriended Toktamish. Vassili fled to Kostromo and from there, as from a place of safety, he wrote the Metropolitan asking him to take the famous ikon of the Virgin from Vladimir to Moscow to comfort the people and avert their peril. Outside the city the holy picture was met by a procession of clergy and grandees, and was placed in the Cathedral of the Assumption. Strange to say, just at this juncture the Tartars retired. The country was bare, winter was approaching, and the Russian Army was gathering in the distance. The Tartars probably thought that in these circumstances prudence was the better part of valour; but it would have been vain to suggest to the Muscovites that such prosaic considerations as these accounted for their enemies' disappearance. They were convinced that their safety was due to the wonder-working power of the ikon, and the Church endorsed their conviction by appointing the 26th August—the day of the ikon's reception—as one of the chief festivals of the Russian year.

Taking advantage of the internal troubles of the Tartars, Vassili began to refuse homage on the ground that he did not know to which of the rival Khans he ought to offer it; but in 1409 Pulad Khan resolved to attack Lithuania, and demanded Vassili's assistance. Vasssili refused it, whereupon Pulad dispatched his general, Idiku, to reduce him to a more humble frame of mind. Idiku arrived before Moscow in December 1410, and once more Vassili fled. The citizens shut themselves up behind their fortifications, and the Tartars proceeded to reduce Moscow by siege. At this crisis, however, Pulad was threatened by a formidable rival, and Idiku had to be recalled. Before leaving, he exacted from Moscow the sum of 3000 roubles, and when he reached the frontier he threatened further penalties in the event of further disloyalty.

The principle of hereditary succession to the dignity of Grand Prince was now established by custom, inasmuch as for nearly a century there was no doubt who the next ruler ought to be, but when Vassili died in 1425, and when his son, also named Vassili, a boy of ten, claimed his father's dignity, Yuri, his father's brother, dragged the old law of succession by seniority out of the oblivion into which it had fallen, and claimed the vacant post as his right. The Metropolitan Photius supported Vassili, threatened Yuri with excommunication if he dared to take action, and finally arranged an armistice until the dispute was settled by the Tartars. In 1431 the Khan decided in favour of the prince's son, and he was crowned as Vassili II. in presence of a Tartar commissioner.

CHAPTER X

VASSILI II.

VASSILI II. made a bad start as Grand Prince, and all through his reign of thirty-seven years he was dogged by misfortune. When his marriage took place, an unfortunate incident increased the number of his enemies. Yuri's two sons, Vassili the Squinter and Chemiaka, were in the palace, when Sophia, the mother of Vassili the bridegroom, saw that Vassili the Squinter was wearing a golden girdle, once the property of Dimitri Donskoi. There and then she charged him with stealing it, and tried to take it from him by force. Furious at this insult, the brothers left Moscow. Their father, Yuri, then set his army in motion, captured Vassili, deposed him, and declared himself to be Grand Prince. But when he entered Moscow the Metropolitan Photius, with his clergy and a multitude of citizens, left it. Photius also threatened him with the curse of the Church for daring to disturb the public peace, and a pestilence which occurred just then was generally understood to betoken the wrath of the heavenly powers. Yuri therefore left Moscow, and Vassili came back to it amid great jubilation. Civil war had, however, begun, and in 1426 Vassili the Squinter fell into the hands of Vassili of Moscow, who blinded him. His cruelty did not go unavenged. When he was worshipping in the Troitska Lavra, Chemiaka, with a band of soldiers, burst into the church, seized him, and put out his eyes.

In spite of his sorrows and sufferings, Vassili II. made a bold stand for the Church and saved the interests of Orthodoxy at a crisis when they were seriously threatened. On the death of Photius in 1431, he selected Jonah, Bishop of Riazanm, and sent him to receive consecration, but Jonah delayed setting out, and spent so much time on the journey that when he did reach Constantinople in 1434, he found that the Patriarch Joseph had already consecrated Isidore.

Isidore was a Greek. At the time of his consecration he was Bishop of Illyria, and hegumen of the monastery of St. Dimitri. He was not unknown in the West. Pope Eugenius IV., much against his will, had found himself compelled to call together the Council of Basel (1431–43), and when he found that it disagreed with him on several questions, of which one of the chief was, whether he or it was the ultimate spiritual authority, he dissolved it. It refused to consider itself dissolved, and went on with its work, whereupon Eugenius summoned another Council, which met at Ferrara in January 1438, and was transferred to Florence the year afterwards. The main purposes of this Council were to endorse the Pope's claim to be the Head of the Church, exalted above all other authorities, secular or ecclesiastical, to meet the growing desire of the Greeks for the union of the Churches of the East and the West, and to combine the princes of Europe in a campaign against the Turks. Isidore was active at the Council of Basel. He was strongly in favour of the union of the Greek and Latin Churches, and he was not disposed to remain quietly in Russia when matters in which he was so deeply interested were being discussed in Italy.

The Greek Emperor, John Palæologus, was also anxious about the results of the Council. His Empire was in its last agony. The Turks were in the vicinity of his capital, and his only hope of saving it lay in the armies of united Christendom. He therefore went to Florence, taking with him the Patriarch Joseph, three vicars of the other Patriarchal Sees, seventeen Metropolitans, and a multitude of bishops, and he pressed his suit to the utmost of his ability. His appeals fell on deaf ears, for the Council was deep in the discussion of doctrinal matters—the procession of the Holy Spirit, Purgatory, the use of unleavened bread, and the Supremacy of the Pope. While debates on these were going on, Isidore appeared.

Vassili and the boyars were not displeased that he should

attend the Council as their delegate. They hoped that the proposed union of the Christian powers against the Turks would materialise for Russia's benefit, and they thought it not impossible that the union of the Eastern and Western Churches might be effected on Orthodox terms. But they were not sure of Isidore's trustworthiness, for his behaviour at Basel was known to them, and his sympathy with Latin Christendom was unmistakable. Vassili, therefore, gave him injunctions to stand firm for Orthodoxy, injunctions which the event proved were needed. Travelling round by Riga and Lubec he reached Florence in August 1438. As the discussions went on he became convinced that unless union were effected on the basis of the Pope's supremacy, there would be no union at all, and along with Bessarion, famous as a scholar, a patron of letters and a friend of the Renaissance, who came in the Emperor's train, he pressed his conviction on the Council. On the other side, Mark, Bishop of Ephesus, poured out vehement invectives against Western doctrine and against union with those who held it. The Emperor, who was in despair about his capital, at last persuaded most of the Greeks to sign a formula vague enough to cover all their beliefs, and to assent to a statement that the Pope is the sovereign Pontiff, the Vicar of Christ, shepherd and teacher of all Christians, appointed to guide and rule the whole Church of God, without prejudice to the rights and privileges of the other patriarchs. The decree of the Council was published in July 1439.

The Council has been made much of by the Romish Church, but it was really a disappointment to every one who took part in it. The Emperor got promises that the Western powers would defend Constantinople. All they actually sent him was two war galleys and three hundred soldiers. The Pope got the modified recognition of his supremacy, but the whole Eastern Church outside the Council chamber refused to acknowledge it, and the antagonism to Rome became positive enmity. When Isidore, who had been made a Cardinal and a legate of the Holy See in Russia, reached Moscow, he found black looks

awaiting him. The other commissioners had reached the
city before him, and had reported what they had seen and
heard. Vassili therefore knew what to expect, but the
common people were not prepared for what was about to
take place. In March 1441 a great congregation gathered
in the Cathedral of the Assumption. Through the open
door, borne on high, there came a Latin cross. Following
it through the startled crowd marched a procession of
clergy, in which the principal figure was Isidore clad in his
cardinal's robes. As the service went on the people heard
with astonishment the name of the Pope mentioned before
that of the Patriarch in the prayers. This feeling became
hot indignation when, towards the close of the service, the
deacon, standing beside Isidore's throne, recited the Acts of
the Council, and intimated that they had been signed by
Isidore in ratification of the union which had been
consummated between the Orthodox and the Catholic
Churches.

Vassili, in a rage, jumped to his feet, overwhelmed
Isidore with reproaches, and denounced him as a traitor.
Four days afterwards he caused Isidore to be brought
before a Council of boyars and clergy, who denounced him
with equal energy, deposed him, confiscated all his property,
and ordered him to be shut up in the Chudov monastery.
It might have gone hard with him in his imprisonment, but,
probably with the connivance of his jailers, he escaped, and
Vassili forbade him to be pursued. He found refuge in
Rome, and after a visit to the East in the Papal interest
he was comforted with the title, Patriarch of Constantinople;
but he did not venture to leave the Pope's side to enjoy his
empty dignity.

After Isidore's expulsion the Russian Church remained
without a Metropolitan for eight years. During this period
he did everything in his power to detach Kiev from Orthodoxy. Kiev was now in the hands of the Polish king,
Casimir, a zealous Catholic, and Isidore entertained the
hope that the king's influence would help him to accomplish
his design. He succeeded so far that he persuaded
Gregory Mammas, the Patriarch who had been ejected

from Constantinople because of his Latin sympathies, and
who was living in Rome, to appoint a monk named Gregory
Metropolitan of Lithuania. The appointment was never
recognised, and in 1459 a Council of Russian bishops held
in Moscow intimated the division of the Church into two
sections—one under the jurisdiction of Moscow and the
other under Kiev. To fill up the vacancy occasioned by
Isidore's departure, Chemiaka nominated Jonah as Metropolitan. When Chemiaka fell from power, and Vassili
once more sat upon the throne, he confirmed the act of
his predecessor, and proposed as usual to send Jonah to
Constantinople for consecration. But as rumours became
current that the clergy of Constantinople were coquetting
with Latin heresies, Vassili detained Jonah in the hope
that the Orthodoxy of the Metropolitan would be shown
to be unimpeachable. At last, tired of waiting, he
summoned a Synod of Russian bishops and commanded
them to consecrate Jonah by their own authority. When
Constantinople fell in 1453, Jonah sent the Patriarch a gift
of money and asked for his blessing. It was given, and at
the same time the Patriarch intimated that the right of
appointing its own Metropolitan was definitely accorded
to the Russian Church. From that time, therefore, the
dependence of Moscow upon Constantinople ceased.

During this period the Church played an important
part in deciding the right of succession to the Russian
throne. In 1447 Vassili called together five bishops and
three archimandrites and asked them as a Synod to decide
between his eldest son on the one hand and all possible
candidates on the other. They assigned the right of
suzerainty to Vassili and his house exclusively, and declared that if his uncle Yuri or his cousin Chemiaka, or any
other, made a claim to it they would be repeating the sin
of Adam who, after listening to the tempter, tried to make
himself equal with God. They also declared in defiance of
history that succession in the direct descending line, and not
succession by seniority, had always been the custom of the
land. Jonah endorsed this decision by an encyclical, in
which he ordered all who aided Chemiaka to rekindle the

fires of civil strife to be expelled from every Orthodox Church and from the fellowship of all Orthodox believers.

Vassili therefore associated with himself his eldest son, Ivan, a boy of ten. There is a curious story about Ivan's birth. At the time it happened, a monk in Novgorod said he had a revelation, which he communicated to his arch-bishop in these words : " Truly it is to-day that the Grand Prince triumphs. God has given him an heir. I behold this child making himself illustrious. He will subdue princes and peoples, but woe to Novgorod. Novgorod will fall at his feet never to rise again." The prediction was fulfilled in Ivan's career.

CHAPTER XI

IVAN III.

A NEW era opens with the accession of Ivan III. His reign began in 1462 and lasted till 1505, and its supreme importance is unquestionable. Its leading features are—the rise of the Grand Prince of Moscow above the other Russian princes to the position of their sovereign, the union of the principalities into one great kingdom, and the assumption that this kingdom was the direct heir of the Eastern Empire and, as such, the defender of the Orthodox faith.

At the beginning of Ivan's reign the Russian plain was shadowed by two great powers—Lithuania on the one hand and the Tartars on the other. Under their overlordship were the principalities of Moscow, Tver, Tchernigov, Suzdal, Riazan, Rostov, and Yaroslavl. There were also several semi-independent commonwealths, of which Novgorod was the chief. Moscow was neither the largest nor the strongest of these, nor was it the most advantageously placed. In point of military power it was inferior to Lithuania. In acreage Novgorod surpassed it. Besides, " Moscow lay at no great distance from the outskirts of three non-friendly principalities. Eighty versts to the north of the city there began the principality of Tver, the most hostile of Moscow's enemies, while a hundred versts to the south the Muscovite outpost line confronted her most restless foe, the Tartar. Lastly, a hundred versts or more to the west stood Lithuania, the most pressingly dangerous of Moscow's opponents. Thus from north, south, and west a hostile force had but a few stages to cover to reach the Muscovite capital, a disadvantage in the external position of the city of which we must never lose sight." [1]

[1] Kluchevski, ii. 3.

Ivan was, however, the man whom the hour required. He was no warrior delighting in the clash of arms. He was careful of himself to the point of cowardice, and he preferred overawing his enemies by a display of force to risking the chances of a pitched battle. He was a statesman, clear-sighted and shrewd, careful in forming his plans, patient and inflexible in their execution. Stephen of Moldavia said : " Ivan is a strange man. He sits quietly at home and triumphs over his enemies while I, though on horseback, cannot defend my country."

The process employed for conquering the other principalities differed in different cases, but the result was always the same. In 1463 Yaroslavl resigned its independence. In 1471 action was taken against Novgorod. Strife was fomented between the nobles and the common people. Ivan entered, posed as the people's champion, and when those who were their natural protectors were put out of the way, he struck the independence of the city to the dust. On 15th January 1478 Novgorod took the oath of allegiance. Immediately thereafter Ivan confiscated for the benefit of his courtiers most of the lands belonging to the city and to the clergy, and returned to Moscow, carrying with him three hundred cart-loads of gold, silver, jewels, furs, and other valuables, as well as the great bell which had so often summoned the Novgorodians to their tumultuous assemblies. In 1495 he gave the city its finishing blow. Having been insulted by the Hanseatic merchants of Revel, he arrested the representatives of the Hanseatic League whom he found in Novgorod, and carried off booty to the value of forty thousand pounds. Traders were so scared that the commercial importance of the city rapidly declined.

While this was going on in Novgorod, other absorptions were taking place. In 1472 Perm was seized, and the produce of its silver-mines was diverted to Moscow. In 1474 Rostov on the Volga sold its territory to Ivan, and its nobles enrolled themselves among his boyars. In 1485 Tver was taken without a blow. In 1489 Viatka surrendered, while a few years later Smolensk, Tchernigov,

Novgorod Severski, and other smaller principalities were gathered in.

After a similar fashion, he acquired his brother's principalities. Yuri and Boris died without leaving heirs. Ivan seized what they left behind them. Andrei, who had been expecting a share in the inheritance, was accused of intriguing with Lithuania for help to secure it. He was therefore thrown into prison, where he died in 1493. Ivan wept, confessed he had perhaps been needlessly severe, and received an easy absolution from his bishops, but he confiscated Andrei's appanage. The remaining brother was glad to escape a similar fate by acknowledging Ivan as his overlord. The undivided plain in this way came to be ruled by one sceptre, and the sentiment of a common nationality began to materialize as solid fact.

During this time also the omens became favourable for an attempt to throw off the yoke of the Tartars. They were now divided into the rival Khanates of the Crimea, Kazan, and Astrakhan. Ivan made overtures to the Khan of the Crimea, and the two became fast and lifelong friends. He then began to defy the Golden Horde. He ejected the Tartar merchants from the Kremlin and put to death the commissioners sent to collect the Tartar tribute. The Horde dispatched an army against him. Ivan advanced with his forces to the river Oka, but at the imminent prospect of battle his courage failed him, and he retired with great speed to Moscow. The common people received him with loud reproaches. The boyars and the bishops were equally demonstrative. At last the vigorous denunciations of Vassian, Archbishop of Rostov, and of Gerontius the Metropolitan, overcame his pusillanimity, and he returned to the front. For a fortnight nothing happened, and then, strange to say, on 23rd June panic seized the Russians and the Tartars at the same time, and they fled in opposite directions. This was, however, claimed as a great Russian victory, and the Metropolitan fixed the day to be kept as a yearly festival in memory of the fact that on 23rd June 1480 the Tartars were overthrown.

Having thus relieved himself of the Golden Horde, Ivan next got rid of the Tartars of Kazan. In 1487 his troops stormed the city and took the Khan prisoner. On his triumphal return to Moscow, Ivan led his captive in chains through the streets, and the spectacle intimated to the world that the Tartar domination was gone for ever.

Lithuania was, however, his most formidable foe, and although busy in other directions he was carrying on a protracted struggle with it. He began his operations with his usual coolness, continued them pertinaciously, and finally achieved his purpose. After a campaign in which the Khan of the Crimea, the Turkish Sultan Bajazet, Matthias Corvinus of Hungary, and Stephen of Moldavia helped him greatly, he was victorious, and peace was signed in January 1494. In order to cement it, Alexander of Lithuania married Ivan's daughter, Helena.

Ivan's zeal for Orthodoxy manifested itself in the provisions on which he insisted in his daughter's marriage settlement. Although her husband was a Catholic, and the majority of the Lithuanians were Catholics, Ivan stipulated that Helena should not be asked to renounce Orthodoxy. She was to have an Orthodox Church in the palace, Orthodox priests to give her ghostly counsel, and Orthodox cooks in her kitchen. Further, all who adhered to the Orthodox faith were to be assured of complete religious toleration. Complete toleration was, of course, impossible, and Ivan probably calculated that this would give him another opportunity of interfering in Lithuanian affairs. His calculations were accurate. Besides, he stirred up strife in Alexander's household to such an extent that Helena begged him to desist. Ivan turned a deaf ear to her complaints. Alexander wreaked his passion not only on her but also on his Orthodox subjects, and made them both suffer acutely. Ivan posed as their champion, and in July 1500 war was begun.

Alexander formed an alliance with the Livonian Knights and inflicted a heavy blow on the Russians near Izborsk in 1501. The Tartars from Serai also came to his help, and the campaign would have ended disastrously for Ivan

had not the Khan of the Crimea made a furious attack on
the Golden Horde and reduced Serai, its capital, to a heap
of smoking ruins. In 1503 a truce was arranged. In
the negotiations which ensued, Ivan regained all that had
been filched from Russia by Guedimin and Vitoft, and
thereby fulfilled his declaration that he would never rest
till he had gathered into one all the territories that had
belonged to Russia from the beginning of time. In this
way he earned for himself the designation Reuniter of the
Russian lands.

As his power increased Ivan began to hold himself
more and more aloof from his boyars, and after his second
marriage he greatly emphasised the distance which separated him from them. He surrounded himself with officials
graded like a hierarchy, and he arranged a court ceremonial
on the complex Byzantine model which made approach
to his person a matter of considerable difficulty. He
removed questions of public policy from the control and
even from the cognisance of the mass meetings of boyars
which had been accustomed to discuss them, and settled
them with a small and select council in his private apartments. This was a decided innovation on ancient custom,
and those who were excluded from this group of favourites
were naturally resentful. But if any one complained in
Ivan's presence that he and his fellows were getting less
consideration than they deserved, he was peremptorily
told that he ought to submit without a murmur to the will
of his sovereign. One outspoken boyar was dismissed from
Court with the contemptuous words, " Begone, boor, I
have no need of thee."

As Ivan's control over his own dominions increased the
control of Byzantium over the Russian clergy declined.
Theoretically the Russian Metropolitan was selected and
consecrated by the Patriarch, and was of equal rank with
the Tsar. But it was always difficult to maintain the
theory in practice. Even before the fall of Constantinople
the journey was tedious and dangerous, and after its capture
by the Turks the Patriarch was sometimes a fugitive whom
it was impossible to reach. Besides, the Grand Dukes

had often already refused to wait for the Patriarch's
selection, and had appointed a Metropolitan of their own.
Therefore on the death of the Metropolitan Gerontius in
1491 Ivan on his own authority appointed Zozimus, archimandrite of the Simonov monastery. Zozimus, however,
proved to be a wolf in sheep's clothing.[1] Between 1470
and 1480 a Jewish scholar named Zacharias began a secret
propaganda in Novgorod. He attacked the doctrines of the
Trinity, the Person of Christ, the Sacraments, and the
Resurrection. He also denounced the worship of ikons and
of the saints. He was accused of cursing the Saviour and
the Virgin, of spitting on the crucifix, and of preaching
Jewish doctrines based on the Kabbala. In Novgorod he
secured the adhesion of two prominent priests who made
Ivan's acquaintance in 1480, and who were brought by
him to Moscow. Through their influence the heresy spread
rapidly, especially in the higher circles of society, and it
even infected members of the Tsar's family. Zozimus
also became sympathetic, and used his influence to protect
those who were going astray. When the mischief was discovered, the wrath of the Orthodox clergy knew no bounds.
Gennadius, Archbishop of Novgorod, whom Ivan at a later
date deposed for simony, mounted the heretics whom he
captured on horseback, with their faces to the horses'
tails, and their garments turned inside out, and he placed
on their heads hats ornamented with tassels of tow, and
crowns of straw, with the inscription " The Army of Satan."
He then paraded them through the streets to be jeered at
and spat on. Joseph of Volokolamsk distinguished himself
by the energy with which he denounced the Judaisers, and
demanded their extermination. Ivan, however, was more
tolerant than might have been expected. He contented
himself with executing a few of the less prominent members
of the sect, and with ordering Zozimus to retire to the
monastery from which he came.

Ivan then appointed as Metropolitan Simon, hegumen
of the Troitska Lavra. The consecration was arranged
for 21st September 1495, and the higher clergy, the nobles,

[1] Karamsin, vi. 245; Howorth, ii. 332.

and representatives of the people were invited to be present. Gennadius refused to appear because he objected to Ivan's invasion of the Church's liberty and of the rights of the Byzantine Patriarch, but he sent a letter stating that he would recognise the Metropolitan in his new capacity.

In 1499 Gennadius rendered the Church a distinct service by issuing the complete Bible compiled from the various Slavonic translations. It was first printed complete by Ivan Feodorov at Ostrog in 1581.

Ivan treated Gennadius' protest as of no practical account, and went on with his schemes for the Church's welfare and for his own aggrandisement. In the early years of his reign, with the assistance of Aristotle of Bologna, and on the site of the wooden building erected by Ivan I., he built the stone cathedral of the Assumption, and adorned it in the Byzantine style. At its corners he laid the remains of the great prelates Peter, Theognostes, Cyprian, Photius, and Jonah, which had found a resting-place in the former sanctuary. He also built the cathedrals of the Annunciation and of the archangel Michael.

In some respects his activities were far from pleasing the clergy. The State needed money, and it seemed to him that the Church was not doing its fair share in providing it. Besides, he wished to award some of the lands and hereditaments of the monasteries of Moscow and Novgorod to his boyars for military service and to take some for himself, and it seemed to him that he had a plausible case. The Church lands were vast in extent, and were being continually added to, and as they were free from taxation, every acre by which they were increased made the burden on the taxpayers proportionally heavier. Ivan began to consider whether this immunity from taxation should be allowed to continue, and whether the Church should be allowed to possess land at all.

To pave the way for future action he forbade any further donations of lands to monasteries, and because Prince Uchtomski and the archimandrite of the Chudov monastery disobeyed this prohibition, he caused them both to be publicly flogged.

In 1503 he commanded the Metropolitan, the Archbishops, and the Bishops to meet together and consider
the question of monasterial land ownership, and to correct
some abuses.   Two opposing views at once appeared.
On the one side, a party led by Nilus of Bielozersk and
Paisius of Yaroslav maintained that the monastic life
implies a remaking of the inner man by solitude, meditation,
and prayer, that a monk's bodily wants should be supplied
by the labour of his own hands, and that the management
of property is a hindrance to the sanctification of the soul.
This party therefore besought Ivan to break up the great
monastic establishments and scatter their inmates over
Russia, so that in quietness they might give themselves to
spiritual discipline.

On the other hand, Joseph of Volokolamsk argued that
this self-regarding view of the monastic life was a false
one.   He held that monasteries were organised for the
public good, for the relief of the poor, and for the carrying
of Christian truth to the ignorant and the heathen.   He
also maintained that the existing system was essential
to the stability of the Church.   After quoting instances
to prove that the holding of land by monasteries was no
recent thing, he went on to say : " If monasteries shall
not possess lands how shall men of honour and of noble
birth assume the vows ?   And if there be not monks of
noble birth whence shall ye obtain men for bishops and
other offices of authority in the Church ?   If there be no
monks of honour and of noble birth then assuredly will
the faith be shaken."

In support of Joseph's position the Metropolitan sent
a letter saying that from the time of Vladimir monasteries
had possessed lands, and he cursed those who laid sacrilegi-
ous hand on the Church property.   He also referred to the
charters of possession and of immunity from taxation
granted by the Tartars, and declared that the Church
could not surrender to the secular power property that
belonged to God.

In the end the Council drew up a report in which it
skilfully mixed up the question of monasterial ownership

with the entirely different question of archiepiscopal land-ownership and with other matters with little connection with the subject in hand. Ivan saw that if he took drastic action he might raise a storm which he could not calm, and with his usual prudence he shelved the project for a time. He decreed, however, that any member of a family who wished to buy back from the clergy the whole or any part of an estate bequeathed to the Church by a parental testator, might be allowed to do so.

Russia was now a great power, and Ivan resolved that his Empire should step into the place which the fall of the Eastern Empire had left vacant, that Moscow should become the successor of Byzantium, and that he himself should be recognised as the vanished Emperor's heir. An opportunity of indicating what was in his mind was furnished at the consecration of the Metropolitan Simeon in September 1495. The ceremonial was arranged on the Byzantine model. At the door of the cathedral Simeon was handed over to the bishops, and when they had finished their function and the act of ordination was over, Ivan rose, as the Byzantine Emperors were wont to do, and delivered an ordination charge, to which Simeon, standing on the steps of the throne, made a suitable reply.

For the same end he made an adroit move in connection with his second marriage. When he was considering the question of a successor to his deceased wife, Maria Borisovna, a Romish ecclesiastic of his court suggested a Byzantine princess who seemed suitable. This was Zoe Palaeologus. When Constantinople fell in 1453, Thomas Palaeologus, brother of the Emperor John who had perished, fled to the west, and found refuge in Rome. He died there, leaving his daughter Zoe to the care of the Pope Sixtus IV. Zoe was said to be beautiful, witty, and clever, and although Ivan knew that any one associated with the Roman Pontiff was suspect in the eyes of his Orthodox subjects, he convinced himself that the possession of Zoe as her husband would justify him in posing as the heir of her uncle in all his rights and privileges. The Pope thought that Zoe might be helpful in uniting the Orthodox Church with that under his own jurisdiction. Zoe was ambitious, and though the position as wife of a mere Grand Prince was not imperial, it was not despicable. Negotiations were therefore easy, and in due course Zoe travelled to Russia by way of Bologna, Nuremberg, Lubec, and Pskov. She entered Moscow in great pomp, with a long retinue, and after her, though not as members of her suite, there came a mixed multitude of Greeks and Italians, who brought with them Greek art and science, Greek MSS., and traditions of Greek ritual and churchmanship.

Zoe had scarcely crossed the frontiers before she disappointed the hopes which the Pope had built on her. She changed her name to Sophia, and declared herself Russian and Orthodox. Anthony, the Papal legate who travelled with her, intended to enter Moscow in solemn procession with a Latin cross borne before him, but when the Metropolitan heard of it he said that if the Latin cross came in by one gate he would go out by another. Zoe approved the stand which the Metropolitan had taken, and the cross was smuggled into the city in a sledge.

After the wedding, which took place in 1472, Ivan intimated not only that the dignity of the great imperial throne from which his consort sprang was transferred to himself, but that the Orthodox Church which the Emperors of Byzantium had patronised, was now his peculiar care. With Zoe's ardent approval, if not at her direct instigation, he appropriated the double-headed eagle of Byzantium as the emblem of Russia, and he began to style himself in his foreign correspondence Tsar—the Russian form of Cæsar—a style hitherto used only in documents relating to internal administration. In other respects also Zoe stimulated Ivan's energies. In particular she spurred him on in his efforts to throw off the yoke of the Tartars, asking repeatedly how long was she, an imperial princess, to be subject to these barbarians.

Zoe died in 1503, and in the same year Ivan made his will. It is a remarkable document, scheduling his possessions, public and private, with business-like precision. With regard to the succession to his throne he wavered.

His eldest son, also named Ivan, the son of his first wife, died in 1490, leaving a boy named Dimitri. Ivan therefore nominated Dimitri, and had him solemnly proclaimed in the Cathedral of the Assumption, investing him with a cap of gold and a collar of pearls, and causing him to be saluted by the Metropolitan as " Mighty Tsar and Autocrat." Nevertheless, it was not long till he found fault with Dimitri, deposed him, imprisoned him, and nominated as the heir Vassili, his own son by Zoe. To Vassili he assigned the greater portion of the revenues of the State. The other members of his family received only trifling annuities. To Vassili also was given supreme jurisdiction in all civil and criminal cases, and when he ascended the throne he showed himself more of an autocrat and supreme lord than his father had been.

Ivan himself died in 1505, after a reign of forty-three years. From a moral point of view his character was not admirable, for he was quite unscrupulous in carrying out his purposes ; but the benefits he conferred on Russia are undeniable. He found it a congeries of independent and often mutually hostile appanages. He left it a firmly united empire. He found it under the shadow of tyrannical overlords, who threatened it incessantly both on the east and the west. He left it with their power broken and with his vast realm gathering to itself the glories of the Eastern Empire which had passed away. He well deserves the designation Ivan the Great.

CHAPTER XII

VASSILI III.

IVAN III. was succeeded by his son Vassili, who was
born 25th August 1479. His coronation took place
in October 1506. He was the first who assumed the title
" Tsar and Autocrat of All the Russias."

In all directions he carried on the work which his father
had left unfinished. Three principalities still preserved
their independence—Pskov, Riazan, and Novgorod Severski.
In 1510 he compelled Pskov to surrender. In 1521 he seized
the Prince of Riazan on a charge of treason. The prince,
however, escaped, and Vassili annexed the territory he
had left behind him. In 1523 the Prince of Novgorod
Severski was seized on a similar charge and thrown into
prison, where he died. This was the end of the appanage
system, and in Russia Vassili reigned supreme.

Foreign foes also had to be reckoned with. On the
one side were the Tartars, whose power, though shattered,
was not yet destroyed. On the other side was Poland.
The dispute with the Tartars resolved itself into a dispute
with the Khan of the Crimea for the possession of Kazan.
In 1521 the Khan marched into Russia and reached Moscow,
whereupon Vassili signed a humiliating treaty, in which
he acknowledged himself the Khan's vassal. A little later
he seized an opportunity of getting back what he considered
his own, and he fitted out two expeditions—one in 1523 and
the other in 1524. Both of these were unsuccessful. In
1530 a third army took the field, besieged Kazan, stormed
it, and forced the survivors of a terrible massacre to sue
for peace.

On the west, war and peace alternated till 1509, when
an arrangement was agreed to. But no arrangement
between Muscovy and Poland could be permanent, and in

1512 Vassili attacked Smolensk. By this time the issue
of the conflict was a matter of importance to a large part
of Europe. Sigismund enlisted in his support the Tartars
of the Crimea, the Kossacks of the Dnieper, and the Swedes.
Vassili's allies were the Teutonic Orders of Knights, the
King of Denmark, Maximilian, Emperor of Austria, the
Hospidar of Wallachia, and the Sultan Selim.[1]

The Emperor, however, was anxious to avert war, and he
sent Sigismund, Baron von Herberstein, as his ambassador
to the Muscovite Court. He reached Moscow in April 1517,
and returned in 1518 without effecting much. But the
first-hand knowledge he obtained enabled him to write
his famous book, *Rerum Moscoviticarum Commentarii*, in
which he gives a graphic account of Russia and Moscow
and Vassili's Court.

The general impression created by the book was not
favourable to the people it described. The powers in the
West concluded that the Russians were a savage nation
which should be confined within its own borders, and
should certainly be denied access to the sea. In spite of
this, Pope Leo X. resolved to see what he could do to bring
Russia into touch with the rest of Europe. Through the
instrumentality of the Grandmaster of the Teutonic Knights
he suggested to Vassili that, on the death of Sigismund,
Poland and Lithuania might choose him as their sovereign
if he were at peace with them ; further, that as the son of
Zoe Palaeologus he might, with the consent of the Christian
princes, become the Emperor of Constantinople if he were
united to them by the sacred bonds of religion ; and once
again that the Metropolitan of Moscow might reach the
higher dignity of Patriarch of the whole Eastern Church.
In conclusion, the Pope declared it was his most ardent
desire to set on the head of the Tsar of Russia the crown
of a Christian monarch, and he cherished this desire from
no terrestrial motive, but simply for the glory of God.

Vassili remembered that in 1514 the Pope had celebrated
a victory of Sigismund over the Russians, whom he had
characterised as heretics. He therefore replied that while

[1] Mouravieff, 175.

6

he was glad to stand on friendly relations with the occupant of the Holy See on the subject of European politics, he and his people would remain attached to the Christian religion in its simplicity and purity.

As his power increased, Vassili increased the splendour of his Court and the loftiness of his own demeanour. When he received foreign ambassadors he did his utmost to impress them with his greatness and glory. In the hall of audience they found the monarch sitting on his throne; the boyars, clothed in robes garnished with pearls, sat on benches round the wall, and profound silence reigned until the Tsar was pleased to speak. The banquets on these occasions were scenes of barbaric prodigality. The tables shone with gold and silver plate. The feast began with brandy and roasted swans, each guest receiving four pieces. The beverages included Malmsey, Greek wines, and different kinds of mead. When the Tsar wished to honour any one he sent him a piece of bread. As a mark of special honour he sent him a portion of salt. The recipient of these gifts was required to bow first to the Tsar, then to the Councillors, and then to the remainder of those at table. When ambassadors received the gifts, not only the ambassadors, but all the rest of the company, were expected to rise and bow. After the banquet, drinking was prolonged far into the night, for it was believed that the guests had not been hospitably treated unless they were sent home helplessly intoxicated.[1]

To enhance his dignity, Vassili formed a bodyguard of young nobles. They wore cloaks of white satin and carried little silver axes. In public they walked before the Tsar. In his palace, standing by the throne, they seemed to strangers like angels descended from heaven. In war they took charge of the Tsar's arms. In addition to these, there were swarms of officials, household domestics, and servants, and the general result was that the Tsar was inaccessible. The older boyars, who had been offended by the aloofness which Ivan III. began to cultivate, were highly incensed when they found that Vassili was carrying

[1] Karamsin, vii. 227.

his father's policy to heights of which his father had scarcely dreamed.

Against such an overpowering potentate the Metropolitan was unable to assert himself. Barlaam, who succeeded Simon, retired after ten years of fruitless struggle to the monastery of Simonov. Porphyry, who succeeded him, was loaded with fetters and imprisoned because he was not sufficiently obsequious, but in Daniel, Bishop of Volokalamsk, Vassili found everything he wished for in the way of servility. Herberstein describes him unflatteringly as " a man of about thirty years of age, of a large and corpulent frame and a red face, who, lest he should be thought to be more given to gluttony than to fasting, vigils, and prayers, used on all occasions when he had to perform any public ceremony to expose his face to the fumes of sulphur to make himself pale."

At the same time, Vassili's pretentions to autocratic authority over the Church did not interfere with its missionary activity, and a considerable number of monasteries was planted among the wild tribes of the frozen north.

During Vassili's reign, Western Europe was stirred to its depths by the Reformation, but the mass of the Russian people and clergy was unaware that it was taking place, and the most enlightened of them could see in it nothing but a conflict raised on the one hand by the worldly ambition of the Pope, and on the other by innovations introduced into religion by human passion. There was equally little interest in the Renaissance. Classical erudition did not exist, tradition was enthroned, ignorance was universal and profound. Fortunately for Russia, however, the scholars who came in Zoe's train, and others after them, brought MSS. and copies of the sacred books, which found a resting-place in monastic libraries, and one day Vassili happened to see a number of these lying neglected and covered with mould. He sought to find in Moscow a man able to select the best of them and to translate them into Slavonic. Not succeeding, he appealed for help to the Patriarch, who sent him Maximus. Maximus was a monk of Mount Athos. He had been educated at Paris, Florence, and Venice, and had a wide acquaintance with Western culture. He was, in fact, one of the most distinguished men of his time, notable alike for his scholarship, his character, and his piety.[1]

On his arrival at Moscow he was astonished at the material in the Royal libraries, and declared that neither Greece nor Italy had anything to equal it. He then set himself to classify the MSS., to correct their text, to harmonise the ritual of divine service with the best Byzantine models, and to translate the Greek annotated version of the Psalter. When his work was finished he asked permission to leave the country, but Vassili was so charmed with him that this permission was invariably refused. He was, in fact, kept in a state of honourable captivity.

On several occasions he used his influence with the Tsar to secure lenient treatment for nobles who had fallen into disgrace, and by so doing roused the jealousy of the Metropolitan Daniel. Daniel therefore set himself to destroy Maximus by starting a campaign of slander. He and his monks accused Maximus both to the prince and to the people of corrupting the sacred books, and they cried heresy long and loudly. On Vassili they made no impression, until Maximus himself gave them the opening they needed. In spite of his efforts to keep out of politics, Maximus' cell had become the rendezvous of boyars who resented the Tsar's innovations. Daniel therefore charged him with carrying on secret intrigues, until he roused in the prince a feeling of doubt which passed into disfavour. Maximus felt the cold wind rising, and renewed his request for permission to retire from the country. It was again refused. A courtier told him bluntly that he knew too much to be allowed to leave.

The crisis came when he protested against Vassili's conduct to his wife. They had been married for twenty-one years, but had no children. It is said that one day Vassili saw a nest in a tree, and exclaimed, " The birds are happier than I am. They have little ones." Then turning to his attendants, he said, " Who is to succeed me on the

[1] Karamsin, vii. 247.

throne of Russia?" "Sire," they replied, "a barren
fig tree is cut down and another takes its place in the
orchard." Daniel, ever ready to please his master, consented to dissolve the bond of matrimony on condition that
Solomonia went into a convent, whereupon in 1526 Vassili
repudiated her and shut her up in Suzdal. Two months
later he married Helena Glinskaia.

"When the Metropolitan, on her arrival at the convent
weeping and sobbing, cut off her hair and then offered to
put on the hood she was so angry that she took it and
hurled it to the ground and stamped upon it with her foot.
One of the chief councillors, irritated at the sight of this
indignity, not only reviled her bitterly, but beat her with
a scourge and asked her, ' Darest thou resist the will of
my lord, and delayest thou to obey his commands?' When
Solomonia asked him in return by what authority he beat
her, he replied by the will of her lord, upon which she,
broken-hearted, protested in the presence of all that she
took the veil unwillingly and under compulsion, and invoked
the vengeance of God on her behalf for so great an injury." [1]

The whole business was infamous, and Maximus and
Vassian Kossoi denounced it. Vassian was a man of
princely blood whom Ivan III. had compelled to become
a monk. He was imprisoned in Volokolamsk. Maximus
was imprisoned in Tver. For many years he was strictly
confined to his cell, but when Daniel was deposed during
the minority of Ivan IV. he was allowed to leave it and
to retire to the Troitska Lavra, where, after twenty more
years of neglect and weariness, he died.

Vassili had scarcely married Helena when a rumour
became current that Solomonia had been delivered of a
male child, but no justification of it was ever forthcoming.
To the great chagrin of the royal couple this second alliance
seemed likely to prove as barren as the first, and Helena
and her husband went on a round of pilgrimages to
monasteries famous for their sanctity, and offered prayers
at many shrines and gave lavish alms to the poor. At
length on 25th August 1530, to the accompaniment of a

[1] Herberstein, i. 51.

terrible thunderstorm, Helena became the mother of a son.
The infant prince was baptized in the Troitska Lavra,
and Vassili, with tears of joy in his eyes, laid him on the
tomb of St. Sergius, praying the saint to guide and preserve
the child through the perils of life.

In December 1534, when on a hunting expedition,
Vassili was seized by a painful malady.   Suffering intensely,
he was borne on a sledge through falling snow to Moscow,
and with difficulty got into his palace.   After giving
directions about the government and his family, he asked
for the monastic habit that he might die in the odour of
sanctity.   Then a strange scene took place round his
death-bed.   On the one hand, Prince Andrei and the
boyars who were present pled with him to follow the
example of his father and of his ancestors who had departed
this life without relinquishing their royal dignity, and
begged him to die as he had lived, Tsar of All the Russias.
On the other hand, Daniel resisted them, declaring angrily :
" No one shall take his soul away from me.   A vessel of
silver is good, but one of gold is better," and in spite of
protests and resistance he gave Vassili the tonsure, wrapped
him in a monk's cloak, and bestowed on him the name
Barlaam.   Immediately afterwards Vassili died, and
Helena became Regent.

CHAPTER XIII

IVAN IV.

AFTER the death of Vassili, Helena found her position difficult, but she put down opposition to her will with such severity that the people began to think a tigress and not a woman sat on the throne. Suddenly, on 3rd April 1538, she died. Herberstein reports the general conviction that she was poisoned.[1]

A period of confusion and strife instantly ensued. One party of boyars after another got possession of the young prince and pandered to his lowest instincts in the hope of keeping him quiet, and of blinding him to the fact that they were reducing him to a nonentity. He indulged himself in vice and cruelty to the limit of their desires, but he saw that everything that was done was done in his name. He also saw that he himself was ignored and humiliated on every possible occasion. Hatred to the boyars as a class therefore took shape in his mind, and it became the passion of his later years. When he was thirteen years old he suddenly asserted himself, charged them with destroying men's lives unjustly, and with hurrying the country to destruction, and there and then, by his express orders, Andrei Shuiski was torn to pieces by huge dogs. This bold act filled the boyars with alarm, and they heaved a sigh of relief when he returned to his brutal pleasures.

In his eighteenth year he was crowned in Moscow. The crown used on this occasion was said to have been brought from Constantinople by Monomachus, and to have been bequeathed to Yuri Dolgorouki with instructions that it was to be reserved till God sent Russia a monarch worthy to wear it. It has been used at the coronation of every

[1] Herberstein, i. 53.

Tsar from that date.   In order to add lustre to his dignity, a genealogy was invented for him.   It not only traced his pedigree to Ruric, but went further back to a mythical brother of Cæsar Augustus, who is said to have settled in Lithuania.   The outrageous fiction was endorsed by the Patriarch of Constantinople, by the Metropolitan of Moscow, and by others of the clergy.

Immediately after his coronation, Ivan married Anastasia Zakharin Koshkin, one of a family which, in the thirteenth century, came from Lithuania to Moscow. The wedding took place on 3rd February 1547. Anastasia made him an excellent wife, and he loved and respected her as much as it was possible for a man of his rapidly corrupting character to do.   But neither his coronation nor his marriage made any improvement in his conduct. Anastasia besieged heaven with prayers for his reformation, the boyars trembled and kept silent, the people were on the brink of rebellion, when Ivan was pulled up as if by a miracle.

In April 1547 a fire broke out in Moscow.   Other fires followed in May.   The most destructive of all took place in June.   It reduced to ashes a large portion of the Kremlin and of the city, and it destroyed a multitude of the inhabitants.   The Shuiskis denounced the Glinskis as the authors of the calamity. Riots ensued. Yuri Glinski, Ivan's uncle, was murdered in one of the churches, and his servants were also slain.   At this crisis, however, a monk from Novgorod, named Sylvester, appeared on the scene and transformed it.   In the style of a Hebrew prophet he declared the fires were due to no earthly cause, but were a divine punishment for the sins of the prince and the people, and he exhorted Ivan to lay to heart the warning lest a worse thing should happen to him.   Ivan listened, and turned over a new leaf.

At this point the second period of his reign begins, and if he had died at the end of it he would have left behind him the reputation of a monarch who, in spite of glaring faults, was on the whole enlightened, progressive, and devoted to the interests of his people.   He soon found that his inexperience required guidance, and for this he betook himself to Sylvester, and to Alexis Adashev, a young noble of inferior rank who was already a favourite. Sylvester took charge of ecclesiastical business, Adashev became practically Minister of the Interior, and these two gathered round themselves an unofficial cabinet of able men with whom they tackled the problems of government.

In 1550, by their advice, Ivan summoned a Council to revise the laws and the arrangements for local government. Those who attended were not appointed by the people, they were nominated by the Tsar, but they included representatives of the Church, of the nobles and landowners, and of the merchants, and they were perhaps as satisfactory a body as could have been expected in those days. Many of them would willingly have stayed at home, for travelling was slow and dangerous, as well as expensive, but they were compelled to appear.

Local government was in a very confused state, and the Council resolved to introduce a system based on the unity of the Empire. It divided the country into districts, in each of which committees were made responsible for the collection of taxes, for the administration of justice, and for the men, horses, and equipment needed by the army. The scheme was wrecked, however, by the difficulty of getting members to serve on the district committees, and the control of business drifted into the hands of officials sent from Moscow.

In 1551 a similar Council was convened to regulate the affairs of the Church. It met in the Kremlin on 15th February, and is called the Council of the Hundred Chapters because its decisions were recorded under a hundred heads. There were present the Metropolitan, nine bishops, all the archimandrites, and nobles of high rank. Ivan opened the proceedings with an address in which he intimated his desire to establish public schools where the clergy should instruct the children in reading and in their religious duties. He also submitted the code of laws as revised in the previous year, and asked the Council to endorse it by their signatures. Among the most important matters discussed were the ceremonies of the Church, the chants, the ikons, the sign of the Cross, the correction of the sacred books, and the purification of Russian Christianity from the paganism which still clung to it.   But the main question was how to correct the morals of the clergy and how to prevent the Church from becoming proprietor of the whole of the Russian land.

The Church lands were held by the monasteries, and these were of two sorts—the Urban and the Desert.   The urban monasteries followed the population, the desert monasteries preceded it.   The urban monasteries were sometimes founded by princes, sometimes by Churchmen, sometimes by rich boyars, and sometimes by the united efforts of a community.   The desert monasteries began with a single individual who, with his own hands, built a rude cell and supported himself.   Other monks came to his neighbourhood and founded the nucleus of a colony. By and by a common life was introduced under a common roof.   Then the community applied for a charter and was recognised by the civil power as a corporation with authority to hold land and other property.   Outside the walls of the monastery the monks became agriculturists, cattle-breeders, fishermen, hunters, trappers, bee-keepers, and so forth, employing peasants as servants in numbers that often reached large dimensions.

The land held by the monasteries was acquired by arrangement with the temporal power, by private donations, by negotiations with laymen who thought that residence in a monastery would give them a better chance of entering heaven, or by purchase in the open market where the monks' wealth enabled them to outbid all competitors.   The general result was that by the middle of the sixteenth century they were reputed to own one-third of all the agrarian property in Russia.   For example, the Troitska Lavra had the best land in twenty-five districts.   It had a hundred thousand peasants under its control, and its annual income was a hundred thousand roubles (four million roubles in modern currency). Similarly the monastery of St. Cyril in Bielozero owned

more than fifty-seven thousand acres of arable land, not to
mention waste land and forests.[1]

Monastic life thus became far removed from its original
ideal. The monks were really the managers of great
corporations, and their time was taken up with secular
business. Of course many of them still gave themselves
to the practice of piety as they understood it, and some of
them as missionaries carried the torch of divine truth into
the dark regions round them. These were the salt of the
monastic order. The remainder carried into their daily
life the habits and even the vices of the world. Wealth
bred luxury and indolence. Saints' days, commemoration
days, and the like were made the occasions for feasts, and
there were monasteries in which the inmates had scarcely
time to recover from one surfeit of eating and drinking
before they were called on to face another. In the year-
book of the monastery of Volokolamsk no fewer than fifty-
one days were set apart for banqueting. In the Solovetski
monastery about 1650 the number had risen to 191, more
than one for every second day in the year, and as the
monasteries were well supplied with the produce of the
fields, the forests, and the rivers, and as they were the
principal manufactories of strong liquor, the festivities did
not lack the elements of good cheer.[2]

In consequence of this, the religious influence of the
monasteries had declined. Ivan IV. himself lamented
that " men do take the vows not for the saving of their
souls, but for the ease of their bodies, and that they may
feast continually." Except in rare instances the fruits of
the Spirit seldom appeared, while indulgence in the lusts
of the flesh was manifest.

As might have been expected, the ignorance of the
monks was profound : " In the sixteenth century Gennadius
of Novgorod notes with sorrow that the men presented
to him for ordination could neither read nor write. . . .
The monasteries, to be sure, went on collecting books. . . .
But what books ! In the monastic libraries a place, and
even a place of honour, was given to the Apocrypha, Adam's

[1] Kluchevski, ii. 187.　　　　　[2] *Ibid.*, 184.

MS. confided to the devil, the Last Will of Moses, the Vision of Isaac. . . . These enjoyed the same credit as the canonical books. The catalogue of the library of the Troitska Lavra in the seventeenth century is still in our hands. . . . We find 101 Bibles, 46 liturgical works, 58 collections of the Fathers of the Church, 17 books on ecclesiastical law, and one solitary book on philosophy. The works on asceticism are the most numerous of all. Until the seventeenth century the ancient Greek and Latin authors were unknown to Russian readers. In profane literature Chronicles were the favourite reading, but what Chronicles—those of Malala with his quotations from Orpheus, or the still more popular chronicle of George the Hamartolian. . . . The authorities on geography and cosmography were George Pissides and above all Cosmas Indicopleustes, whose conclusions as to the dimensions of the earth founded on the form of Moses' tabernacle were undoubtedly accepted. . . . But the book of all read up till the eighteenth century was the *Bee,* an incoherent compilation of scripture quotations, extracts from the Fathers of the Church, and a medley of detached thoughts from Aristotle, Socrates, Epicurus, Diodorus, and Cato. Books on mathematics, arithmetic, astronomy, geography, and music were proscribed as impious, and the Knijnik was shut up within a narrow horizon above which the light of European science could not rise, and was forced to trample the same ground ever and always, far from the current on which his Western neighbours were being borne onward." [1]

The morals of the monks were on the whole deplorable. Ivan, himself no pattern saint, laid before the Council a demand for their reformation couched in a series of questions, in which he specified the monks' shortcomings. These constituted nearly half of all the Council was asked to discuss, and formed a detailed indictment, the truth of which the monks could not deny.

Unfortunately the Council was not disposed to tackle the tremendous task which Ivan had set them, and in

[1] Walizewski, *Ivan the Terrible,* p. 64.

place of dealing with his questions individually they treated them as a whole and wandered off into problems and difficulties connected with asceticism. They also spent much time in lamenting the increase of sodomy among the laity. In other words, they side-tracked what they were expected to deal with, and they stereotyped errors and perpetuated abuses which they were meant to correct. Ivan's well-meant efforts effected little or nothing.

The attempt to deal with Church lands was equally futile. It cannot be said that Ivan's motives were altogether disinterested, for he meant to seize some estates belonging to the monks of Moscow, and to use this as a precedent for extending State control over Church lands everywhere. He was supported by Artemi, soon to be appointed Prior of the Troitska, who boldly demanded the secularisation of all monastic property, and also by Cassian, Bishop of Riazan, who denounced the corruption of morals rampant among the monastic clergy. On the other hand, Macarius the Metropolitan opposed the Tsar's designs and was supported by the whole body of the clergy, so that all that Ivan secured was the annulling of gifts made to the Church during his minority, the restitution of all freehold lands ceded to the monasteries without his consent, and the prohibition of the monastic practice of acquiring the patrimonial estates of ancient appanaged princes.

In many respects Ivan was more progressive than the clergy. For example, under his protection, a printing-press was set up. It was brought from Denmark, and was the first seen in Moscow. At it the deacons Feodorov and Peter Mstislavets printed the Acts of the Apostles, a description of Moscow, and the Book of Hours, and they designed to issue a text of the Service books corrected by the best MSS. that could be secured. Unfortunately, they did not know what texts were correct, and the scribes, who realised that their craft was in danger, reviled the press as an instrument of the devil, while the priests and monks, who mistook the corrections for perversions, raised the cry of heresy with such vehemence that the press was forced to remain idle till after the death of Macarius.

Ivan now turned his attention to foreign affairs and undertook an expedition against the Tartars.   His objective was Kazan, which he entered in triumph on 3rd October 1552.   The capture of Kazan was a turning-point in Russian history.   It not only marked the final overthrow of the Tartar power, it constituted the first step of the advance of Russia over Central Asia, which has continued to the present day.   It also marked the point at which the Crescent began to retreat before the Cross, and the final repulse of that militant Mohammedanism which had so long threatened to submerge the Christianity of Eastern Europe.   The instinct of the Russian people has, therefore, marked the event with special emphasis.   A new diocese was created, and the Bishop of Kazan was given precedence next to the Archbishop of Novgorod, and a tithe of the revenue of the conquered province and of certain other districts was ear-marked for his support.   In 1556 Astrakhan was conquered, and the Volga from its source to its mouth became a Russian river.   By a slower process the Tartars were pushed off the fertile black soil towards the Crimea, and a triple line of fortified towns destroyed the chance of their return.   Immigrants from more congested districts settled in the regions which the Tartars had vacated, whilst bands of rovers patrolled the frontiers and scoured the steppes and became known as the Cossacks.

In 1553 Ivan had a serious illness in course of which his conviction that the boyars were disloyal to him was confirmed.   Fearing that death was approaching, he asked them to swear allegiance to his young son Dimitri.   But the boyars as a class claimed a traditional right to share with the Tsar the responsibilities of government, and they resented the manner in which he was thrusting them aside.   Besides, they detested Dimitri's family connections. Therefore they refused to take the oath required of them, and supported the claim to succession put forward by Ivan's cousin, Vladimir.   Furious discussions raged even at Ivan's bedside.   In his distress he turned to Sylvester and Adashev.   To his consternation they also failed him. Then after making a pitiful appeal to the handful of nobles who remained faithful to him, begging them not to abandon his wife and child to their enemies, he fell into a stupor in which he remained for two days. Suddenly he regained consciousness and recovered. Vladimir's supporters made haste to pledge themselves to Dimitri, and Vladimir himself followed their example; but Ivan marked them all down for punishment, and the anguish of these days and nights determined his policy toward the boyars till the end of his life.

From this time onward he was obsessed by three fixed ideas. First, that he was exalted to the throne by divine choice, that he held his position independent of his subjects' approval, and that his will was law, which they were bound to obey. Second, he was convinced that the boyars were eager to rob him of his power, and were not to be trusted. Third, that severity was necessary to secure the safety of his person and the stability of his throne. On these themes he harped continually.

In fulfilment of a vow he made on his sick-bed, Ivan took his wife and son on a pilgrimage to the monastery of St. Cyril. On the way he visited the Troitska. Maximus, who was still living there, besought him to return, pleading the hardships of the journey and the tender age of the child. Ivan turned a deaf ear, and on the way Dimitri died. With great lack of discretion and of sympathetic feeling, Sylvester is said to have told the sorrowing father that the child's death was Heaven's punishment for rejecting good advice. At the monastery of Pesnocha, Ivan met Vassian, formerly Bishop of Kolomna, who had been deposed for perfidy and cruelty. This wicked old man gave him advice which exactly suited his inclinations. " If you wish to be a real autocrat, seek for no councillors wiser than yourself. Accept no advice. Give it. Always command, never obey. Then you will be a real sovereign and a terror to the boyars. Remember that the wisest councillor of a prince ends by becoming his master." Ivan raised Vassian's hand to his lips, saying, " My father could not have given advice that is more salutary."

From this point the third section of Ivan's reign begins, and in it he earned the designation, The Terrible.

In the meantime intercourse was beginning with the
West. In 1547 a Saxon named Schlitt told Ivan of the
progress in science and art which had been made in Germany, and was commissioned to secure artificers, apothe-
caries, doctors, printers, scholars, and others, and bring
them to Russia. In the attempt to do this he was stopped
by the Hanseatic League and imprisoned at Lubec, while
his companions were scattered. In 1557, however, he
reached Moscow, and others who had eluded the frontier
guards appeared in Russia about the same time.

Trading intercourse was begun by the arrival of a ship
from England commanded by Richard Chancellor. Accompanied by other two ships which were wrecked on the coast
of Norway, Chancellor left London in 1553, rounded the
North Cape, entered the White Sea, and when he came
to anchor at Fort St. Nicholas, found to his astonishment
that he was in Russia. He went up to Moscow, saw Ivan,
and returned to London with a letter to Edward VI. In
1555 he made a second voyage, and on his homeward
journey carried with him a charter from Ivan giving the
English company which he represented the sole right of
trading on Russian soil, and that without payment of
taxes. In May 1597 he was followed by Anthony Jenkin-
son, who, after reaching Moscow, crossed the Caspian Sea
and finished his journey at Bokhara. In recognition of
the service he had rendered Russia by opening these
Eastern regions to commerce, Ivan authorised the English
merchants to trade on all the rivers of the north and to
establish depots in the principal Russian towns.

But, although communication with England had begun,
intercourse with the Western nations of Europe was still
difficult, and Ivan and his advisers came into angry collision
on questions of policy. Sylvester and Adashev thought
that the Tartars should be finally destroyed before any
other enterprise of magnitude was started, and in this they
were supported by many boyars. Ivan thought otherwise. He was determined to open the way to the West at
once, and in 1558 he picked a quarrel with Livonia, captured
Dorpat, Narva, and other towns, and forced the Teutonic

Knights to ask help from Poland. Ivan's success extended the frontiers, which had to be guarded, and added much to Russia's danger. If harmony had existed between Ivan and his advisers, victory might have been possible, but they and their friends did everything they could to prevent the success of the war, and they exasperated Ivan by their animosity to his wife. His temper, always bad, became so savage that Sylvester thought it wise to flee to the monastery of St. Cyril. Ivan, however, ordered him away to the inhospitable solitude of the Solovetski. Adashev was imprisoned in Dorpat, and died there, probably by Ivan's orders. His mistress and five of his sons were executed. His brother, with his twelve-year-old son, his father-in-law, and several other relatives were also put to death. There is a story that when one of these was being roasted over a slow fire, Ivan himself raked the glowing coals together below the quivering body with his iron-tipped staff.

In the same year, exhausted by endless worry, Anastasia died. Ivan swore the boyars had poisoned her. He may have been right, but we cannot tell. What is certain is that he took a bloody revenge.

The event which let loose all his fury was the defection of Kurbski, a prince who boasted the blood of Ruric. In 1562 he had mismanaged an expedition against Livonia, and fearing Ivan's wrath, he committed the unpardonable sin of entering the service of Russia's chief enemy, Poland. He then wrote a letter justifying his desertion, and denouncing Ivan's cruelties. Legend says that Ivan, with his iron-tipped staff, nailed the letter-carrier's foot to the red staircase and kept it there while the letter was being read. Ivan replied, and the correspondence was carried on at intervals from 1564 till 1579. Kurbski wrote four letters. Ivan wrote two. Kurbski, not without reason, complained that Ivan had set aside the boyars' counsel, and had usurped an autocratic authority which did not belong to him. Ivan retorted that he had a divinely-given right to do what he pleased with his slaves. The expression of these opinions on both sides was accompanied with floods of virulent personal abuse.

7

Ivan now felt that if he did not master the boyars, the boyars would master him, and as he did not know how to reduce them to political impotence the only course that seemed open was to wipe them out. For this he needed a free hand, and he got it. On 3rd December 1564 he suddenly betook himself with his family to Alexandrov, a village seventy miles from Moscow, and on 3rd January 1565 he sent back two letters which filled the capital with consternation. One of these accused the boyars of neglecting the affairs of State, and of conspiring to rob him of his divinely-given authority. Because of this, he said he laid his anger on them and went to reside wherever God called him. In the other letter he simply assured the common people of his continued goodwill. The citizens of Moscow were now in a serious dilemma. They had to choose between the rule of an oligarchy, corrupt and cruel, and that of an autocrat who was certainly not less cruel. At last, spurred by the memory of their sufferings during Ivan's minority, they besought him to come back and govern as he pleased. He consented on conditions, and summoned them to meet him in February 1566 in the Red Square. He said if he were to continue as their Tsar he must be allowed to punish all who were disloyal, and to execute certain persons whom he named. Besides, he must not be troubled any longer by the intercession of the clergy. The people agreed to the terms he imposed.

On the following day he began operations. He beheaded six of Kurbski's adherents, and impaled a seventh. He then set about collecting a body of picked men, afterwards increased to six thousand, to act as the instruments of his will. They were clothed in black and armed to the teeth, and they carried a dog's head and a broom at their saddles, to show they were to worry the Tsar's enemies and sweep them off the earth. For their lodgings they were assigned certain streets in Moscow and other places, from which, although it was the depth of winter, the inhabitants were turned out. For their maintenance, districts were appropriated, and these embraced almost half the area of the country. This band was called the

Oprichniki. The estates and all pertaining to them were the Oprichnina. The section of the country left under the control of the district councils was called the Zemstchina, and Ivan did not interfere with these except by reserving power to revise and, if he thought fit, to cancel their decisions.

As his headquarters he created a special abode which from the devilry that went on in it might have been called Satan's seat. In the forests round Alexandrov he cleared a space, enclosed it with a wall and a moat, and on all the roads leading to it he placed gibbets to warn travellers of their fate if they ventured too near. Inside the wall he built a palace, a monastery, a chapel, rooms for his servants, and torture-chambers and dungeons for his prisoners. For company he selected three hundred of the Oprichniki, and formed them into a parody of a monastic brotherhood. He clothed them in black cassocks and skull-caps, assumed the title of their abbot, appointed one as sacristan and another as cellarer. If ever there were men who had a form of godliness but denied its power, it was Ivan and his black brotherhood. He may have deceived himself into thinking that he was religious, but whether his blasphemies were unconscious or deliberate, a more unholy confraternity has scarcely existed on earth.

The routine of the establishment was as follows. At 3 a.m. Ivan himself rang the bell for matins. The service lasted for hours, during which Ivan read the Scriptures, chanted prayers, and prostrated himself with such vigour that he sometimes bruised his head on the floor. At 8 a.m. the company met again to hear Mass. At 10 a.m. they sat down to table. While they were eating, Ivan read with a loud voice extracts from books of devotion. When the others had finished, Ivan dined alone, recited the Paternoster, and then went to superintend the torturing of the prisoners. Happy were those to whom death came quickly. Nothing pleased him better than to see men and women grovelling at his feet imploring mercy. Nothing maddened him so much as to see them defying him to do his worst. When their agony was more than usually awful, he left the torture chamber with a beaming face and returned to the church to resume his prayers. At 10 p.m. he retired to his bedchamber, usually dragging with him the weeping wife or daughter of one of his victims. If he could not sleep, he got three blind old men to tell him stories, or he drank himself into unconsciousness.

From their headquarters the Oprichniki scoured the country, and the more ferociously they behaved the higher they rose in their master's favour. Macarius, the Metropolitan, ventured very cautiously to intercede for some of those who were arrested. After his death in 1564 Athanasius succeeded him, but overcome by horror at the cruelties he had to witness, he retired after a year and cut himself off from the world. Ivan then compelled Germanus, Archbishop of Kazan, to assume office. In a private interview he tried to turn the Tsar from the bloody path he was pursuing. Ivan in a fury declared his See vacant, and summoned to Moscow, Philip, one of the most saintly men in Russia. He belonged to a noble family, and had known Ivan in youth. After ten years' residence in the Solovetski monastery, he became its abbot, and by his energy and wisdom conferred many blessings on it. At the same time he diffused the light of Christianity among the heathen tribes round the White Sea. When he discovered what was going on in the south he was astounded, and refused to accept office till the Oprichniki were disbanded. He also urged the bishops to support him in his stand for righteousness, justice, and mercy. But they failed him, and with great reluctance he yielded to Ivan's will.

After he accepted office it was not long till he felt compelled to speak out. At first he dealt with Ivan privately, till Ivan began to avoid seeing him. On one occasion there was a dramatic public encounter. On 31st May 1568, when Philip was conducting service in the Cathedral, Ivan entered with a band of Oprichniki dressed as monks and approached the Prelate for his blessing. Philip ignored him. A second and a third time he approached. Some one said, " The Tsar is here." Philip replied, " I do not recognise the Tsar in any such dress. I do not recognise him either in the acts of his government. What hast thou done, O Tsar, to put off from thee thine honour ? Fear the judgment of God. Here we are offering the bloodless sacrifice to the Lord, while behind the altar there is flowing the innocent blood of Christian men." Ivan in vain tried to silence him. " If living men were to hold their peace," said Philip, " the very stones would cry out." " Hold thy tongue," shouted Ivan, " and give me thy blessing. My subjects and my kinsmen rose against me and plotted my ruin." Philip retorted, " I never asked to be put into this See. Why didst thou call me from my hermitage ? " In a blazing passion Ivan cried, " I have been too pious. Now I will give thee and thy clergy something to complain of." The following day Prince Vassili Pronski was put to death with frightful torture, and for three weeks thereafter hell was let loose in Moscow and the neighbourhood.

Ivan took his revenge on Philip in June. Calling together the bishops of Novgorod, Riazan, and Suzdal, he ordered them to try Philip on the charge of embezzling the funds of the Solovetski monastery ; and the hegumen of the monastery, to his shame be it said, consented to act as prosecutor. Knowing that his condemnation was determined on, Philip boldly declared his innocence, divested himself of his mitre and cope, and walked towards the door of the court-room. Ivan called him back and ordered him to say Mass in the Cathedral the following day. While he was proceeding with the ritual, the Oprichniki rushed in, seized him, stripped him to his shirt, threw a tattered monk's frock round him, dragged him to a sledge and drove off, sweeping with their brooms the ground over which they passed. Two days later Philip was sent to Tver to be kept in close confinement. Two years later, when Ivan was on his way to Novgorod, he sent Maliuta Skuratov, the chief of the Oprichniki, to Tver. When he left the Metropolitan's cell, Philip was dead.

In pursuance of his policy of exterminating his enemies, Ivan struck a heavy blow at Novgorod. Novgorod was known to be fretting at its subjection to Moscow, and a criminal whom its magistrates had punished took his revenge by forging a letter in the name of the Archbishop and some of the leading citizens, offering to place the city in the King of Poland's hands. Then he guided the Tsar's police to the place where the letter was hidden. Ivan, without making any inquiries, set out with a large force, sacked and burned Tver and Klin as he passed them, and reached Moscow on the Feast of the Epiphany in 1570. The signal for massacre was given at a banquet, and the bloody work went on unceasingly for five weeks. The number of the victims has been set as high as sixty thousand. It is no doubt an exaggerated figure, but it indicates the awful things that were done. When there were no more human beings worth murdering, the monasteries and churches and many dwelling-houses were reduced to ruins. The trembling survivors of multiplied horrors were finally collected and commanded to pray for the prosperity of the Tsar and his family.[1]

On the homeward journey, Pskov was saved from a similar fate by a monk half-imbecile and half-fanatic. It was Lent, and he offered Ivan flesh to eat. The Tsar refused it, saying he did not eat flesh at Lent. " Thou doest worse," said the monk. " Thou eatest human flesh and blood, forgetting not Lent, but Christ Himself." Then he threatened Ivan with destruction by a thunderbolt if he harmed a hair of a child's head in the city.

On reaching Moscow, Ivan set about arresting all whom he suspected of disloyalty. After some months he was convinced he had got most of them into his net, and on 25th January 1570 three hundred miserable survivors of awful tortures were taken to the Red Square. Gibbets were ready for them, and furnaces and cauldrons of boiling water, and red-hot pincers and needles, and claws for tearing their flesh, and other devilish implements. But so far as spectators were concerned, the Square was empty. The people had hidden themselves. They were therefore hunted out and compelled to listen to a long harangue on

[1] Horsey, 162.

the old theme of disloyalty to the Tsar himself and danger
to the State. Ivan finished by saying he would show his
clemency by sparing some of the rebels, but the rest must
die. Then one hundred and twenty died in agony.

By these methods Ivan ruined about twelve thousand
boyar and noble families, but he did nothing to displace
the boyars as a class from their constitutional position.
He simply reduced the number of those who could assist
in the government of the country, and weakened its
administrative strength.

That Ivan's conduct was not the outcome of mere
homicidal mania is shown in various ways. For one
thing, he kept a record of his victims. Long as it is, it is
not exhaustive. In the monastery of St. Cyril there is a
list of 3470 names in his own handwriting. Many of
these are followed by such phrases as " With his wife and
children," " With his daughters," " With his sons." Under
the head of Novgorod we read, " Remember, Lord, the
souls of thy servants, inhabitants of this town, to the
number of 1505 persons." In similar documents preserved
elsewhere he simply mentions, " A number of men, women,
and children whose names are known only to God." In
none of the lists is there the slightest indication of remorse
for his guilt in connection with them.

Another indication that his mind was clear is given by
the fact that a day or two after the scenes in the Red
Square he took part in a full dress theological debate. It
happened that one of the members of a Polish Embassy
then in the country was John Rokita, one of the Confraternity of the Bohemian Brethren. Audience was granted
to him on 8th February 1570. There was a large company.
Ivan spoke first, and he was not one whom an opponent
could afford to despise. He was exceedingly well read,
in fact he was one of the most learned men in Russia in his
day. He knew by heart long passages of Scripture. He
was familiar with such Greek Fathers as Basil, Gregory,
and Chrysostom. He was acquainted with the Greek
Chronicles accepted as history, and he knew something
about classical antiquity. His arguments were rambling,

and his language was both vehement and abusive ; but he had ready wit, great powers of sarcasm, and he was full of zeal. He attacked the Reformed doctrines in a speech to which Rokita replied, laying emphasis on the errors of Rome. Ivan closed the debate in another speech in which he complimented Rokita on his learning and eloquence, and summarised his answers to what Rokita had said. When Rokita left the country Ivan had this summary written down, and enclosed in a richly-bound volume which he offered as a parting gift.

During this time of terror war was going on with Poland. In 1556 a truce was arranged, and Ivan assembled the Great Council to consider what should be done. It decided that the war should continue, but Russia was not able to continue it, partly because the Tartars and the Swedes were menacing the country, and partly because Ivan's excesses were shattering his nerves. In 1569 the Tartars crossed the Volga. In 1571 they reached Moscow, stormed it, and burned almost the whole of it except the Kremlin. As many as 800,000 men and women are said to have perished, and 150,000 more were carried into captivity. After all deductions are made from these figures, it is plain that the blow to Russia's prestige and strength was great. After the Tartars retired, Ivan, who had fled for his life, reconstructed his army. While he was doing this, the Tartar Khan sent him an insulting letter charging him with cowardice and demanding the surrender of Astrakhan. Ivan replied humbly, but learning that he was gathering his forces together, the Tartars advanced a second time. On this occasion they were successfully repulsed, and Ivan at once became as scornful as he had been servile.

The Tartar menace on the east was made more dangerous by the Polish menace on the west. The Congress of Lublin in 1569 placed a large number of Orthodox Russians under Polish rule, and left them at the mercy of the Catholic Church, with the result that they were miserably persecuted. They appealed to Russia for help, and when Sigismund Augustus II. died in 1572 without leaving issue, and ending the dynasty of Jagiello, and when the Polish nobles invited candidates for the vacant throne, Ivan suggested that he himself would make them an excellent sovereign. The Poles were, however, afraid of losing their national identity, and they chose Henry of Valois, younger brother of Charles IX. of France. Six months afterward Charles IX. died, and Henry promptly returned to Paris. In 1575 the Poles set Stephen Batory on the throne, and he proved himself one of the best rulers they ever had.

As Batory declared his intention of recapturing all that Russia had seized, Ivan attacked him in 1576 when he was unable to defend himself effectually, and made extensive conquests in the Baltic provinces. Then when complete victory was within his grasp, he faltered and fled to his gloomy stronghold of Alexandrov to drown care in debauchery. In 1579, when he repeated the attack, Batory not only cast out the Russians from the Baltic provinces, but invaded Russia itself. Ivan, in a panic, sought the mediation of Pope Gregory XIII. The Pope was delighted, and in May 1581 commissioned Anthony Possevin, a Jesuit who was credited with great skill in converting heretics, to go to Moscow, giving him instructions to effect a truce between Russia and Poland in such a way as to convince Ivan that he owed it to the powerful influence of Rome, to secure the concession of a free route through Russia to the East, to obtain permission for priests to reside in Russia, and to build churches, to bring Russia into alliance with the Western powers against the Turks, and chiefly to use every effort to unite the Orthodox Church of Russia with the Catholic Church of the West.

On 18th August Possevin was received by the Tsar and presented him with the Pontiff's gifts : a crucifix carved in rock crystal, a rosary of precious stones mounted in gold, a copy of the Records of the Council of Florence, and also a letter to the Tsarina Anastasia, who had been dead for years, and whose place had already been filled several times. In a special letter Gregory assured Ivan of his goodwill, promised to secure peace with Batory, and to recover everything which Russia had lost. In recom-

pense for this he hoped that Ivan would restore peace
to the Church by uniting the Orthodox with the Catholics.
Possevin added verbally that when peace was concluded
the Pope suggested an alliance of the Christians against
the Turks, and promised 50,000 soldiers as his contribution
to the expedition.

Ivan thanked the Pope for his kindness, praised the
proposed alliance, gave Italian merchants permission to
trade and to worship God privately after their own fashion,
but said bluntly that Russia did not want Catholic Churches,
and made it plain that the whole success of Possevin's
mission depended on the issue of the negotiations with
Batory.   Possevin then went off to see what could be done.

During Possevin's absence an incident occurred which
had far-reaching influence on the nation's fortunes, and
was for Ivan himself the beginning of the end.   He is said
to have seen the wife of his son Ivan in the palace much
more scantily clad than became a woman in her condition,
and to have beaten her so savagely that she miscarried on
the following day.   The Tsarevitch vehemently reproached
his father, whereupon Ivan struck him on the head with
his iron-tipped staff and felled him to the ground.   Four
days afterwards, on 10th November 1581, the young
man died.   For three days the Tsar sat beside the
corpse, taking neither nourishment nor sleep.   After the
burial he spent his nights in weeping and giving way to
hysterical remorse.   One morning he called his boyars
together, told them that the hand of God was heavy on
him, and that the only thing left for him was to end his
days in a monastery.   Further, he said that Feodor,
his second son, was not fit to govern, and could not live
long, so he begged them to choose a worthy successor to
whom he could resign the crown.   Fearing that he was
only seeking a pretext to send them down the bloody road,
which so many of their order had already travelled, they
begged him to continue as their sovereign.   He yielded,
and in token of his grief sent ten thousand roubles to
the Patriarchs of Constantinople, Antioch, Alexandria, and
Jerusalem, asking them to pray for the repose of his son's soul.

In February 1582 Possevin reappeared in Moscow, and indicated the arrangement he had concluded with Batory. It could not have been more humiliating to Russia if it had been drawn up after defeat in a decisive battle. Poland was allowed to recover all it had lost during twenty-four years, while Ivan had to content himself with the bare fact that he had obtained a truce.

Possevin then begged for an audience in which to set forth his views on the reunion of the Churches. Ivan consented to hear him, but only in presence of his councillors. He also hoped there would be no discussion, for he desired peace. On 21st February Possevin entered the throne-room. After the usual compliments, Ivan begged him not to raise the question of religion. Said he, " I am now fifty-one years of age. I was brought up in the Orthodox Church, and I cannot turn traitor to it at the end of my life." Possevin assured him that if he would study the Acts of the First Councils, and specially the decision of the Council of Florence, his difficulties would vanish like clouds before the sunshine of truth, and he would not only contract an alliance with the most powerful monarchs of Europe, but would regain Kiev and become master of the whole Byzantine Empire which God had taken from the Greeks as a punishment for their schism and disobedience to Jesus Christ.

Ivan replied quietly that he had not written to the Pope about religion, he left questions about religion to the clergy. He promised protection to foreign merchants and even to Latin priests on condition that they did not proselytise among the Russian people; but he ignored Possevin's reference to the Council of Florence and the Crusade against the Turks. Possevin then set out to prove that the Russians were novices in the Christian faith, and that Rome was its metropolis. Ivan lost his temper. " I will not," said he, " debate with you on dogma, but I will ask you one question. I see that you shave. Neither ecclesiastics nor laymen are commanded to do this. From what text is this custom taken ? " Then he went on, " I am told they carry the Pope on a throne as if he were an angel on a cloud, and, kneeling, the people kiss his foot, on the sole of whose shoe the crucifixion is embroidered." Possevin answered that these honours were paid to the Pope as the representative of St. Peter, and that all true Christians recognised him as such. Ivan replied, " Our subjects give us obedience and respect as they did to our ancestors. To potentates belong the honour due to potentates, to prelates the honour due to Christ. The Popes who have obeyed the commandments of Christ and have walked according to the Apostles and the teaching of the seven Great Councils have been truly equal to the Apostles, but a Pope who acts contrary to the doctrine of Christ and Holy Scripture is not a pastor, but a wolf." Possevin replied, " If the Pope be a wolf, I have nothing more to say but this, Why didst thou send to him to succour thee ? Why didst thou style him pastor of the Church ? " At this retort Ivan rose in fury, brandishing his staff and shouting, " Wast thou brought up among peasants that thou darest to use such language to us ? " Knowing what Ivan was capable of doing, Possevin trembled, but the Tsar restrained himself and said, " I told you religious discussion could scarcely terminate without something disagreeable."

Further interviews made no change in the situation. In getting peace with Batory, Ivan had got all he wanted, and he did not care how soon the Romish envoy left the country. After a farewell audience he made his exit from Moscow on 15th March, and for many years direct relations between the courts of Russia and of Rome ceased.

The misfortunes of Russia in the West were to some extent balanced by its expansion in the East. The free-booter Yermak captured the Tartar capital in Siberia in October 1581. Further successes raised the question how was the conquered country to be retained under Russian authority. Yermak solved it by the bold expedient of sending his comrade Koltso direct to Ivan with a letter expressing profound regret for all his past misdeeds, and offering the vast and wealthy region he had subdued as a gift to the Russian crown. Ivan, overjoyed, received the messenger graciously, sent Yermak a free pardon, and bestowed on him the title Prince of Siberia. After Ivan's death Yermak went on with his conquests, till in August 1584 he, and practically all his followers, were slain in a surprise night attack on the banks of the river Irtish. He has left behind him a deathless name, and is one of the greatest of Russia's popular heroes.

In the summer of 1581 an English doctor named Robert Jacobi arrived in Moscow with a letter of introduction from Queen Elizabeth. Ivan, who had already been repeatedly married, asked if there were any women in England worthy of the hand of a sovereign. Jacobi named Lady Mary Hasting, Elizabeth's niece, and in 1582 a messenger was sent to England to see her. In case Elizabeth raised the objection that Ivan had a wife already, the messenger was to say that Ivan was tired of her, and was ready to dismiss her. Lady Mary was at first interested in the proposal, but finally rejected it. On his departure from England the messenger took with him Jerome Bowes as Elizabeth's ambassador, with full powers to settle the political relations between the two countries. Ivan found, to his chagrin, that Bowes would not commit England to an alliance in which all the advantage would be on the side of Russia, and in a rage ordered Bowes and his suite to leave Moscow. But he really admired the Englishman's sturdy loyalty to his Queen and his country, and not only recalled him after each dismissal, but said to his courtiers, " Would to God my servants were as faithful to me."

Ivan's health was now failing. His body, weakened by excess and bloated by corruption, had become loathsome, and was filled with pain. His mind, haunted by gloomy memories, looked into the future with foreboding, and a great comet blazing in the sky filled him with superstitious terror. He had long passed the point at which he could appreciate the consolations of the Christian faith, and like Saul who, in the night of his despair, betook himself to the Witch of Endor, he sent to Finland for sorcerers. With some difficulty seventy of these were brought to Moscow. They gave him no comfort, they only foretold the day of his death. Sir Jerome Horsey, the English ambassador, gives a striking account of one of the closing scenes when Ivan caused himself to be carried to the Treasury and displayed his precious jewels to his attendants, and descanted on their virtues.

On 18th March 1584, the date which the sorcerers had specified, he sent to tell them that he was as heartwhole as ever he was, and that he meant to burn them all alive for their lies. " Be not so wrathful," was the Finns' reply, " the day ends with the setting of the sun." [1] Soon afterwards, as he sat in bed playing chess with Boris Godounov, he suddenly closed his eyes and fell back in a swoon. Doctors were instantly summoned, the Metropolitan threw a monk's cloak round him, gave him the name Jonah, and read the prayers for the dying; but Ivan was already beyond all they could do. He was standing before his heavenly Judge to give an account of his dreadful career on earth.

The Russian is a strange mixture, and perhaps we err on the side of severity when we judge him by Western standards. One and the same man will display a desire after holiness taking the form of ascetic self-martyrdom, and will at another time display an almost unbelievable ferocity and bestiality. Through the lips of one of his characters, Mitia Karamazov, Dostoievsky says : " I cannot bear to see how a man with a heart above the ordinary, and a superior mind, begins by setting up a Madonna as his ideal, and ends by descending to the depths of Sodom. And what seems to me more awful still is that with the thought of Sodom in his feelings, he finds a place in his heart for the vision of the Madonna, and is burning for her, really and truly burning, as at the time when he was an innocent youth." The problem of uniting these two extremes is presented in its most difficult form by the character of Ivan the Terrible, with this qualification that, if he ever had a vision of the Madonna, it never made a real appeal to him.

[1] Horsey, pp. 200–1.

CHAPTER XIV

FEODOR I., GODOUNOV, AND THE FALSE DIMITRI

FEODOR, who ascended the throne at the age of twenty-seven, resembled his father in nothing. He had neither his imposing presence, his mental ability, his iron will, nor his ferocious cruelty. He was slender of stature, pale, and thin. A timid smile hovered on his lips, but his features were expressionless. His one passion was to take part in Church services, and his one amusement was to ring church bells.

Knowing Feodor's incapacity, Ivan in his will appointed a Council of five to carry on the government. One of these was Boris Godounov, whose sister, Irene, Feodor had married. The Council promptly took measures to secure the public peace, and in pursuance of this policy it sent Ivan's widow, Maria Nagoi, with her young son Dimitri, and others of the family, to Ouglitch.

The members of the Council then began to intrigue against each other until Godounov succeeded in removing his rivals from his path. Feodor was ruler of Russia in name. Godounov was ruler in reality. His management of foreign affairs was so successful that he regained for Russia all the territory that Ivan had lost, and if he had been bold enough to make a definite alliance with Sweden he might have made more extensive conquests, but he tried to play off Sweden against Poland, and finished by alienating both. His management of internal affairs did much to assist the nation's development in art and science. He added a new section to Moscow, fortified Archangel and other important towns, revised the system of taxation, and peopled empty districts with settlers from other parts of the country.

Two events of importance are associated with his reign
—the binding of the peasants to the soil and the institution
of the Patriarchate.

It is open to question whether the binding of the peasants
to the soil was the inspiring motive of Godounov's policy.
The problem he had to face arose largely from the fact that
the peasants were not remaining on their locations. Their
obligations to the landowners were so heavy, and the
burden of taxation was so crushing, that many of them
absconded and hid themselves. As it was the commune
that was taxed, and not the individual, the responsibilities
of those they left behind them were made the heavier by
their departure, and Godounov saw that unless something
were done to keep the number of peasants in each commune
at a steady and normal figure, rebellion on a large scale
was inevitable, and the economic system of the country
would collapse. Therefore he decreed that any absconding
peasant who was found in any part of the country within
ten years of his disappearance from his original place of
abode must be brought back to it, and must resume the
financial obligations from which he thought he had shaken
himself free. Further, in order to check the abduction of
peasants from communes by fraud or by violence, which
was practised by the bailiffs of the monasteries and by the
agents of the great landowners, he issued an Order on 8th
November 1601 which allowed none but small landowners
to abduct peasants, and not more than two at a time.
Another Order, dated November 1602, added that peasants
who had removed from one place to another, and who
had been counted taxpayers in the place they left, were to
be counted taxpayers in the place to which they went.
A third Order, dated February 1606, forbade the reduction
of the taxpaying peasant to the level of a slave who paid
no taxes, and, with the intention of holding the tyranny
of the landowners in check, a fourth Order specified the
maximum of the obligations by which the peasants were
to be bound. It seems certain that the maximum was
fixed too high, and as the landowners treated it as the
minimum the position of the peasants was made more

desperate than it had been before. The practical result of Godounov's legislation was that the peasants ceased to be able to move about the country at their pleasure, and that they could not ease themselves of the fiscal load which was laid on their backs.

The institution of the Patriarchate was brought about not so much by definite plan as by an accident. In 1586 Joachim, Patriarch of Antioch, came to Moscow on a begging expedition, and at Feodor's request Godounov sounded him on the subject of creating a Russian Patriarchate. Joachim replied that he must consult the other Patriarchs before giving a definite answer. In July 1588 Jeremiah, Patriarch of Constantinople, came to Moscow also in quest of subscriptions. The Church which he represented had fallen on evil days, and its poverty was not entirely due to Turkish rapacity. Shortly before Jeremiah's appearance in Moscow there were four rivals for the Patriarchal throne, Metrophanes, Pachomius, Theolept, and Jeremiah, and the struggle between them was fierce. Jeremiah was thrown into prison, then he was banished to Rhodes, and Pachomius was made Patriarch. Soon afterwards the Sultan banished Pachomius and installed Jeremiah in his place. Then through the intrigues of Greek eunuchs and women of the seraglio, and as the result of enormous bribes, Jeremiah was dismissed in favour of Theolept. By similar means Jeremiah ousted him in his turn and got possession of the Patriarchal dignity once more. One result of all this was that the coffers of the Church were empty. It could not pay its tribute to the Sultan, and was in danger of being suppressed. The rivals called a truce, and Theolept went to Georgia and Persia to raise funds. Pachomius went to Cyprus and Egypt. Jeremiah, with Dositheus and Arsenius, bishops of Monembasa and Ellason respectively, went to Russia.

Feodor, overjoyed at their arrival, proposed that Jeremiah should escape from all his troubles by remaining in Russia and setting up his Patriarchal throne in the city of Vladimir. Jeremiah, however, refused on the ground that the creation of a new Patriarchate must be the act of a

8

Synod, and Dositheus and Arsenius supported him. Pressure of various sorts was then brought to bear on him, until, in spite of the protests of his companions, he yielded and agreed to create a separate Russian Patriarchate.

The Russian bishops were convened to Moscow, and they agreed to submit three names to the Tsar. Feodor immediately selected Godounov's friend Job, who was at that time Metropolitan of Moscow, and whose name was first on the list. On the 23rd January 1589, as Job was conducting service in the Cathedral, and was standing with a lighted candle in his hand, one of the clergy approached him and said with a loud voice, " The Orthodox Tsar, the Œcumenical Patriarch, and the Sacred Council raise thee to the Patriarchal throne of Vladimir and of Moscow and of all Russia." Job replied, " I am an unworthy sinner, but since the Tsar, the Œcumenical Patriarch, and the Sacred Council raise me to this important dignity, I accept with thanks." The consecration took place on 26th January, and when the ceremony was ended Job received from Feodor a precious cross, a mantle of green velvet embroidered with pearls, and a white mitre. He was also commanded to style himself " Chief of the bishops, Father of the fathers, and Patriarch of all the Western countries by the grace of God and the will of the Tsar." At the close of these proceedings, mounted on an ass and followed by an imposing procession, he went round the Kremlin, sprinkling its walls with holy water and reciting prayers for the preservation of the city. The day closed with a great banquet.

A document was afterwards prepared and sealed with the Tsar's seal in which the first Œcumenical Prelate was declared to be the Patriarch of Constantinople, the second that of Alexandria, the third that of Moscow and Russia, the fourth that of Antioch, and the fifth that of Jerusalem. It declared that in all time coming the Russian Patriarch was to be chosen and consecrated without reference to the consent or approbation of the Greeks. Feodor was resolved that from the first the Patriarch of Moscow should be recognised not only as independent of his brother of Con-

stantinople, but also as equal to him. Job was therefore
ordered to kiss the lips of Jeremiah, and not to lay aside his
crozier unless Jeremiah did so too ; to sit side by side with
him on an elevated platform, and to retire from it by a
different door. To these marks of distinction others were
added. When the Patriarch left the church a lamp was
to be borne before him, and his exit was to be accompanied
with the ringing of bells. He was to wear on weekdays
a cowl embroidered with crosses and seraphim, and a silk
mantle with stripes. When he went out of doors he was
to carry his cross and his crozier, and his coach was to be
drawn by six horses.

Some days afterwards Feodor increased the number
of the Russian Metropolitans to four—those of Novgorod,
Kazan, Rostov, and Kroutitsk ; raised six bishoprics to
the rank of archbishoprics—those of Vologda, Suzdal,
Nijni-Novgorod, Smolensk, Riazan, and Tver ; resuscitated
the Bishopric of Kolomna and Bransk, and added to them
five new ones—those of Pskov, Kiev, Oustiog, Bielozero,
and Dimitrov.

As difficulties might have arisen from the fact that the
Patriarchate of Moscow was constituted by Jeremiah alone,
steps were taken to regularise his proceedings. On his
return to Constantinople he called a Council which met in
February 1591. This Council confirmed what had been
done at Moscow, acknowledged the Patriarch of Russia
as taking the place of the Roman bishop who had fallen
into heresy, but it assigned him the fifth place in rank,
i.e. next after the Patriarch of Jerusalem. The document
embodying this finding bore the signatures of the Patriarchs
of Constantinople, of Antioch, and of Jerusalem (the
Patriarch of Alexandria was dead), as well as of forty-two
Eastern Metropolitans, nineteen archbishops, and twenty
bishops, and of the other clergy who were present at the
Council. It was taken to Moscow by Dionysius, Metropolitan of Tirnoff and all Bulgaria. Feodor was disappointed
that the Russian Metropolitan was only fifth on the list, but
he gave Dionysius a large subscription for the erection of
a new building in Constantinople to replace the ancient

Church of the Almighty Ruler which had been seized by the Sultan.

The fabric of the autocracy was now beyond attack; but Godounov's position was far from secure, for his safety depended on the life of the Tsar. One of his most deadly enemies was the Metropolitan Dionysius, who conspired with the princes of the house of Shuiski to persuade Feodor to divorce his wife because of her sterility, and to espouse another. Godounov perceived that if Feodor did this, his own tenure of office would be short. What made his prospects even more threatening was the fact that Dimitri, the heir to the throne after Feodor, still lived, and Dimitri's relatives were only waiting till he succeeded his brother to hurl him to political perdition. From Godounov's point of view it was desirable that Dimitri should disappear, and in May 1591 Moscow was electrified by the news that the boy had died at Ouglitch. It is said that a brawl occurred, in which the boy was killed, that his relatives and the townsfolk endeavoured to avenge his death, and that fighting took place in which some of Godounov's retainers lost their lives. Popular excitement rose to such a height that Godounov sent a commission to Ouglitch to inquire what had taken place. It reported that Dimitri had fallen on a knife in a fit of epilepsy. The report was received with universal scepticism. Dimitri's death suited Godounov's purpose so well that he was believed to have arranged it, and the subsequent proceedings strengthened that belief. On the charge of creating the riot, Dimitri's mother was forced to take the veil, her relatives were brought to Moscow, tortured and banished. Two hundred of the citizens of Ouglitch were put to death. The remainder were deported wholesale to Siberia and the town was destroyed. Then, when all who could have given testimony as to the real cause of the prince's death were put out of the way, the Patriarch Job made a solemn declaration that Dimitri had died according to the will of God, and for the time being the incident seemed to be closed.

Godounov now composed himself to wait till, in the

natural course of events, Feodor passed away ; and at last on 7th January 1598 Feodor died leaving no child, and with him the line of princes descended from Ruric came to a end.

Godounov had only one step more to take, but he was unwilling to take it without the approbation of the people. That approbation, stimulated by the threats and blows of his agents, was given. On 17th February 1598 an assembly held in the Kremlin commissioned the Patriarch Job to wait on him and declare his election to the vacant throne. After protesting his unworthiness, Godounov said piously, " Let the will of the Lord be done." [1]

He began his career with vigour in his foreign policy, and with clemency at home, but he failed to win the confidence of his subjects, and as the proofs of their disaffection increased, so also did his severity. One after another of the boyars was got rid of by imprisonment, exile, or execution. Among these was Feodor Nikita, head of the house of Romanov, who was compelled to become a monk, and to change his name to Philaret. But Godounov still failed to find the security he desired, and news from Poland convinced him that the dangers of the past were about to be doubled by the dangers that menaced him in the future.

The efforts of the Polish king to establish the Catholic faith in his own dominions and to propagate it in Russia were strenuously assisted by the Jesuits. They were first introduced into the diocese of Vilna, and their success there was made easy by the corruption of the Orthodox clergy. Besides, the Royal influence was strongly in their favour, and one after another of the great families which had accepted Calvinism abjured it. Some of the highest clergy followed their example, and Terletski, Bishop of Loutsk, Potief, Bishop of Vladimir, and Ragoza, Metropolitan of Kiev, arranged to hold a Synod at Brest Litovsk to offer the submission of the Orthodox Church in these regions to the Pope.[2] The Synod met early in 1595, and Terletski and Potief were sent to inform Pope Clement VIII. that their Church was willing to acknowledge the supremacy of Rome on condition that its doctrine and

[1] Ralston, p. 214. [2] Mouravieff, p. 140.

ceremonies and discipline were left intact. They were received by His Holiness who, in the beginning of 1596, published the Bull, *Magnus Dominus et Laudabilis Nimis*, proclaiming the consummation of the union. He also ordered *Te Deums* to be sung and medals to be struck in honour of the happy event. Thus the Uniate Church began.

The Synod of Brest had, however, acted without the knowledge of the common people, and when they discovered what had been done in their name, they were furious. A second Synod was held at Brest in October 1596, at which the Uniate bishops excommunicated those who refused to follow them. At the same time the Orthodox bishops excommunicated those who had allied themselves with Rome, and Nicephorus, the Patriarch's deputy, placed the Uniates under the malediction of Constantinople.

In these borderlands the Orthodox Church was now rent in twain. In doctrine, in discipline, in ceremonial, and in the language used in the services, the two sections were identical. The difference was that one section was united to Rome, while the other remained in communion with Moscow and Constantinople. The hostility between the two was bitter, and the King of Poland, who was determined to secure the triumph of Catholicism, tried to strike a blow at the heart of Orthodoxy by patronising a pretender to the Russian throne. Whether or not there was a formal contract is doubtful. The practical arrangement was that the Poles and the Uniates supported the Pretender, and the Pretender supported them.[1]

The Pretender first appeared in Lithuania, at Bragin, in the house of Prince Adam Wisnowieski, where he was employed as a menial. During an illness which seemed likely to be fatal he revealed to his confessor what he said was his origin. He declared himself to be the Prince Dimitri, who was said to have died at Ouglitch, but who had really escaped. His confessor repeated the story to the prince, who accepted it, and infected others with his belief in its truth. The Pretender rose rapidly in favour, and was betrothed to Marina, daughter of Prince George Niszek,

[1] Howe, *False Dimitri*, p. 284.

Palatine of Sandomir, to whom he made promises whose fulfilment was contingent on his reaching the Russian throne. At the same time he made himself agreeable to the Jesuits by a letter to Pope Clement VIII., dated 24th April 1604, in which he declared his entrance to the Roman communion as one of the flock of the chief pastor of Christendom. The Papal legate at once took him under his protection. The King of Poland gave him forty thousand crowns, acknowledged him Tsar of Russia, and allowed Polish nobles and gentry to come to his aid with all the retainers they could collect.

Godounov, alarmed by the news of the attack that was preparing, sent Sigismund a letter in September 1604 upbraiding him for espousing the Pretender's cause and giving the official Russian version of the Pretender's origin and character. According to Godounov the so-called Dimitri was a monk named Grishka Otrepiev, who had been a deacon in the Chudov Monastery, from which he had fled, fearing punishment for bad conduct. He then joined the Cossacks and thereafter he had entered the service of Prince Wisnowieski. The Patriarch Job endorsed Godounov's letter, but the people who knew how much blood Godounov had shed not only remained sceptical of the truth of these official statements, but convinced themselves that the Pretender's claim rested on a firmer basis than Godounov allowed.

After baffling an attempt to kidnap him, the Pretender crossed the frontiers of Russia. Town after town received him, and his onward march resembled a triumphal progress. Godounov's army interposed repeated checks, and it might have routed his forces completely had not the whole situation been suddenly changed by Godounov's death on 13th April 1605. The cause of his death is uncertain. He rose from dinner in his usual health. Two hours afterwards he just had time to don a monk's frock and assume the name Bogolep before he expired.

Nothing could have been more fortunate for Dimitri's interest. Godounov's army went over to his side, and everywhere the people rose in his favour. On the other hand, the Patriarch Job denounced their disloyalty to Orthodoxy and their lack of patriotism, with the result that when he was conducting the service in the Cathedral of the Assumption, he was seized, stripped of his robes, and thrown into a cart on which he was dragged to the Staritsky Monastery. The mob at the same time burst into the palace, seized Godounov's wife, his son Feodor, and his daughter Xenia. Ten days afterward Feodor was cut to pieces, his mother was strangled, and his sister was condemned to perpetual imprisonment.

On the 30th June 1605 Dimitri entered Moscow amid the acclamations of the people. He began his reign with moderation, he shed no blood, but he banished the surviving members of Godounov's family. He recalled Philaret Romanov and made him Metropolitan of Pskov, he also recalled Philaret's wife and their young son, Michael. He brought back the coffins of the Nagois to Moscow and buried them with honour, but the coffin of Godounov was lifted from the Church of the Archangel and was buried in the monastery of Barsonophiev, where it remained till the reign of Shuiski, when it was once more lifted and buried for the last time in the Troitska Lavra. He pardoned those who had fought against him ; and when the widow of Ivan IV. acknowledged him as her son in a dramatic interview, Moscow was convinced that the rightful heir had reached the throne. He was crowned on the 30th July.

Almost at once his troubles began. If he was really a Russian and the son of Ivan IV. there was little to suggest it There was, in fact, much in his conduct that contradicted every Russian tradition, and day after day he outraged public sentiment. When he approached the city, the clergy went out to meet him. He drowned their *Te Deum* by the noise of his military band. When the bishops talked solemnly about the seven Œcumenical Councils, he said flippantly that there might be an eighth. He deposed the Patriarch Job, who, with all his faults, was Russian, and appointed Ignatius, who was a Greek. In defiance of general hostility to everything Roman, he welcomed the visits of the Papal legate. In contempt of

the claims of the Russian nobles he filled his Court with
Poles, and he told the boyars that their wits would be
sharpened by education, and their manners improved by
foreign travel.   He refused to wear the usual Russian robes,
or to dress his hair in the usual Russian style.   He ate
veal, a prohibited food, and instead of sleeping off the
effects of his dinner, he walked about or he rode at a furious
gallop.   Worst of all, he called the monks lazy, made
annoying inquiries into their wealth, confiscated a large
part of it for a proposed expedition against the Turks, and
left them only a bare subsistence.   The people began to
question whether, after all, he was really Ivan's son, and
the question has never been answered.   It can scarcely be
denied that a real Russian, trained in the customs and
traditions of his country, would not have acted as Dimitri
did unless he had a singular lack of common sense, and it
is on his amazing behaviour that the case against him is
founded.

When Marina, his bride, arrived on 12th May 1606, it
seemed as if she had set herself to increase the exasperation
of popular feeling.   She brought with her a numerous
body of Polish nobles and gentry.   These were accompanied by their retainers, and they were not dressed like
guests going to a wedding.   They were clad in steel, and
armed as if they were about to begin a campaign.   Marina
herself was lodged in a nunnery, and she laughed its regulations to scorn.   She refused to receive instruction in
the Orthodox faith, she ridiculed the long prayers of the
priests, and amused herself with masquerades.   She refused
to wear the conventional dress of a Russian bride, and
insisted, although in vain, on wearing robes of a modern
fashion.   She refused to be baptized into the Orthodox
Church, and finally she arranged to be married on what
was called an unlucky day, Friday the 18th May, the eve
of the Festival of St. Nicholas.   The Poles who escorted
her to church behaved themselves during the ceremonial
with scandalous irreverence.   Up till the last moment
the people waited patiently, expecting to hear her abjure
the Latin faith, but they waited in vain.   In the eyes of

patriotic and pious Russians she left the church as she
entered it, a dangerous foreigner and an obstinate heretic.
The wedding was followed by a banquet in the palace, but
there was perplexity and wrath in the city.   The drunken
Poles returning to their lodgings insulted the women they
met on the streets, and drew swords on those who tried to
protect them.

In these circumstances there was no difficulty in foment-
ing rebellion.   Eleven days after the wedding there was a
riot.   Soon afterwards Shuiski and the boyars effected a
coup d'état.   Shuiski made a violent speech, then raising
a sword in one hand and carrying a cross in the other, he
led the way to the Tsar's apartments, shouting, " Death to
the heretic."   Dimitri jumped from a window, broke his
leg in the fall, and as he lay helpless, was stabbed to death.
Marina was imprisoned.   For three days Dimitri's body
lay in the public square, naked and exposed to outrage.
After it was buried, reports began to circulate that strange
lights had been seen flickering over the grave.   These were
taken to prove that Dimitri was a sorcerer.   The body
was therefore disinterred and burnt to ashes, and the ashes
were blown to the winds from a cannon's mouth.   The
meteoric reign which closed in this way lasted scarcely
eleven months.

A great massacre followed, in which twelve hundred
Poles perished.   Vassili Shuiski was then proclaimed Tsar
by a small party of boyars who, before they allowed him
to ascend the throne, compelled him to renounce the right
of arbitrary punishment without proof of guilt, the right of
confiscating the property of those who had been condemned,
and the right of secret trial with torture.   Most important
of all, he had to agree not to take any decision of importance
without consulting his nobles.   On 4th June 1606 he sent
a letter to James I. of England announcing his succession,
and asserting that the fallen Pretender was no son of Ivan,
but was really the monk Otrepiev.   Then began the period
of Troubles.   There was discontent and confusion everywhere, and in 1608, in the hope of securing relief from
oppressive taxation and vindicating their personal liberty,

a large number of peasants and others rose in rebellion
under a man who is sometimes called the second Dimitri,
and who, like his predecessor, claimed to be Ivan's son.
He defeated Shuiski's forces on 24th April 1608, intercepted
Marina on her way to Poland, and induced her to marry
him, whereupon almost all Russia swung round to his side.

Shuiski's position was now desperate. He had neither
men nor money, and while the discontented peasants were
gathering round the second Pretender's banner at the
village of Tushina in preparation for an attack on Moscow,
the King of Poland sent one section of his army against
Smolensk and another against Moscow in the confident
expectation of capturing the whole country for himself.
In 1609 the force which Shuiski sent to relieve Smolensk
was utterly defeated, and the country became the prey of
gangs of armed men, some of them Russians, some Cossacks,
and some Poles. In 1610 riots broke out in Moscow itself,
Shuiski was deposed and forced to become a monk, and
the boyars who adhered to him were scattered. The way
was now open for the second Pretender, "The Thief of
Tushina," to march right into Moscow; but the advance
of the King of Poland's forces terrified him and he fled to
Kaluga, leaving his supporters to make the best of a bad
situation. In despair they offered the crown of Russia to
the son and heir of the Polish king on condition that he
would support the Orthodox faith and become a member
of the Orthodox Church. An agreement was reached in
August 1610, and the leading citizens of Moscow took the
oath of allegiance. Their example was followed in Suzdal,
Vladimir, Rostov, and other places. On 2nd September
a Polish garrison entered the Kremlin, and it seemed for
a moment as if the doom of Russia as an independent State
was sealed, and as if the Empire of the Tsars was about
to become a Polish province.

It should be noted, however, that it was not the common
people of Moscow or the peasantry in the country that
bowed the neck to the Polish yoke. The common people
everywhere were horrified and angered by what had taken
place, and the Orthodox clergy did all in their power to

raise that anger to white heat.   Believing that as soon as the Polish supremacy was established the next thing would be the destruction of Orthodoxy, the clergy urged the people to let no foreign heretic sit on the Russian throne.   The Patriarch Hermogenes distinguished himself by his untiring efforts to stir up revolt.   The Poles therefore threw him into prison.   Nevertheless, he succeeded in sending out letters urging the people to stand fast in the defence of their country and their faith, and these circulated far and wide.   As a punishment the Poles starved him to death. A violent outbreak was only a question of time.   In Passion Week 1611 a brawl took place in Moscow.   The Poles construed it as a signal for insurrection and massacred seven thousand persons.   Then a fire broke out and destroyed the greater part of the city.   In June the Poles captured Smolensk, seized Shuiski and sent him to Warsaw, where he died in confinement.   At the same time the Swedes raided the Baltic provinces and seized Novgorod. Then, to crown their miseries, there came to Russia a winter of frightful severity, in which multitudes died of cold and hunger.

All this time Polish soldiers and Catholic priests were pouring over Russia like a flood.   But there was one spot that remained unsubmerged.   Rising above the waves of invasion like a rock, the great fortress monastery of the Troitska Lavra held out unconquered and unconquerable, and its clergy did not fail their country's cause in the hour of need.   The hegumen Dionysius was not only as bitter a foe of Catholicism as Hermogenes had been, he was an equally ardent patriot, and when a Polish force of thirty thousand men with ninety guns besieged the monastery, he armed his monks, his servants, and his serfs, and lined the ramparts to repel the assault.   For six weeks the guns roared, but no practicable breach was made in the walls, and at last the besiegers lost heart and retired.

While the siege was going on, Dionysius sent out burning appeals to his fellow-countrymen to save the Empire and the true religion, and his dauntless courage revived their drooping spirits.   The first definite blow for liberty was

struck at Nijni-Novgorod.   The Mayor of the city, Kosmas
Minin Suchoruk, by occupation a butcher, poured forth
torrents of patriotic eloquence.   At the same time a wave
of religious revival swept over the whole district, and it was
agreed that before anything else was done the people must
repent of their sins and get right with God.   In order to accomplish this, a fast of three days' duration was proclaimed
and was strictly observed.   To provide money every man
offered his third coin, *i.e.* a third part of his income.   Arms
were purchased, mercenaries were hired, and a small body
of troops was placed under the command of a country
squire, Prince Pojarski.   Sweden was kept quiet by astute
negotiations.   Other towns joined Nijni-Novgorod, and an
offensive was begun.   In a series of fierce struggles the
Polish forces in the field were defeated.   The garrison in
the Kremlin was compelled to capitulate.   On the 24th
October 1612 the flag of Poland was hauled down, and on
the following day the triumphant Russians, preceded by
the clergy with banners and ikons, celebrated their victory
in the Cathedral of the Assumption.   The prisoners whom
the Poles were holding in captivity were released, and
among them was the young Michael Romanov.   The
period of the Troubles had reached its close.

These events have had a profound effect upon Russia's
subsequent history.   They filled the whole country with
the conviction that a patriotic Russian must be Orthodox,
and that a Catholic must be a traitor.   Further, they showed
up the Polish State and the Romish Church in the guise
of enemies with whom Russia could never make terms, and
again they made it evident that the Orthodox clergy were
the last line of Russia's defence.   They were a bulwark
which could not be overthrown.   Any one who left their
fellowship was to be looked on with suspicion, and heresy
became a crime which was put on a level with treason.

CHAPTER XV

MICHAEL

AS soon as the Russians realised that the Polish power was broken, the Council which was managing State affairs sent out letters far and near inviting deputies to assemble in Moscow to appoint a new Tsar, and on 21st May 1613, after three days of fasting and prayer, a great meeting was held in the Red Square of the Kremlin. Several candidates were proposed for the vacant throne, but the boyars could not agree on any of them, while the lower gentry and the common people were solid for Michael Romanov. They remembered with respect his grandmother, Anastasia Romanov, the first wife of Ivan IV., and his grandfather, Nikita, one of Ivan's bravest captains. They counted his father, Philaret, and his mother, now the nun Martha, although both were still alive, as saints who had suffered martyrdom for their country and their faith, and with one voice they shouted, " Let Michael Romanov be Tsar." After negotiations, and the promise of concessions limiting the Tsar's prerogatives, the boyars withdrew their opposition and Michael's election was then a matter of course.

Michael, however, was nowhere to be found. He was only a youth of sixteen, neither strong in body nor vigorous in mind, and the task awaiting him was terrible. The time of troubles, though it lasted only fifteen years, had been almost fatal to Russia's prosperity. When it ceased, the country was bleeding at every pore. Commerce and agriculture were both alike in ruins. Brigands roamed everywhere, and those whom they spared perished of hunger and cold. Under the pressure of foreign foes the frontiers of the Empire were shrinking. Sweden and Poland between them already possessed one-half of the whole area of Russian soil, and they were preparing further invasions. Michael therefore hid himself, and it was only after long search that he was discovered with his mother in the Ipatievsky Convent near Kostroma. After much resistance he yielded to the entreaties of the Commissioners and was crowned in July. He styled himself autocrat. It remained to be seen whether he would emphasise his autocracy or would regulate his policy by the will of the people expressed through constitutional channels.

He began by calling to his aid an assembly of the people. During the first two years of his reign this assembly virtually took the whole business of government into his own hands, and during the remaining twenty-two years it met no less than ten times. It might have become the real ruler of the country, but it did not know how to make itself indispensable by retaining control of the national purse, and as the Tsar and the boyars established themselves more and more securely, it became decreasingly important, and finally ceased to function. Russia was not yet ready for representative government. The vast distances, the isolation of the villages, and the difficulties and dangers of travelling made it practically impossible to group the people into constituencies, and their political ignorance was so profound that it was better to have State affairs managed by men who had a wider range of vision, who knew what ought to be done, and who had authority and power to do it.

The problems before Michael and his advisers were numerous and embarrassing, but evidently the first thing needed was order. With the assistance of the clergy, who denounced all who refused assistance, a band of trained men was equipped and organised. By their efforts one troop of brigands after another was caught and punished. Among these was a Cossack who had not only proclaimed himself to be the true Dimitri—the third who had done so—and who had terrorised Moscow by his cruelties, but who had also persuaded Marina, the widow of the first, and afterwards also of the second pseudo Dimitri, to marry him. After being tortured he was impaled on July 1614. Marina and her four-year-old son were sent to Astrakhan, where the mother died in prison and the child was hanged.

It was almost equally important to raise money, for the treasury was empty. A census of the whole nation was therefore begun in 1619 to discover the number and status of possible taxpayers. The work proceeded slowly, and the records were partially destroyed by fire in 1626, but a conclusion was reached in 1628. This census completed the process of binding the peasants to the soil. It reduced them all to the level of serfs, and the owner of the land on which they laboured was held responsible for the payment of their taxes. As a compensation, the landowner was allowed to put upon them any burdens that he chose. He naturally exploited them to the utmost. Their discontent naturally expressed itself in violent outbreaks.

An effort was also made to get at those who evaded taxation by taking shelter under the wing of the great monasteries or landowners. In 1619 it was proposed that all who had renounced their freedom and had become serfs to landowners or dependants of ecclesiastical establishments should be replaced in their former fiscal position, and if they did not pay their taxes directly their superiors should pay for them. If this measure had been carried through, the monasteries, which had by far the greatest numbers of serfs and dependants, would have been mulcted of considerable sums of money, so they joined their forces and delayed realisation of the purpose for thirty years.

While these internal reforms were going on, foreign foes were being dealt with. As Poland, a Roman Catholic State, encroached on Russia, Sweden, now a Protestant State, did the same. It even dreamed of a great Scandinavian Empire with its capital on Russian soil. Sweden, being the less formidable of the two, was dealt with first. Through the mediation of John Merrick, Ambassador of King James of England, a treaty was signed at Stolbovo on 10th March 1617, in which Sweden gave up all claim to Ladoga, Novgorod, and some smaller towns. On the other hand, Russia gave Sweden two thousand roubles and surrendered its claim to Livonia, and to the coast on both sides of the Neva. It therefore lost the access to the Baltic, which it was on the point of securing, and although it was agreed that immigrants from the West should be allowed to pass through Swedish territory to the Tsar's dominions, Sweden retained the power to stop them at any moment. When Gustavus Adolphus met the Riksdag at the close of the negotiations he boasted he had left Russia no standing-ground from which to jump the brook (the Baltic).

A settlement was also come to with Poland. In spite of what had taken place the Poles maintained that the King of Poland was also Tsar of Russia. The Russians maintained that he was not. War ensued, and in October 1618 the Polish Army reached Moscow. A siege was begun. But the Poles feared the winter which was approaching, while Michael feared the spread of disaffection in his capital, so that both were easily persuaded to think of peace. In February 1619, at the village Duelino, near the Troitska Lavra, a treaty was signed, and the best that can be said for it is that for fourteen years afterwards hostilities ceased.

After the treaty was signed there was an exchange of prisoners. Among those who were restored to Russia was Michael's father, Philaret, Metropolitan of Rostov. Michael met him on the outskirts of Moscow in the middle of June. Ten days later he was consecrated Patriarch by Theophanes, Patriarch of Jerusalem, who was then in Russia, and who had received from the Patriarch of Constantinople authority to act in his name. From that day forward, till the bond between father and son was broken by the death of Philaret in 1633, the Government of Russia was a diarchy, and the mediæval idea that Church and State are different aspects of one and the same organism, and that the governing powers of each are complementary to each other, was practically realised. At all public ceremonials the Tsar and the Patriarch appeared together. The Tsar sat on his throne with the Patriarch on his right in a golden chair, and ambassadors addressed each of them in turn. When gifts were presented both made suitable replies. In official documents the Tsar's name preceded that of the Patriarch, but in the transaction of business, even though purely secular, the Patriarch sometimes issued orders and acted alone. At the same time each had his own court and his own servants.

Philaret took part in all manner of political affairs, and it was during his tenure of office that negotiations for the first Franco-Russian treaty were entered into with Louis XIII. He was strictly Orthodox and conservative, to such a degree that he insisted on the re-baptism of Catholics, and he believed that in religious matters Russia had nothing to learn. At the same time he saw that in other respects the West could be Russia's teacher, and he did much to introduce to his countrymen the learning and science by which he thought they could profit. He himself had a knowledge of the Latin language, an unusual accomplishment in those days, and he established in Moscow an academy where Greek and Latin were taught. He also edited and distributed new editions of liturgical works, and he ordered the bishops to open schools in their dioceses. He encouraged immigrants, and they came in large numbers —iron miners, copper smelters, spinners of wire, weavers of velvet, carriage builders and upholsterers, goldsmiths, and lapidaries. Iron foundries, tanneries, chemical works for the manufacture of potash and glass, and factories of various sorts came into being. Bellmakers arrived to cast the bells for the churches, and permission to settle was granted to all on condition that they taught their crafts to Russian workmen. In addition to these, technical experts, physicians, geographers, astronomers, actors, and others began to drift into the country. In course of time a distinct section of Moscow was assigned to the foreigners. In 1638 at least a thousand families were said to reside in it, and in 1660 their number was so great that the foreign quarter contained three Lutheran churches, one Reformed church, and one German school.

Another service which Philaret rendered the country was the improvement of the army by the help of foreign officers. Many of them were Scots, among whom the most conspicuous were Leslie and Keith and Mathieson.

There were also the Englishmen, Fox and Sanderson, and the Germans, Samuel and Jacob Scharl. In 1624 there were in the Russian Army 445 foreign officers, and in the end of 1631 there were about sixty thousand mercenaries of all ranks; but in training and equipment they were far below the Western standard, and in the second Polish war the Russian Army was heavily defeated.

This was the golden age of the Patriarchate, and its splendour was increased not only by the honour which Michael conferred on his father, but by the privileges granted to the clergy. Ivan IV. had decreed that all the officers, serfs, and servants of the Metropolitan should be free from Government imposts, and from the jurisdiction of civil courts, except in the case of crimes against life which the ecclesiastical authorities had certified. In 1559 Godounov renewed this privilege to the Patriarch Job. Michael further ordained that, in addition to the civil immunity which the clergy enjoyed, the Patriarch should, except in capital cases, have unchallengeable jurisdiction over all the clergy of his province, that he should be allowed to impose taxes on them without interference, and that civil suits in connection with the lands and dependencies of churches and monasteries which belonged to the Patriarch should not come before the lower courts of the realm, but should be judged by the sovereign in person. At the same time Michael endorsed the edicts of Ivan IV. which forbade churches and monasteries to acquire either by gift or purchase any real property.

Philaret's zeal for antiquity was greatly stimulated by a present which he received from Shah Abbas of Persia. It was the seamless coat of our Saviour which, according to tradition, was brought into Georgia by one of the soldiers who divided Christ's garments at the foot of the Cross, and which was preserved for many years in the church of a small village to the north of Tiflis. Philaret placed it in the Cathedral of the Assumption, where it was soon credited with power to work miracles.

Shortly before Philaret's return to Moscow, an incident took place which indicates the ignorance and bigotry of

some of the Orthodox clergy.   Through the carelessness of
transcribers, and through other causes, errors had crept into
the ritual.   Michael therefore collected the printers who
had been scattered by the Poles, set up the presses, and
appointed a commission to revise the Trebnik and publish
an accurate text.   The President of this commission was
Dionysius, the famous archimandrite of the Troitska, who
had defended it against the Poles, and whose scholarship
was equal to his courage and piety.   The work of revision
occupied a year and a half, and while it was going on
Dionysius and his collaborators had to deal with the
formula used in the Blessing of the Waters.   In the Trebnik
in common use it ran, " Come, O Lord, and sanctify this
water with Thy Holy Spirit and with fire."   They found
that the phrase " and with fire " occurred in only two
copies of the old Slav version, and in no Greek copy at all.
Therefore they considered it an interpolation and struck
it out.   In the Troitska Lavra, however, the chief cantor
Login, who is said to have regarded the arts of reading and
writing as almost heretical, and the choirmaster were
Dionysius' bitter enemies.   One day he had rebuked them
for scandalous irreverence during divine worship, and they
took their revenge by raising the cry of heresy :   " He does
not confess that the Holy Spirit comes with fire."   In
1618 Dionysius was brought to trial, and his judges were
of the same type as his accusers.   He was condemned to
be stripped to the shirt, loaded with fetters, led through
a jeering crowd, and imprisoned in the Novospassky
Monastery.   In the meantime his enemies spread the
alarming report that he wished to banish fire from Russia.
After Philaret's return, however, the case was reopened,
and Dionysius was triumphantly restored to his former
dignity.

Philaret died in 1633, and the withdrawal of his firm
hand from the reins of government soon became apparent.
For twelve years more Michael reigned in comparative peace.
The closing months of his life were shadowed by the death
of his two sons, Ivan and Vassili, and by his failure to marry
his daughter Irene to Waldemar, Prince of Denmark.

When the young man arrived in Moscow to claim his bride, he found to his surprise that he was expected to abjure the Lutheran faith and to accept Orthodoxy. Although plied with argument, entreaty, and threatening, he refused to do this, and when he asked permission to return to his own country Michael refused to let him go.

Michael's death occurred suddenly on 12th July 1645. While he was attending Mass at the Court Chapel he fell down in a fit, and was just able to nominate his son Alexis as his successor before he expired. A month later his wife, Eudoxia, also died, and Alexis was left to bear the burden of the Russian crown alone.

CHAPTER XVI

ALEXIS

AFTER the death of Michael a meeting of representatives was held, and for the second time in Russian history the Tsar was placed on the throne by popular election. A unanimous choice fell on Alexis, Michael's son, a youth of sixteen, whose engaging manner seemed to promise that he would be a mild and gracious sovereign.

As he was inexperienced in political affairs his advisers had no difficulty in keeping him in the dark as to the state of the country, and in using his authority for their private ends. In combination with the landowners and lesser boyars they imposed burdens on the serfs and the mercantile classes far heavier than were justifiable.

Popular indignation expressed itself in riots, one of which took place at Moscow. In May 1648, when Alexis was returning from the Troitska, he was stopped by a mob whose spokesman, seizing the horse's bridle, expounded the people's grievances and demanded redress. Alexis made a pacific reply, and was moving on quietly when some of his attendants began to flog the people with their whips. Instantly there was a savage attack. Two judges, whose corruption was notorious, were murdered in the street, and five days elapsed before the tumult ceased.

Alexis then did the best thing he could have done. He summoned a national Council, comprising representatives of all classes except the serfs, and instructed it to revise and codify the laws of the Empire, and draw up regulations which would secure justice. The Council reported the result of its labours in January 1649, and although composed so hastily the excellence of this new code kept it in force till 1833.

Further, in order to lighten the burden of taxation by

increasing the area of the taxpayers, Alexis made a strong effort to inscribe the serfs and servants of the monasteries, of whom there were tens of thousands, and the dependants, real or nominal, of the great landowners. As this would have implied payment of money in large sums, the monasteries joined the landowners in resisting the Tsar's efforts, and all he succeeded in obtaining was a description of the lands and heritages possessed by the monasteries at that date. This, though excellent in itself, had no immediate pacific effect. The people remained as poor as before, and the discontent and the rioting continued. Misery was in fact reducing the people to despair. Many of the peasants sought escape by flight. Some found refuge in the forests, some went as far as Siberia, some joined the Cossacks of the Dnieper and the Don and roamed over the Steppes. Finally, in 1667, a band of them threatened the heart of Russia itself.

The leader was Stenka Razin, a bold man who began his career as a pirate on the Volga. He posed as the peasants' champion, and thousands flocked to his banner. In August 1669 he stormed Astrakhan, and converted it into a Cossack republic. He did the same at Samara and Saratov. Town after town received him with jubilation, and wherever he went the peasants butchered the landowners and burned their houses, till in the region between the Volga, the Oka, and the Dwina there was nothing but desolation. In April 1671 his progress was stopped near Simbirsk. Soon afterwards he was captured and taken to Moscow where, after enduring unspeakable torments, he was burned alive. His followers were dispersed, their strongholds were razed to the ground, the rivers were cleared of their boats, and order was restored. The rebellion therefore failed, and the burdens laid on the serfs were made more crushing than they had been before.

In Little Russia also the position of the peasants was intolerable. The Poles, their masters, looked on them with contempt, robbed them of their lands and liberty, and proscribed their religion. Orthodox churches were seized, and when they were not destroyed they were farmed out

to Jews who allowed the Orthodox clergy to conduct
Divine worship only on payment of heavy fees. The
peasants turned for help to the Cossacks, and a rising was
organised by Bogdan Khmelnitsky, a well-educated Cossack
who had been shamefully handled in his person and his
family by a Polish noble. Receiving no redress from the
Polish king, he took sword in hand to avenge himself.
The Orthodox clergy came to his aid, and he speedily
gathered an army. The cause which moved him to revolt
was not, he said, that the Poles had robbed the people of
the land, nor that they had imposed heavy burdens, but
that he and his friends were being compelled to apostatise
from Orthodoxy, and were being forced into Catholic heresy.

In the war which followed, Khmelnitsky swept over
the Ukraine, hunting down Polish landlords, Catholic
priests, and Jews, and putting them to agonising deaths.
Three times in succession he defeated the Polish Army and
seemed on the point of overthrowing the Polish throne
when the Polish king, Vladislas, died, and his brother,
John Casimir, was elected in his stead. John Casimir
was a Cardinal, in whom the three dynasties of Jagiello,
Vasa, and Hapsburg were united. In order to ascend the
throne, he was released from his ecclesiastical vows, and,
with the view of saving the country the expense of supporting two queens, he married his brother's widow. He
speedily discovered that he must come to terms with the
rebels, and in 1649 he promised to restore to its former
owners the property of the Orthodox which had been
confiscated, to give the Metropolitan of Kiev a seat in
the Polish Senate, and to close the Jesuit schools. The
promise was not kept, and war broke out again.

In the meantime, however, Khmelnitsky's ally, the
Khan of the Crimea, deserted him, and the Cossacks discovered that they could not maintain their liberty without
foreign assistance. Therefore, on Khmelnitsky's suggestion, they offered their submission to Alexis in the hope
that he would defend them. By the advice of his Council,
Alexis refused their offer. In 1652 they repeated it, and
told Alexis that if he refused a second time they would

forthwith ally themselves with his enemy, the Sultan. The
Council was still disposed to refuse, but under pressure from
the Patriarch Nikon, Poland was warned that if justice
was not granted to the Orthodox in the Ukraine, Russia
would declare war. The Poles replied that Russia had no
right to interfere in a purely Polish affair. Then on 1st
October 1653 the Russian Council resolved that for the sake
of the Orthodox faith the Cossack Hetman, with all his
forces, should be received under the sceptre of the Russian
sovereign. In the war which followed the Russians went
from victory to victory. At the same time the Swedes
under Charles Vasa attacked Poland on the other side,
and if its enemies had been wise enough to act in concert
Poland would have been crushed between them. But
Alexis and his Council feared that if Sweden became
strong at Poland's expense, the footing on the mainland
which it obtained would make it dangerous to Russia,
and therefore peace with Poland was rapidly patched up.

As Sweden was a formidable power, Alexis could not
rid himself of the idea that it must be dealt with. Therefore with the strenuous support of Nikon, but against the
advice of his Council, he invaded the Baltic dominions of
the Swedish king. After some initial successes he was
severely defeated, and despairing of ultimate success he
signed the Treaty of Andrussova in January 1667. Thanks
to the skill of his representative, Nastchokin, Russia
received not only the provinces of Smolensk, Tchernigov,
and Novgorod Severski, but also regained the region to the
west of the Dnieper which included Kiev. Russia thus
became master of the whole of the Ukraine, and there can
be no doubt of the satisfaction with which the Tsar entered
into possession of what had been the cradle of the Russian
State.

In spite of disorder and warfare, the stream of im-
migration from Western Europe continued to flow. Its
volume was not large, but its influence was great. The
enlightenment these incomers brought with them convinced
many leading Russians that if their country was to take
its place among the great powers it must open its arms to

learning, literature, and science. On the other hand, the common people and the clergy, who were both profoundly ignorant and stupendously self-conceited, were convinced that Russia had nothing to learn from any one, and that the whole duty of a patriot and a churchman was to maintain intact the customs received from his ancestors.

The vague terrors which filled men's minds with regard to change expressed themselves openly on the occasion of the Tsar's second marriage. One of his boyars named Matveef had married a Scottish lady named Hamilton, who not only took care that none of the drunken orgies which were common in other houses were permitted under her roof, but asserted her emancipation from the bondage in which Russian ladies were confined by establishing a salon, mixing freely with her guests, and engaging in conversation with them. Matveef and his wife adopted a beautiful girl, one of his nieces named Natalia Naryschkine, and gave her a liberal education. She was therefore a refreshing contrast to the inhabitants of the ordinary Russian terem. The Tsar met her repeatedly in Matveef's house, fell in love with her, and when the news was circulated that he proposed to marry her there was a loud outcry that the pious old order was about to be abolished. Nikon's reforms were already convulsing the country, and the outcry seemed to be justified. Nevertheless the wedding took place in 1671.

By his first wife, Maria Miloslavski, Alexis had two sons, Feodor, born in 1662, and Ivan, born in 1666, as well as six daughters, of whom Sophia was one. By his second wife he had one son, Peter, born in 1672, and two daughters. In 1674 he nominated Feodor as his successor, and committed Peter to the care of Matveef, his wife's uncle. In 1676 he died.

More than a decade before the wedding occurred, the great movement with which the name of Nikon is identified came to a head, and it rent the Orthodox Church of Russia into two sections. The movement has nothing in common with the movement for reform in which Luther and others figured prominently. That movement was essentially religious. The movement in Russia had no religious significance. In Western Europe the Romish Church claimed to mediate between God and man. It organised a hierarchy to offer sacrifice to God on the sinner's behalf, and to receive from God and transmit to men the grace of which they had need. On the other hand, Luther and his associates held that the sinner's access to God is mediated by Christ alone, that the sacrifice of Himself which Christ offered cannot be continued or repeated, that forgiveness and all other blessings are made over to believers in immediate response to their faith, and that their duty is determined not by the Church or its priests, but by the will of God revealed in Holy Scripture. They denounced the Romish Church because it assumed a position to which it was not entitled, claimed an authority which it did not possess, and pretended to exercise powers which were not entrusted to it. If the Reformers were right, there was no room in Christendom for the Romish hierarchy. If Rome were right, there was no room for the Reformers.

In Russia, however, the points at issue were quite different. The conservative section, afterwards known as the Old Believers, insisted that the errors in the service-books should not be corrected, that the eighth article of the Creed should read, " and in the Holy Ghost, the *True* Lord and Giver of Life," that the name of the Saviour should be spelt Isus and not Iisus, that Hallelujah should be sung twice, and not thrice, at a certain part of the rituals, that two and not three fingers should be used in making the sign of the Cross, that Church processions should go with the sun and not against it, that the only cross to be honoured should be that which has eight points, and that seven prosphoræ and not five must be used in the sacrament of the altar. Over such trivialities as these the Church was split, and while there was a great uproar over the correction of the service-books it was perhaps the dispute about the proper way of making the sign of the Cross which created the most intense feeling.

Nikon, who was largely responsible for the split, is one of the most outstanding characters in Russian history.

He was the son of a peasant, and was born in 1605 in the Province of Nijni-Novgorod.   He learned to read in the village school, and at the age of twelve he entered the monastery of Zheltovody in the same government.   When he was twenty his parents persuaded him to leave it and to marry.   As a means of livelihood he took charge of a church in Moscow where, after ten years of quiet labour, his three children died.   Taking this as a call from heaven to change his mode of life he persuaded his wife to enter a nunnery, while he became a monk at Anzer on the White Sea.   Five years later he became hegumen of another monastery in the same region.   In 1645, when he was visiting Moscow and attending a Council, the Tsar, impressed by his capacity for business, transferred him to the Novospassky Monastery.   Once a week thereafter, and sometimes oftener, Alexis had long conversations with him on public affairs, and in 1649 appointed him Archbishop of Novgorod.

Before accepting office Nikon showed the position he meant to maintain with regard to the Church's freedom from external control.   He stipulated that the section of the new legal code which set up the monastery court, and dealt with monastic property, should not apply to his diocese.   Alexis consented, and also empowered Nikon to decide not only the spiritual matters that came before him, but also civil causes affecting the monks, the popes, or the domains of the Church.   In addition, he authorised Nikon to revise the decisions of the civil and criminal courts, and to alter them if he thought fit, so that in the province of Novgorod Nikon became the final authority.   He took his responsibilities seriously, and acted with vigour.

As might have been expected, he met with opposition. Most of the clergy desired to be let alone.   They were ignorant and lazy, and as sleeping dogs growl when they are disturbed, so when Nikon stirred up the popes to greater fidelity in the discharge of their duties, and his methods were not gentle, there was in every parish in his diocese groaning and complaint.

While he annoyed the popes, he irritated the people.

Up to this time the Mir was accustomed to appoint the pope, to prescribe his duties, and fix his salary, and it did so without regard to his religious qualifications, " Indeed the free election of the pope, even when it was a reality, formed no spiritual tie between pastor and flock, just because they exacted of him no gifts of teaching or knowledge. They wanted Mass to be sung regularly, and the Sacraments administered, especially to the dying, and no more. Consequently they used their right of election to procure a pope as cheaply as possible, and they wanted in their deacon just one gifted with a big voice for the responses. His function was that of a deep-tongued bell. He also served them as a clerk to keep accounts, etc., but he was in any case a luxury, the gift of a rich elder, like the chorister of to-day." [1] The pope and his parishioners were therefore united mainly by a cash nexus, and they held that if they were satisfied with each other no third party had a right to interfere. Nikon denied this. He said that the pope is the servant of the Church, and is responsible to the bishop. The Mir might choose him and pay him, but he must take his orders from the bishop, and account for his conduct to the bishop. This infraction of traditional practice was so generally distasteful that when at last Nikon carried his point many of the popes, and many of the Mirs along with them, left the State Church and became dissenters.

Another difficulty arose from the excessive veneration for antiquity. Nikon and his opponents both appealed to antiquity, and if antiquity decides anything, Nikon and his supporters were right, and his opponents were wrong. The antiquity to which the latter appealed went back less than three centuries. Nikon went back to the earliest Christian days, and to his arguments his opponents could make no satisfactory reply. Therefore they fell back on slander and abuse.

The demands he made upon his clergy irritated them still further. He himself lived austerely. He ordered them to do the same, and there was undeniable need for

[1] Conybeare, p. 75.

this, for in almost every case they failed to live soberly, righteously, and in a godly fashion, setting an example which their flocks could follow. Further, the ignorance of the clergy was unbelievable. Not one in four of the popes could read a syllable. They repeated the ritual by rote, and inevitably introduced variations into the standard texts, and these variations were accepted in preference to the original. Nikon therefore insisted that all candidates for Holy Orders must have at least the rudiments of education, and he himself ordained none but those who could read what he set before them. He was vehemently denounced for his unreasonableness.

In connection with the services he put down a practice which was evidently the outcome of irreverence. The churches were cold, the ritual was long, there were no seats, and before the end was reached the worshippers were weary. Therefore the service was divided into sections, and all went on simultaneously. While one official was reading the lessons, another was singing a psalm and another was offering prayer. The result was babel. Nikon ordered that only one voice should be heard at one time. He also improved the music by introducing choirs who sang in harmony, and from his time the musical part of divine worship in the Russian Church, especially in the great cathedrals, has been unsurpassed for dignity and impressiveness. He also made an attempt to introduce preaching. He himself was accustomed to preach, but few of the popes could face an audience. The boldest contented themselves with reading a homily from one of the Fathers. Most of them were entirely of Pobie-donostseff's [1] opinion that the service was well enough without a sermon. The people on their part maintained that listening to sermons was no part of their religious duty, and even Nikon's energy had little immediate effect in establishing the practice.

These reforms, justifiable in themselves, although badly received, were all meant to rescue the Church from the contempt into which it was falling in the eyes of the

[1] *Reflections*, p. 214.

enlightened section of society, and they led up to a dramatic incident in which the Tsar himself was persuaded to take part. In 1652, while he was still Archbishop of Novgorod, Nikon proposed that the relics of the Metropolitan Philip, who was murdered by Ivan IV., should be brought back to Moscow. He was therefore commissioned to go himself to the Solovetski Monastery where they had been preserved, and to take with him and lay on the Saint's tomb a letter in which Alexis implored pardon for his predecessor's wickedness. In due time he returned with his precious burden and laid it, with imposing ceremonial, in a shrine specially prepared for its reception in the Cathedral of the Assumption. While absent on this journey the Patriarch Joseph died, and a Synod was held to elect a successor. As the Tsar strongly favoured Nikon, he was unanimously appointed to the vacant office. When it was offered him, to the surprise of every one, he positively refused to accept it, and even after he was brought into the Cathedral he remained obdurate, till the whole assembly fell at his feet imploring him to yield to its wishes. There is no need to suppose that a sense of unworthiness oppressed him. He was simply determined to get his own terms, and he knew he must get them now or never. In the course of a long address he said : " If it please you to choose me as your Patriarch, give me your word and make a covenant before God and our Saviour and his Most Pure Mother and before the Angels and the Saints that ye will keep the evangelic dogmas and the canons of the Holy Fathers and of the Apostles and the laws of the pious Emperors, and if you promise to obey me also as your chief pastor and Father in everything which I shall teach you concerning the divine dogmas and canons, then will I according to your wish accept this great Patriarchate." [1] The whole assembly swore as he demanded, and he was consecrated on 4th August 1652. As Patriarch, Nikon was now able to extend his radius of action over the whole Church, and he proceeded to do so in connection with the service-books. He first realised the need of this correction in 1652 when

[1] Palmer, iii. 383.

he was examining the letters of the Patriarch Jeremiah in connection with the appointment of the Patriarch Job.[1] He also happened to compare a copy of the Creed worked in pearls on a sakkos with a copy of the same Creed in some Church books, and found a discrepancy between them. Further investigation disclosed discrepancies. Therefore in July 1653 he commanded all the monasteries to send him all their oldest books, and in 1654 he persuaded Alexis to summon a Council to consider the propriety of making such corrections as might be found necessary. He also dispatched Arsenius Sukhanov to Mount Athos with a large sum of money, and with a letter to the Superior of the Convent requesting him to send whatever he could command in the way of old Greek books.[2] In order to give the Council greater authority he secured the attendance of the Patriarchs of Antioch and of Serbia, and of the Metropolitans of Moldavia and Nicæa. This Council resolved that the books and the ritual ought to be brought into conformity with the most ancient standards. Thereafter Paisius, Patriarch of Constantinople, convened a Council of Greek bishops and endorsed the Russian Council's decision.

In January 1655 Arsenius returned with a great collection of books, some of them very ancient. The Patriarchs of Alexandria and of Antioch also sent a substantial number of volumes. Nikon himself had a wonderful library, and he seems to have thought that his critical apparatus was now complete.

He committed the work of revision in the first place to certain monks in whom he had confidence. They did their work so carelessly, and made changes so needlessly, that they roused great feeling against them. " Recent liturgical scholars in Russia have shown that of the five hundred Greek MSS. brought to Moscow by Sukhanov for Nikon's use from the East, only seven were consulted in editing the service-books afresh." [3] The revised books might have been accepted without serious opposition if they had not been associated with the change which the Council ordered

---

[1] Palmer, iii. 419.   [2] *Ibid.* ii. 170.   [3] Conybeare, p. 47.

in making the sign of the Cross. Paisius and the Greek Council said in regard to it : " We all have the ancient custom and tradition of doing our reverence by putting together the first three fingers to symbolise the Holy Trinity." In answer to the question, How ought bishops and priests to bless, he replied : " The Church blesses all figuring by the hand of the priest, the name of the Messiah, namely, IC, XC. With whatever fingers any one figures these four letters there will be no difference, so long as he that blesses and he that is blessed have it in their thought that a blessing comes from Jesus Christ by the hand of the priest. However, it is proper to put together the second and third fingers so as to make the IC, and the first, the fourth, and the fifth so as to make the XC." [1]

Now every living Russian, even Nikon himself, had been taught from his infancy to make the sign of the Cross with two fingers so that the decree of Nikon's Council which was based on the recommendation of Paisius was the condemnation of a universal practice. The Patriarch of Antioch gave the condemnation a sharper edge by declaring that those who made the sign of the Cross in the old way were heretics, and the Metropolitan of Nicæa said that they drew on them the curse of the Holy Trinity. The question became urgent. What was an Orthodox believer to do ? Was he to cross himself in the old way which had been followed by the saints of previous ages or in the new way which was now imposed upon him ?

The question was answered by the party of the protopops, a group of bold men which included Stephen Vonafitev, the Tsar's Confessor, Paul Bishop of Kolomna, Nerinov, protopop of the Kazan Cathedral in Moscow, Daniel of Kostromo, Longinus of Murom, and Avakum, protopop of the Yurievetsky Convent on the Volga. These banded themselves together to resist all changes on the ground that change was heretical and ruinous. They all had a reputation for piety, as well as zeal for Orthodoxy, but Avakum was the most conspicuous. He had every quality required in a leader of men, a hero, and a saint. Un-

[1] Palmer, ii. 210.

fortunately he was invincibly ignorant and impervious to argument. This group besought the Tsar to forbid innovations. The Tsar handed their petition to Nikon, and they and their adherents were punished. The people became interested and asked an explanation. The answers they received did not satisfy them. They refused to believe that men of such piety could be heretics, and in many cases showed their sympathy with the sufferers by joining them.

When Avakum returned from his first Siberian captivity he found there was a reaction against Nikon, and with Nikon's enemies he became a great favourite. He was admitted to the houses of great nobles, he was even received into Court circles, and the Tsar's sister-in-law, the wealthy boyarina Feodosia Morozov, her sister Eudocia, and others of almost equal rank became his converts. If he had been reasonable some *modus vivendi* might have been found, but he and his followers raised such disturbances that, in the interests of order, they had to be dealt with. Avakum was the first to be seized, and he was banished to a lonely spot on the White Sea near Archangel. Other banishments and executions followed.

In 1666 an effort was made to prevent the disruption that was threatening. It failed. In May 1667 a Council was held for the same purpose. In the interval between the two the Tsar himself endeavoured personally to placate Avakum and Feodosia Morozov. He had no success. Therefore the Council excommunicated and degraded Avakum, cursed all who adhered to him, cut them off from the fellowship of the Church as heretics and rebels, and consigned their souls to eternal torment, along with the souls of the traitor Judas and of the Jews who crucified our Lord. As this Council was attended by three Patriarchs, fourteen Metropolitans, eight archbishops, five bishops, twenty-five archimandrites, eight hegumens, and thirteen protopops, its decision may be taken as the final judgment of the Orthodox Church on the Old Believers, and as the point at which the disruption of the Church begins.[1]

After this the persecution of the Old Believers became

[1] Palmer, iii. 342.

incessant and pitiless. Avakum and his three chief associates were condemned to have their tongues cut out, and to be banished to Pustozerk on the Petchora, the most northerly town in European Russia. Through the intercession of the Tsarina, Avakum's tongue was spared, but for fourteen years his sufferings were almost incredible. Nevertheless, he sent out secretly letters and appeals which nerved his followers to endurance almost equal to his own, and he wrote an autobiography which is said to be one of the most moving compositions in the Russian language. On 1st April 1681 he was burned alive.

The boyarina Morozov was treated with similar severity. She was stripped of all her property, reduced to rags, and thrown into an underground dungeon. In order to compel her to yield she and her sister Eudocia were forced to witness the torture of their maids. As this had no effect, they were themselves scourged, first on the back and then on the stomach. They were racked, frozen, roasted, but not a syllable of recantation passed their lips. Finally they were starved to death. A similar fate befel many others less well known to fame. They were all martyrs. The infinitely pathetic thing is, they were martyrs by mistake.

In this connection, there occurred the persecution of the monks of Solovetski. This great establishment was founded about 1220 in one of the most desolate regions of the north. Winter reigns there for more than half the year. As might have been expected, those who of their own choice betook themselves to it became famous for their austerity, and of all the Russian monks they were perhaps the least inclined to tolerate departures from tradition. In 1666 they sent a petition to the Tsar asking him to allow them to worship according to the ancient rule, and stating that they were ready not only to suffer privations and pains, but also to seal with their blood their devotion to the old ordinances. So far from securing the Tsar's favour, their petition only increased his wrath. He sent several messengers to bring them to repentance, but without success, and eventually he ordered Ignatius Volkhoff to take a hundred men and compel the monks to accept the new order.   This force was quite inadequate to the work to which it was set, and although it worried and harassed the monks for four seasons it did nothing effective against them.   Volkhoff was therefore recalled, and Clement Jobleff, with a thousand men, took his place. By killing all the monks' horses and cattle, by burning the huts they used for hunting and fishing, by destroying their implements and tools, and by wrecking the out-buildings of the monastery, he reduced the monks to straits, but could not force his way through the monastery gates. After two years of vain effort he died, and Ivan Mencherinoff, with thirteen hundred men and some artillery, made a fresh attack.   The monks had already supplied themselves with Dutch guns, from which they expected great things, but their position became more and more desperate, and some of them began to speak about surrendering.   Their more resolute brethren locked them up and went on fighting.   At last a monk named Theoctistus escaped by night and showed the besiegers how to enter the monastery by a conduit under the White Tower.   On 22nd January 1676 a body of armed men effected a complete surprise, and massacred all they found within the walls.   Then when the buildings were empty, contingents of monks from other places, on whose obedience the ruling powers thought they could rely, were drafted in, and the work of the monastery began as before.

The siege lasted for eight months, and from the point of view of tactics it was a mistake.   The people in these regions held the monks of Solovetski in the highest reverence, and when they saw them besieged, bombarded, and butchered for holding traditions which had been sanctified by immemorial usage, they concluded that those responsible for the siege and the butchery were agents of Antichrist.   On the other hand, wherever the tale of the monks' heroism was told, they were regarded as saints and martyrs.   They were practically canonised.   Pilgrims came and burned incense at their tombs weekly, monthly, and annually, and were witnesses of the miracles wrought there, especially on the anniversary. [1]

[1] Palmer, ii. 447.

In spite of the resistance of the Old Believers, the movement which Nikon had started was adhered to not only by the Tsar, the nobles, and most of the higher clergy, but also by the majority of the common people, Nikon had therefore conquered, but after six years in the Patriarchate he fell from his high position, and among the causes of his fall his own conduct had a foremost place.

Every one knew that he was a peasant's son, but that did not create friendliness towards him. Those whom he eclipsed in the royal favour became intensely jealous, and poured into the Tsar's ear a stream of misrepresentation and slander. They also took care to prevent a meeting in which misunderstandings might have been cleared up. At last, with the Tsar's approval, the monastery court began to interfere in Church affairs, and Nikon's protests were not listened to.[1] He was also made to suffer personal slights, which he felt keenly. On the 10th July 1658 he took a step which brought matters to a head. At the close of the service in the cathedral he ordered the doors to be shut, as he was about to deliver an address. After a passionate harangue he said : " Since the Tsar's authority has engrossed everything and we are accounted nothing, I shall now go away from this place and city into the wilderness. I commend you to the living God and give you my peace and blessing." [2] Thereafter in presence of the congregation he put off his official patriarchal robes and put on the humblest clerical dress to be found in the vestry. Afterwards he wrote a letter to Alexis containing these words : " I depart because of thy wrath, because the Scripture saith, ' Give place to wrath,' and again, ' If they reject thee in one city go to another, and if they receive thee not, shake off the dust from thy feet as a testimony against them.' " [3] After dispatching it he lingered in the neighbourhood of Moscow, hoping that the Tsar would invite him to return. The invitation was not sent. Bitterly disappointed, he went his way to Voskresensky, a monastery of his own foundation which

---

[1] Palmer, iii. 385. [2] *Ibid.* 384, iv. 127.
[3] *Ibid.* iv. 3. 134.

the Tsar, who was impressed by its beauty, had called in happier days " The New Jerusalem."

Had he abdicated ? Nikon constantly affirmed that he had not. His enemies as constantly affirmed that he had. After much hesitation, Alexis concluded that the Patriarchate was practically vacant, and ordered Pitirim, Metropolitan of Kroutitz, to administer the business belonging to it. At the same time he intimated that he himself was to be regarded as the final authority in all cases whether episcopal or spiritual.

As it was impossible to continue this arrangement indefinitely, Alexis summoned a Synod to meet in Moscow on 16th February 1660. It decided that Nikon had abdicated, and was on the point of declaring that he had forfeited his priest's orders and of deciding that he should be forbidden to discharge any clerical function, when Epiphanius Slavenitsky, one of the most learned men of the time, pointed out that, according to the canons of the Church, Nikon could not be forbidden to exercise priestly function unless he were proved guilty of some crime. The Synod broke up in confusion, and Nikon went back to his monastery, characterising it as not only a Judaical synagogue but even a diabolical one, and comparing himself to the woman in the wilderness who was persecuted by the dragon, and, again, to St. John in Patmos.[1]

After this the bishops were disposed to let Nikon alone, but he did not leave them alone. In Lent 1662 he excommunicated them and all others whom he considered his enemies. At this juncture there came to Moscow a wily Greek named Paisius Ligarides. He arrived on 28th April without credentials and without an invitation. He professed Orthodoxy, but his Orthodoxy was suspected and his morals were said to be not irreproachable. He was born in Scio, and was educated in Rome, where he is reported to have taken Orders as a Jesuit. In 1657, when he was in Moldavia, Nikon asked his help in the reforms he was advocating, but as it was not yet clear whether or not Nikon was to win, Ligarides did not commit himself. He

[1] Palmer, iii. 36.

appeared in Moscow soliciting subscriptions for the diocese
of Gaza, of which he called himself the Metropolitan. On
his arrival, Nikon sent him a letter detailing his sufferings.
On 12th July 1662 Ligarides replied that it was dangerous
to kick against the pricks. Nikon was hugely disappointed,
and declared in a rage that as Paul had appealed to Cæsar,
so he would appeal to Rome.[1] In Lent 1663 Ligarides
suggested that the Patriarch of Constantinople should be
asked to give judgment on the situation, and at the request
of Alexis and of the Council he prepared twenty-five
questions covering the points at issue. Meletius, a Greek
deacon, was commissioned to take these questions to the
four Patriarchs, to state orally that Nikon's case was
involved in them, and to suggest the form in which the
answers should be worded.[2]

On 29th May 1664 the Patriarchs replied to the effect
that in Russia the imperial authority is unlimited, that
the patriarchal authority is not unlimited, that Nikon
had gone beyond his rights in demanding at his election
a vow of obedience to himself, that he was blameworthy
for abandoning his chair, for meddling with affairs of
State, and for introducing changes into divine worship.
In opposition to the opinion of Slavenitsky they said he
could be dealt with by a properly summoned Council of
bishops, and might without sin be deposed from his office
and replaced by another.

Copies of the letters to the Patriarchs fell into Nikon's
hands. In his wrath he took them to the monastery
church, and ordered to be sung over them Psalm 109, one
of the cursing psalms, which contains the passage : " Let
his days be few, and let another take his office. Let his
children be fatherless, and his wife a widow. Let his
children continually be vagabonds and beg, and let his
posterity be cut off." This was reported to Alexis, who
cried in indignation, " Even though I myself have erred,
of what sin have my children been guilty, and wherein
has my wife offended ? " On 17th July 1663 he sent
Ligarides and Prince Nikita Odoefsky to ask Nikon what

[1] Palmer, iii. 51, 68, 314 ; xlv.   [2] Ibid. iii. 500.

he meant by his conduct. Nikon received them haughtily, denied that he had cursed the Tsar, admitted that he had cursed the nobles, declared himself willing to curse them again, and finished by asserting that the Tsar and the boyars were treating him as Herod and Pilate treated Christ.

Alexis then resolved to bring the whole business to an end by the decision of a General Council, and in September 1664 Meletius was sent again to invite the four Patriarchs to come to Moscow.

Nikon, however, had still friends in the capital, and when Meletius was away some of them thought that a conciliation could be effected if the Tsar and the Patriarch could be brought face to face. A boyar named Zeuzin, who had been intimate with Nikon, wrote him a letter containing a suggestion which he said came from Alexis himself, to the effect that Nikon should reappear in the cathedral, and should thereafter be reinstated in his patriarchal dignity.[1] Even if there had been a chance of reconciliation, Nikon wrecked it by his own behaviour. At midnight, on 18th December 1664, he entered Moscow with a train of sledges, drove to the cathedral, and entered it in his full canonicals. The Metropolitan of Rostov was singing Mass, but when he heard the well-known voice ordering him to cease, he obeyed. Nikon then ascended the patriarchal throne, and sent a message to the Tsar to announce that he had arrived and was waiting to begin service. Alexis, thunderstruck by the audacity of the summons, summoned his Council to meet him instantly, and asked what was to be done. On the suggestion of Ligarides a deputation was sent to Nikon, who said to it, " I have come back to my chair as Narcissus, Patriarch of Jerusalem, came back to his chair after twelve years of absence." [2] When this answer was reported, a messenger was sent to Nikon a second time to tell him to depart at once. Nikon then produced a letter to the Tsar, which he asked to be read publicly. It described a vision in which Nikon said an angel appeared to him and com-

[1] Palmer, iv. 514, 516.   [2] *Ibid.* iv. 520.

manded him to return to Moscow. The effect of the letter
was disappointing. He was commanded to leave Moscow
at once if he valued his life. With great reluctance he
obeyed, and as he entered his sledge he said he shook off
the dust of his feet against his enemies. A soldier replied,
" We will sweep it up." Nikon pointed to a comet which
was blazing in the sky and cried furiously : " God will
sweep you all away with a fiery besom." Then grasping
his patriarchal staff, which he regarded as the proof of
his rank, he drove off. Messengers were sent after him to
demand the surrender of the staff, and after two days of
wrangling at Chernovo he gave it up.

On 6th November 1666 the Patriarchs of Antioch and
Alexandria arrived in the capital, and immediately held
long conferences with the Tsar and his Council. On the
3rd December a Synod met. Those present included the
Tsar, the two Patriarchs, the Metropolitans of Novgorod,
Kazan, Kroutitz, Gaza, Serbia, Nicæa, Amasia, Iconium,
Trebizond, and Kios, the Archbishops of Sinai, Vologda,
Smolensk, Riazan, Tver, Astrakhan, and Pskov, several
bishops, and many nobles and grandees. In answer to a
summons Nikon himself appeared, and after several stormy
passages the Synod gave its decision to the effect that
Nikon had slandered the Tsar, and the Council, and the
Patriarch, that he had behaved in a disorderly fashion
by stripping himself in public in the cathedral, and that
he had been guilty of injustice, rapine, and cruelty. Therefore it resolved to strip him of all episcopal honour, and
reduce him to the level of a simple monk.[1]

The act of degradation took place on 12th December
in a small chapel over the gate of the Chudov Monastery.
After the sentence had been read, the two Patriarchs
present ordered Nikon to take off his headdress, which
was richly embroidered with pearls, and also the pectoral
and the panagia. Nikon said sarcastically, " I know that
as ye are poor ye will be glad to have some pearls."
The Patriarchs retorted, " Keep them to thine own con-
founded perdition." [2] When he was stepping into the

---

[1] Palmer, iii. 170, 189.   [2] *Ibid.* iii. 196.

sledge which was to take him to prison in the Therapontov Monastery in Bielozero, he sighed and said to himself, " Oh, Nikon, if thou hadst given costly banquets and hadst supped late with thy guests, these things would not have happened." As it would have been awkward for the Patriarchs of Jerusalem and Constantinople to condemn the action of their two colleagues, and as such condemnation might have dried up the stream of donations which they were accustomed to receive, they ratified the proceedings of the Synod and declared its decision to be valid. Thereafter Joasaph, Archimandrite of the Troitska Lavra, was appointed to succeed to the Patriarchate.

Nikon lived fifteen years after this, partly in the Therapontov Monastery, partly in that of Cyrilov. Alexis did not allow antagonism to Nikon's behaviour to diminish his kindly feeling to Nikon personally, and he showed it by sending frequent presents. These, however, did little to assuage Nikon's bitterness, and although Alexis asked forgiveness for the line he felt it his duty to pursue, it was six years before forgiveness was granted. Alexis died in 1676 asking Nikon's blessing, and his death removed Nikon's most powerful friend. Immediately after it took place, the Patriarch Joasaph increased the hardships which Nikon had to endure, and it was only when death had evidently claimed him that he was allowed to travel to his own monastery of Voskresensky. By accident or design he was compelled to start too late, and he expired on the journey on 17th August 1681. His remains were buried in the monastery church, which his own hands had helped to build and decorate.

Nikon's faults lie on the surface of his character and are unmistakable. He was ambitious, overbearing, and so difficult to put up with that even a milder man than Alexis would have found it impossible to remain always on good terms with him, and his harshness and his positive cruelty in dealing with the lower clergy and the common people raised up against him many enemies. But behind all this there was a fundamental divergence of opinion which forbade Nikon and Alexis to live in concord. Alexis stood for autocracy, and posed as the final authority both in Church and State. Nikon stood for the Church's independence, and maintained that the Tsar had no authority in the Church's affairs, and that if either were to be subordinate to the other it was the State that was subordinate to the Church and not the Church to the State.

In reply to Question XXIV. of the Boyar Simeon Streshneff, and the answer given to it by Ligarides, Nikon says, " The Lord God Almighty when he made heaven and earth commanded two great lights, the Sun and the Moon, to shine upon the earth, by the one of which, the Sun, he typified the episcopal, and by the other, the Moon, the imperial or royal authority. The Sun, the greater luminary, shines in the day as the bishop who enlightens souls, but the lesser luminary shines in the night, by which is meant the body. As the moon receives the light from the sun . . . so also the Tsar derives his consecration, unction, and coronation from the bishop. . . . There is just such a parity between these two persons in all Christian society as there is between the sun and the moon in the material world, for the episcopal power is in the day, *i.e.* over souls, but the imperial or royal is in the things of this world, and this power, which is the Tsar's sword, must be ready to act against the enemies of the Orthodox faith." [1]

In the prologue to the anathema which he pronounced on the Synod of 1660 Nikon repudiates the assumption that the Tsar has any right to meddle with the affairs of the Church. " How can men say that the chief care proper for the Tsar is the government of the Church ? Is the Tsar the head of the Church ? No. The Head of the Church is Christ. The Tsar neither is nor can be the head of the Church. He is one of its members, and on this account he can do nothing whatever in the Church, not even what belongs to the order of the lowest reader or clerk. If, contrary to the will of God, the Tsar acts by force, doing violence to the Churches, taking to himself their rights and properties, and judges bishops, archimandrites, and all the sacred order of the clergy, he will

[1] Palmer, iv. 328.

himself be judged for this. . . . Where is there any word of Christ that the Tsar is to have power over the Church ? Christ says, ' All power in heaven and earth is given unto Me.' Again He says, ' Whatsoever ye shall bind on earth shall be bound in heaven.' To whom does He say this, and to whom is this power given ? It is to the Holy Apostles, and after them to their successors the bishops, not to kings. . . . For this reason the priesthood is a vastly greater thing than the Empire." [1]

These were sentiments which no autocrat could tolerate, and the clergy of that day were so subservient to the autocracy that they did not tolerate them either. They found a spokesman in Ligarides. In one of the meetings of the Synod which degraded Nikon he expounded the rights of kings and Tsars in language which contradicted Nikon at every point. He said, " The King is free from law and from all necessity of accountability. He has irresponsible authority. He does as he pleases. He judges without being judged, and being himself living law he changes the customs and laws of his country according to his will and pleasure. As God is to the world so he is to the State." [2]

At the consecration of the Patriarch Joasaph he expounded still further the rights of the Tsar. " As being the common master of science for the Churches he is the director over the synodical judgments. He gives them their force, he regulates the ecclesiastical orders, he legislates for the life and polity of the clergy, he decides the causes of bishops and clerks, determines the elections to vacant churches, and promotes men from less honour to greater in accordance with his own judgment and by his own authority. . . . With the single exception of officiating in sacred things, all the other episcopal privileges are clearly represented by the Tsar. In respect of these he acts lawfully and canonically . . . and seeing that he is also the Lord's Anointed, and that Christ our God both is and is called our High Priest or Bishop, the Tsar also is reasonably adorned with episcopal graces." [3] The Synod

[1] Palmer, iv. 328.   [2] *Ibid*. iii. 226.   [3] *Ibid*. iii. 298.

formally agreed with these sentiments, and from that time forward till the connection between Church and State was cut by the Bolshevists the Church bowed like a slave before the Tsar's feet.

In the great struggle which centred round the service-books Nikon was victorious. In the more important struggle for the liberty of the Church within its own province, as he understood it, he was utterly defeated. He was the strongest champion which the Church's liberty has ever had in Russia, and he was more favourably situated for securing that liberty than any other who might have taken the field in its defence. His fall and failure there-fore implied that the Orthodox Church in Russia became more and more the tool of the secular power, and the results have been pernicious to the best interests of the Empire from that day to this.

CHAPTER XVII

FEODOR II. AND SOPHIA

ALEXIS died on 30th January 1676. Five of his children had predeceased him, but he left behind him Feodor and Ivan and six daughters, of whom Sophia was one, as the fruit of his first marriage, and Peter, Natalia, and Feodora as the fruit of his second. He had already made a will by which he transferred the crown to Feodor. Feodor, who was only in his fifteenth year, was an intelligent lad, alert in mind and well educated, but he was sickly and partly paralysed. During his brief reign of six years a truce was arranged with Poland and with Turkey, and an academy was founded at Moscow for the study of the Greek, Latin, and Slavonic languages, and of all scientific subjects which were not forbidden by the Church.

This academy became a battleground between the progressives and the reactionaries. The former were to some extent Latin in their sympathies and their theology. The latter held by Byzantium. The progressives might have carried all before them had not Dositheus, the Patriarch of Jerusalem, who was in Russia at the time, succeeded in securing for two reactionary Greek monks named Likhudy the post of directors in the new academy. This blow to the progressives was followed by another on the doctrinal point whether the Transubstantiation of the bread into the body of the Lord takes place when the words of Christ instituting the Sacrament are repeated by the priest, or whether it happens at a later point when the Holy Spirit is invoked in prayer. A decision was given by a Council at Kiev in 1690. It condemned the latter view as a heresy, and, fortified by this decision, Joachim, the Patriarch, dismissed all the progressive teachers and introduced others who favoured a stiff Orthodoxy.

Feodor's most notable achievement was the suppression of the Miestnichestvo, a system of hereditary right of precedence which was the source of endless trouble and sometimes of danger. According to this system the descendants of a man of high rank took precedence in all circumstances of the descendants of a man of low rank. The consequence was quarrels which kept the court in turmoil, ruined the discipline of the army, and crippled the civil service. Every noble family had a book of genealogies, and as it based its claims on these books they were preserved with jealous care. Feodor intimated that if the books were brought to him he would settle the question of precedence once for all. He kept his word, but not as those interested expected. When the books were produced he burned them to ashes, then he handed out new documents certifying the rank of the boyars at that date, and he declared that in future precedence would be determined by merit and by the will of the Tsar.

Feodor's first wife, Agatha, died in July 1681, leaving a son, Ilya, who died six days afterwards. On 24th February 1682 Feodor married as his second wife Martha Apraksia, but he himself died on 27th April of the same year without issue, and without nominating a successor. Contrary to all precedent he was nursed by his sister Sophia.

Sophia's appearance outside the terem indicated not only her force of character, but also the length to which in some circles the emancipation of women had gone. The ancient restrictions pressed severely on all women, and specially on the ladies of the Royal house. They passed useless lives behind closed doors, seeing no one and being seen by none. When they dined, they dined alone. The Tsar might sit at his wife's table, but not at that of his daughters. When they travelled abroad they used closed carriages with the blinds down. When they went to church they slipped in by a private gallery and sat behind a curtain.[1] But Sophia asserted herself with such effect that she instituted a salon, and she had long conversations with the guests. One of these was Simeon Polotsi, who

[1] Palmer, v. 221, App.

had studied at Polish academies and had come to Moscow in 1666. Another was Prince Vassili Golitzin, one of the most cultured men of the day. Although Golitzin was a married man, Sophia became infatuated with him, and began to dream of a union which would set him beside her on the throne. But Natalia and Peter stood in the way. She detested the one and saw danger in the other. Therefore when Feodor died, and when the Patriarch and the Council, on the ground that Ivan was physically unable to reign, proclaimed Peter as Tsar and Natalia, his mother, as Regent, she promptly showed her opposition to their decision. On the day of Feodor's funeral she detained Ivan in the palace, and, in defiance of all tradition, walked openly herself behind the coffin, thereby asserting the right of her absent brother. In hot indignation, Natalia and Peter left the church before the conclusion of the funeral service.[1]

Sophia could not indeed annul the proclamation of Peter as Tsar, but she found means of shaking his seat on the throne. When the Streltsi went to Natalia demanding arrears of pay she posed as their champion, and inflated them with the idea that they might seize the supreme power for themselves. They began a massacre of all the boyars they could lay their hands on, killing in all about seventy persons. Thereafter they demanded that Ivan should be first Tsar, that Peter should be second Tsar, and that Sophia should be Regent. Their demands were granted, but knowing that they were hated by the people, they endeavoured to strengthen their position by linking up their cause with that of the overburdened taxpayers, and petitioned the Government that they had created to justify the massacre of the 15th, 16th, and 17th May by allowing them to erect a pillar in the Red Square. Sophia gave them all they asked. Further, to bring the Old Believers to their side the Streltsi endeavoured to bring about a rising in favour of the old faith. Peter and his mother were then dispatched to the village of Præobrajensky, three miles from Moscow, while Ivan was retained

[1] Palmer, v. 926.

in the Kremlin and surrounded with pomp.   Khoviansky,
their leader, also arranged a conference to discuss the
merits of the old as against the new, and on 5th July a
mixed multitude of Streltsi and Old Believers marched
into the Kremlin with crosses and ikons and lighted candles,
and set up a platform from which they expected the
champions of the two sides to address them.   After waiting for some time, they were told that the conference was
to be held in the palace.   When they entered the audience
chamber they expected to see the two Tsars.   To their
intense surprise they found four women waiting them :
Sophia and her Aunt Tatiana sat on the double throne,
her sister Maria and the Tsaritsa Natalia sat below them in
arm-chairs, with the Patriarch Joachim and the bishops
on the right, and some boyars and civil dignitaries on the
left.   Under compulsion from Sophia, the Patriarch spoke
first and rebuked his audience for presuming to condemn
what had been approved by the late Tsar, and by the
œcumenical Patriarchs and the whole Orthodox Church.
A furious altercation ensued, in which Sophia was repeatedly
told to keep within the terem to which she belonged.
In reply, she said that if she had to listen to any more
insolence she and the two Tsars would at once leave Moscow.
As nothing could have been more alarming to the Streltsi
than this threat, for they knew that if the Government
disowned them they were left to the vengeance of their
enemies, they fell foul of each other, and their enthusiasm
for the Old Believers rapidly weakened.   " Do not betray
us and all the Russian Empire for half a dozen monks,"
Sophia said.   They answered : " We have nothing to do
with the faith ; we leave that to the Patriarch and the
Synod."   They were liberally rewarded for these sentiments, and in proof of gratitude they began to beat the
Old Believers who had come with them.   In this way
Sophia broke up an alliance which might have been
dangerous to her authority, and reduced the Old Believers
to impotence.

At the same time, she recognised that her position was
insecure.   She depended on the Streltsi, and they were

reactionary, while she and her friends were progressive. Their relations became strained, and she was in fact compelled to fulfil her threat of taking the Tsar from Moscow. From the Troitska Lavra she arranged the arrest of Khoviansky on a charge of conspiring to upset the Government, to install a new Patriarch, and to suppress the corrected books. He and his son were beheaded on 17th September 1682. The Streltsi in dismay became suddenly submissive, confessed that the massacres of May were a crime, and begged that the pillar in the Red Square should be taken down. Then they accepted as a commander one of Sophia's supporters, and on 6th November she and the court returned to Moscow.[1]

It was not long till she struck the Old Believers also, and the persecution which they endured can be compared to nothing but the pagan persecutions of the early Christians. In 1685 there appeared an edict of appalling severity. In it Sophia commanded her Orthodox subjects in general, and the civil officials in particular, to hunt down the Old Believers and kill them like vermin. Those who were suspected of sympathy with them were to be tortured three times to make them recant. If they refused they were to be burned alive. Those who yielded were to be knouted and set free. All whose names they mentioned in their agonies were to be seized and tortured in their turn, and so on. Any one who abjured his recantation was to be burned alive. Those who failed to betray Old Believers, or who sheltered them even unawares, were to be knouted and fined. Those who tried to alleviate their suffering or even inquired after them were to be knouted at the discretion of the magistrates.

In 1687 another edict commanded the authorities of the northern regions " to look to it carefully that the Raskolniks did not dwell in the woods, and that whenever they were heard of armed men should be dispatched in pursuit so that their refuges might be discovered and destroyed, and their property confiscated, and every man, woman, and child apprehended in order that their abomin-

[1] Palmer, v. 877.

able heresy might be exterminated without any chance of revival." [1] The edict was repeated in 1689, and in 1693 it was amended by instructions that all the buildings of the Old Believers should be burned to the ground, " in order that their companions should nowhere find any refuge."

These edicts remained in force for thirty years, and the Old Believers had no rest day or night. Thousands perished, thousands fled into the depths of the forest or across the frontiers to Sweden, to Poland, to the Caucasus, to the desolate shores of the White Sea, across the Urals to the farthest limits of Siberia, and some of them hid themselves so well that their settlements were not found for a hundred years. As far as possible they were followed, and when caught they were put to painful death ; but the fury of the persecutors was matched by the constancy of the persecuted, and even the weakest of them began to be filled with a spiritual exaltation. They no longer sought to escape death, they rushed to meet it.

If it is true that persecution drives wise men mad, the persecution to which the Old Believers were subjected explains the abnormal mentality which began to appear. Their sufferings are indicated in the following paragraph : " Everywhere blows resound, everywhere thrashings and subjugation to his yoke follow in the train of Nikon's teaching. Everywhere whips and rods are soaked daily in the blood of confessors. The preachers of Nikon's new ideas breathe not the spirit of gentleness but that of fury, wrath, tyranny. Beatings and wounds, such are the methods of their instruction, and not the grace of Christ : guile and evil deceit, and not apostolic humility. With these they would spread their faith, and the outcome of their cruel violence and tyranny is a reign of blood. Village and field are bathed in tears. Wilderness and forest are loud with weeping and moaning and groaning." [2]

Before long a new sect appeared—the Fire Baptists. In Tumen, a town in Western Siberia, after a man and a woman had been knouted in the public square for protesting in church against the new books, a monk named Danilo

[1] Stepniak, p. 415.   [2] Conybeare, p. 89.

gathered three hundred Old Believers and persuaded them to flee with him into the forests. Being surrounded so that they could not escape, they locked themselves into a wooden shed and set it on fire. Every one of them perished.[1] In Lake Ladoga there is a small island on which stands the monastery of Paleostrovsky. In 1688 a party of Old Believers defended themselves in it with success for several months. When the soldiers were advancing to the final assault they assembled in the wooden church, which they had already filled with combustible materials, blocked the windows with boards, nailed up the doors, and set the place on fire. The number of those who immolated themselves on this occasion is said to be not less than 2700. The monastery was rebuilt, stormed again, and the holocaust in the church was repeated. The number of those who died in this second " locking-up " is reported as about 1500.[2] It is reckoned that between the years 1667 and 1700 there were no less than 117 cases of this description, and the total number of victims in this period is said to exceed twenty thousand. As a rule this act of suicide was their only way of escape from the tortures which were waiting them at the hands of their enemies. In one case the agony was for minutes, in the other it was sure to last for hours.[3]

In the nineteenth century there were twenty incidents of this sort. In 1860 fifteen old men burned themselves alive in the government of Olonetz. The last collective suicide that is known took place in the beginning of 1897 in a farm on an estuary of the Dnieper when twenty-four men burned themselves alive. The doctrinal justification was found in a text which was accepted in a corrupt version: " There is one baptism by fire for the remission of sins."

At first the Old Believers were a homogeneous body, united by the conviction that they alone maintained the true faith. Before long, however, differences began to appear on the question of the priesthood. When they broke away from the State Church they took with them a number of priests who had been ordained before the days

[1] Stepniak, p. 417.   [2] *Ibid.*, p. 419.   [3] Wilbois, p. 249.

of Nikon, and the validity of their orders was admitted, but when these priests died there was no one to succeed them. One section maintained that no successors were possible, for grace had vanished from the earth. The future, therefore, held no prospect but that of a priestless Church. They became known as the Bezpopovtsi, *i.e.* the priestless people. The more moderate section held that grace still lingered, and they hit upon the plan of bribing priests of pre-Nikonian ordination to come over to them. They also accepted priests who were ejected from the State Church for any reason. When these devices failed to supply the number required, numbers of respectable men were appointed to hear confessions, to conduct marriages and funerals, to perform Mass, and to baptize.[1]

In this way they carried on till 1846 when they persuaded Ambrose, a bishop of Bosnia, to join them and to establish himself just across the Russian frontier at Belokrinitza in Bukovina. Here he ordained bishops and priests, as many as were required, and consecrated the bread for Communion, and mixed the holy oil. These are called the Popovtsi, *i.e.* the people with priests. They number about four millions, and it is they who are usually referred to when the Old Believers are spoken of.

The history of the Bezpopovtsi is much more tragical than that of their brethren. Torn from their ancient moorings, and launched on an uncharted sea, they broke company with each other and sailed to the farthest limits of extravagance. Their intellectual activity was robbed of its value by their ignorance and their wild fanaticism. They lived for the most part in regions which were empty and desolate. They had no common life, no books except a rare copy of the Bible or a service-book, which few of them could read. They had no spiritual guide except their memory, and what they believed to be their memory was often their imagination.

It is impossible to enumerate all the sections into which they divided; but a few of the more prominent may be mentioned.[2]

[1] Stepniak, p. 447.   [2] *Ibid.*, p. 451.

The Pomortsi, *i.e.* the shore-dwellers, lived on the shores of the White Sea to begin with, but they scattered over the central regions, and are even found in the far south. They are the most moderate of all the Bezpopovtsi, and at an early date they showed a disposition to come to terms with official Orthodoxy. In Peter's time they persuaded themselves that they had made a mistake in regard to the reign of Antichrist, for the great enemy of mankind was not yet come in the flesh. He was only reigning in a spiritual sense, and until he actually appeared they were at liberty to pray for the Tsar and to pay their taxes. In this way they eased themselves of the pressure of persecution, and became fairly comfortable.[1]

The desire of reconciliation with the State did not, however, commend itself to all of them. About 1684 the deacon Theodosius established a more rigid sect near Novgorod. He and his associates refused to pray for the Tsar even in modified terms, or to have intercourse with the State Church either in this world or the next. After the death of their leader in 1711 they split up. Some remained faithful to their principles, others joined the Pomortsi, others drifted into the State Church.[2]

One great difficulty which the Bezpopovtsi encountered arose in connection with marriage. When they were all flying for their lives marriage was not to be thought of. When they began to settle down the problem became acute. Some declared that the unmarried state was the ideal ; but even in their case the flesh was sometimes too strong for the spirit, and there began to appear certain " orphans," *i.e.* boys and girls of unacknowledged parentage, whom it was impossible to explain away. Sometimes the children were brought up by their mother's kinsfolk, sometimes they were simply abandoned.

The Beguni (fugitives) or Stranniki (wanderers) carried their fanaticism a stage further. They appeared mostly in the North. Their leader was a deserter from the Streltsi, named Euphemius, who baptized himself with rain-water so that he might owe nothing to a world which lies

[1] Wilbois, p. 285.

[2] *Ibid.*, p. 245.

in the wicked one. " Antichrist " he said, " is everywhere, and the only way to save one's soul is by incessant flight." Therefore he and his followers tore up their passports, threw away their money, because both were stamped with St. George and the dragon, *i.e.* with the mark of the beast, left their homes, and went wherever they could go, to escape the wrath to come. They may still be found wandering aimlessly, for " Here," they say, " we have no continuing city."

These sects and others which could be named have a relation with the State Church to this extent that they definitely oppose and reject it. There are other sects which get their inspiration from rationalism and from mystical sources. Among these are the Khlysti and the Skoptsi. The origin of the Khlysti is lost in antiquity, and there is nothing in it that gives it a claim to be called Christian, although it has borrowed some ideas from Christianity. The members of it hold that God is present only in man. He was perfectly incarnated for the first time in Jesus Christ. He was incarnated for the second time in the seventeenth century in a peasant named Daniel Philippovitch, who solved the problem of the comparative value of the old and the corrected service-books by the simple method of rejecting both. He collected as many of them as he could find and threw them into a river. In answer to his prayer that the way of salvation might be revealed to him he said that a chariot of fire came down from heaven attended by a cohort of angels, and that God entered into him by his ear. He therefore claimed to be the Living God, and forthwith began to teach that similar, though imperfect, incarnations are continually taking place. His followers call themselves in consequence Christs, Saviours, Redeemers, and so forth, and they pray to each other as they do to the Divine Being.

To enter this society one must resolve to eat no flesh meat, to drink no alcoholic liquor, to fast often, and to attend no worldly entertainments. To reach the condition in which the highest communion with the Divine is possible, it is necessary to stimulate the faculties of body and soul to delirium. This is done by suffering and by the trance. The Khlysti meet in profound secrecy in rooms with the doors and windows closed in such a way that no ray of light escapes into the darkness. These meetings are called " ships," and each ship has two pilots, a man and a woman, a Christ and a Madonna. Clothed in white robes the members of the ship sit round the walls, and the proceedings begin with a simple service in which singing and exhortation have a leading part. Thereafter they begin to dance. Faster and faster they whirl and spin like so many dervishes till they become hysterical. They gabble incoherently, they scourge themselves, they stamp and kick, and leap and shriek till, one after another, they fall on the floor exhausted and often unconscious. It is sometimes said that at this stage the lights are put out, and that an orgy of sensuality begins. The truth of this accusation is, however, doubtful. Similar charges were brought against the Early Christians. Besides, the Khlysti theoretically eschew marriage. They consider a wife married before entrance to the sect as a gift of the devil, and they describe the children born of her as little sins. Nevertheless, after initiation, they take spiritual wives in addition to the living legal wife, and they are expected to live with them in perfect chastity. It is noteworthy that the Khlysti are perhaps the only sect which includes members drawn from all classes of society.

The Skoptsi are an offshoot from the Khlysti. They came into existence about the middle of the seventeenth century, and before the end of it they found a leader in Kondrati Salivanov. Taking Matthew xix. 12 literally he emasculated himself, and began to preach his peculiar doctrines. He made so many converts that Catherine II. ordered him and his more prominent disciples to be knouted and sent to Siberia. The Tsar Paul brought him back to Moscow and shut him up in a lunatic asylum, from which he was released by Alexander I. He began again to preach, and made such a multitude of converts that in 1810 he was forced to sign a promise not to continue his propaganda. He broke his word, and, after being arrested and liberated twice, he was incarcerated in Suzdal, where he died in 1830. Nevertheless, the Skoptsi maintain that he is alive and that he is the Living God.

In their general attitude to religion the Skoptsi resemble the Khlysti. The main point of difference between them is that they regard emasculation as the supreme sacrament. The rite is usually performed in maturity, often after marriage and the birth of children. An attempt is sometimes made to inflict a similar mutilation upon women. The number of the Skoptsi is not large, and the sect cannot increase by natural growth. All the members come into it from the outside, sometimes voluntarily, sometimes compelled by force. As in the case of the Khlysti, they are drawn from all classes, and by the austerity of their lives, their industry, and their thrift they are usually well off and frequently wealthy. They seem to have a peculiar aptitude for making money and for getting into positions demanding fidelity. Their hope for the future life is largely based on a text in the Book of Revelation (xiv. 4): "These are they which were not defiled with women."

There are many other sects with similarly fantastic opinions and practices. They are all small, and they have no importance. Perhaps the best thing that can be said for them is that they supply an extensive field for the study of morbid psychology and religious mania.

CHAPTER XVIII

PETER THE GREAT

DURING the time that Sophia was reigning she was harassed by the thought that when Peter, her half-brother, came of age on his sixteenth birthday, her authority as Regent would cease. To avert this, in January 1684 she married her brother Ivan to Prascovia Soltikoff. The union produced only daughters, and in the meantime Peter was growing up. As far as possible she kept him in obscurity, and did nothing to fit him for the responsible position which he was destined to occupy. In the village of Præobrajenski he lived a boisterous life with youths of his own age, and as his natural disposition was not refined the companions he found for himself fostered what was worst in it. In the hope of weaning him from their influence his mother, Natalia, married him in his seventeenth year to Eudoxia Lopukhia, the daughter of a poor squire ; but the marriage came too late to act as a moral safeguard. For about three years he and his wife lived on peaceable terms, and the fruit of their union was two sons, Alexis, born 18th February 1690, and Alexander, born 3rd October 1691. Alexander died in 1692.

Even before the birth of his children Peter had found his way to the Sloboda, the quarter of Moscow where the foreigners lived. Its first inhabitants were German traders. In Peter's time there were English, Dutch, Danish, Swedish, and other residents, fine houses with flower gardens, schools and churches, a theatre, drinking shops and dancing saloons. There were merchants and traders, teachers and artists, soldiers and scholars, and others much less reputable, in whose society Peter found the low pleasure which he wanted. Among these was a Swiss named Lefort, who became his intimate friend, and Anna Mons, who became his first acknowledged mistress.

When Peter attained his legal majority, Sophia felt that she must act if she was to remain in power. Accordingly, she arranged with some of the Streltsi to kidnap him ; but being warned of his danger he escaped by a hasty flight to the Troitska Lavra, where his mother and sister joined him.[1] Sophia then sent the Patriarch Joachim to plead for her ; but he remained with Peter as one of his friends. She then set out herself to make her peace. On the way she received a peremptory order to return to the capital. There she appealed to the merchants to stand by her. The appeal fell on deaf ears, and when Patrick Gordon arrived with his troops she knew her cause was lost. A few days later Peter entered Moscow in triumph, and compelled Sophia to hide her disappointed ambition and her sore heart under a nun's veil in the monastery of Novodivichy.[2]

As the Tsar Ivan remained Tsar only in name, and as Peter was too young to govern by himself, a Council was formed to take his responsibilities off his shoulders, and while it was busy with the affairs of State he spent his time in drilling soldiers, building ships, and picking up a vast amount of miscellaneous information.

On the 25th January 1694 Natalia died somewhat suddenly, and Peter was affected by his loss. It did not, however, prevent him from arranging a wild extravaganza for his jester's wedding. The bride and the bridegroom were accompanied to church by a motley crowd dressed in outrageous costumes, and riding upon oxen, asses, swine, and dogs. The ceremonial was followed by a banquet which degenerated into a drunken orgy lasting for three days.

On the 29th January 1696 Ivan died, and Peter became sole Tsar. As he was now convinced that Russia must have access to the sea, and as the northern harbours were blocked by ice for more than six months of the year, and as the Baltic was in the hands of the Swedes, he turned his attention to the Black Sea. An expedition sent against Azov, in which he acted as a bombardier, failed completely.

[1] Palmer, v. 937.   [2] *Ibid.* v. 953.

A second expedition, in which he assumed the rank of captain, was more successful. The city was taken and a naval base was established at Taganrog.[1]

Being now on fire to secure for his people all the material benefits which Western Europe could offer him, he sent out bands of young men to Venice, England, and Holland to learn various branches of art and industry. Thereafter he arranged a great embassy to the West to visit the Emperor, the Kings of England and Denmark, the Pope and the States of Holland, the Elector of Brandenburg and the Republic of Venice. The principal figure in it was Lefort. Peter played the part of a private gentleman named Peter Mikhailov. This embassy scandalised the more conservative elements of Russian society, and the Streltsi, whose success with Sophia gave them a false idea of their importance, were loud in denouncing it. They were really a militia, undisciplined and inefficient and conceited to the highest degree. Many even of the rank and file were engaged in trade and agriculture. Soldiering was only one of their occupations, and that a secondary one. They preferred to go to war in the summertime, not too far from home, and when Peter compelled them to drill and dig trenches and build forts incessantly they growled that he was turning them into slaves. In March 1697 the embassy set out. It visited Riga, Königsberg, Berlin, and Amsterdam, where Peter joined it. There he studied surgery and engraving, and took part in the building of a frigate. He also purchased great quantities of books, mechanical models, and natural history specimens, and engaged engineers, sailors, shipwrights, and others for service in Russia. Thereafter he went to England and saw King William, and again engaged in shipbuilding at Deptford. On his way home he visited Vienna, and while there received news that the Streltsi had mutinied. He instantly resolved to finish with them, and on 25th August he reached his capital.

He believed that his half-sister Sophia had inspired the mutiny, but he wanted proof. In order to secure it

[1] Palmer, v. 989.

he built ten torture chambers in Præobrajenski, and in these for days and nights men and women writhed in anguish. They confessed nothing he could lay hold of. Massacre came next. On the 30th September 1698 two hundred of the Streltsi who had survived their torments were led out to the Red Square, where they were forced to kneel by fifties with their necks on a tree-trunk which served as a block. Peter himself began the bloody work. On the 11th October there were 144 fresh executions, 205 on the 12th, 141 on the 13th, 109 on the 17th, 65 on the 18th, and 106 on the 19th. In addition, three of the Streltsi, with copies of a letter to Sophia in their hands, were hung before the window of her cell till their bodies rotted to pieces. Those who fled to the country were hunted down, and in January 1699 those who were caught were executed. On one occasion the Patriarch, attended by the clergy, appeared in Peter's chambers and besought him to be merciful. Drunk with liquor and mad with lust for blood, Peter pointed to the ikon and shouted furiously : " What is that doing here ? Perhaps I do greater honour than you to God and His mother by defending my people against evil-doers."

Contemporaneously with Peter's arrival in Moscow and with all this bloodshed the whirlwind of change began. The first act of it looked like a practical joke, but it really signified his determination to change the people from an Oriental nation into a Western one. When the boyars appeared to welcome him after his return from the West he clipped off their beards with his own hand. The action was an outrage not only on their personal dignity but on their religious prejudices. In Russian eyes the beard was sacred. A man who shaved it off proclaimed himself a heretic who might expect to stand at the Last Day on the left side of the Judge among the damned. But if the boyars thought that this was only a mad freak they were quickly undeceived. On 1st September 1701 he issued a ukaz and repeated it in 1705 commanding all Russians to shave. As multitudes showed themselves ready to submit to the executioner's axe rather than to the barber's razor, a compromise was effected. The recalcitrants were ordered to pay a fine and to wear a medal which bore on one side a beard and moustaches under the words "Money taken for them," and on the other side the date. A similar attack was made on the long flowing robes, and was continued until the people cut their coats according to the Tsar's orders.

While this was going on, Peter gave their moral sense a more serious shock by repudiating his wife. She had long been out of sympathy with him, and he was tired of her. He asked her to take the veil. She refused. He therefore took away her son Alexis, then eight years and seven months old, and dispatched her to Suzdal to be shut up in a convent. In May 1699 he had her tonsured by force.

Another change caused great excitement. On 20th December 1699 he gave orders that the New Year should no longer be reckoned from 1st September, which was believed to be the date of the creation of the world because at that time fruit was ripe on the trees of the Garden of Eden, and should be reckoned as from 1st January. The order was received with horror, and Adrian, the Patriarch, refused to officiate at the service appointed to signalise its coming into force.

Peter's efforts to reach the open sea had not yet met with complete success. Starting from Azov he tried to force his way through the Bosphorus to the Mediterranean. Finding this impossible, he turned his eyes once more to the Baltic and arranged a coalition against Sweden, which included Poland and Denmark. Sweden took its enemies in detail and struck swiftly and hard. Denmark was forced to sign the peace of Traventhal in 1700. The Poles were driven from Riga, and on 30th November 1700 a battle fought on the Narva resulted in Peter's defeat. Happily for Russia, the Swedes went off on a side track, and Peter took advantage of this to perfect his army. By 1702 he had become master of the district through which the river Neva flows from Lake Ladoga to the sea. At its exit from the lake he captured a Swedish fortress

and renamed it Schlusselburg. At its confluence with the
Gulf of Finland he captured another fortress, and on
27th May 1703 laid the foundations of a new stronghold
on a neighbouring island. This afterwards became the
citadel of SS. Peter and Paul. Beside it he began to erect
a new capital. Moscow was hateful to him. It was the
headquarters of reaction and stagnation. Into his new
city he resolved to gather a society which would help him
to introduce new ideas into Russian life.

From many points of view the site he had fixed on was
the worst in his dominions. It lay on the circumference of
Russia as far as possible from the centre. The surrounding
region was barren and empty. It was easy to attack
and difficult to defend. The banks of the river that ran
through it were swampy at all times, and were often laid
under water by storms. The river itself was too shallow
for merchant vessels. It was also frozen over for months
on end, and it was away from the great trade route. Nevertheless, Peter determined that there and nowhere else his
new capital, Petrograd, should stand.

For its construction he pressed into his service prisoners
captured in war. He compelled the nobles to bring their
serfs, but he did nothing to supply them with tools or food.
Many nobles ruined themselves by their outlays, and no
less than 200,000 of the forced labourers perished in the
first year. But canals were cut, streets were laid out, piles
were driven, houses and churches were built, fortifications
were constructed, a harbour was improvised, the island
of Kronslot was armed for defence, and in a twelvemonth
the city was an actual fact. By the simple expedient
of forbidding foreign merchants to import or export hemp,
flax, leather, corn, etc., through Archangel, he directed
so much trade to Petrograd that in 1725 no fewer than
240 vessels entered the port.

In his wars with the Swedes, the Tartars, and the Turks,
Peter became convinced of the pressing need for developing
Russia's resources, and he applied himself to this work
with titanic energy. His reforms were all devised, as it
were, on the spur of the moment, for Peter's vehement

nature made him constitutionally unable to sit down calmly and think out anything, and his riotous habits and his too often prolonged drunkenness made the patient working out of political problems impossible. His general conceptions were often sagacious, as well as bold, but they were not co-ordinated with each other, and they were not developed in detail. Besides, one decree after another came hurrying from his pen so rapidly that the people could not remember them all, and bewilderment became confusion.

To secure the men needed for the army and navy he introduced conscription. To secure money, he taxed everything that was taxable. Unfortunately he did nothing to check the dishonesty of the tax collectors, who, from his favourite Minister, Mentschikov, downwards, embezzled vast sums and reduced the revenues that reached the coffers of the State to a mere fraction of what was wrung from the tax-payers. Nevertheless, when Peter died he did not leave one rouble of public debt. In these circumstances the exhaustion of the tax-paying classes can be imagined, and their resentment against Peter and his policy manifested itself in many directions.

One of his devices for increasing the revenue was a change in the basis of taxation. Between 1718 and 1722 he arranged that the individual, and not the household or the commune, should be reckoned in future the unit of taxation. The name of every serf was therefore to be inscribed on the tax-payers' roll, and from each serf so inscribed a specified sum was exacted. This poll tax, or soul tax, as it was called, created further resentment. In addition, to make sure of its payment, the serfs were forbidden to leave their master's service, and when they tried to flee he closed the frontiers against them and kept them in their cage.

On the other hand, for the purpose of getting some useful work out of the upper classes, he ordered all males of these classes to serve the State in the army, the navy, the civil administration, or the Court. These spheres of service were divided into fourteen grades (tchin), and rank was made dependent on the grade which the official occupied. Previous social status had nothing to do with it. Further, every one entering the service of the State had to begin at the lowest grade and work his way upwards. In the army, for example, the sons of serfs and those of boyars had to stand side by side in the ranks and go through the same drill, and sleep in the same barracks. The sons of the boyars were furious at this, but if they refused to obey they were deprived of their land and forbidden to marry. In the same way the middle classes were divided into sections and graded. In this way Peter created a vast bureaucracy, for whose maintenance he made no adequate provision. The inevitable consequence was that the members of the bureaucracy eked out their scanty official salary by taking bribes, and the corruption, the perversion of justice, and the delay in the dispatch of business which began then continues to the present day.

In 1711 the Senate was created. It was meant to act as a board of supervision while Peter was away on foreign wars, but it became a permanent institution, exercising the largest powers in legislation and finance. In the same year, and on Prussian models, certain ministries or colleges were created. The first of these was the College of Commerce. In 1717 Peter decided that their total number should be ten. In 1722 he issued regulations for the College of the Admiralty, and to save further trouble he commanded that the regulations for the Admiralty should be the pattern for all the others, the only change permitted being that of names. To these colleges he annexed financial areas, ignoring what he had already done for purposes of taxation and producing overlapping and confusion.

As another means of increasing the efficiency of his people, he turned his attention to education. In a ukaz of 28th February 1714 he sketched a magnificent scheme of free and compulsory education. It found little favour. An outcry was raised that if children were withdrawn from work, agriculture and industry would be ruined, and he was forced to confine instruction to the sons of civil servants and of village priests. This by no means contented him, and he started a training college at Petrograd, and another at Moscow, which would turn out men fit to act as officers in his army and navy. Foreign masters were appointed to teach mathematics, navigation, geography, engineering, Latin, French, and German. Scholars were more difficult to secure. Most of those who were brought into these advanced seminaries could neither read nor write. Therefore in 1714 Peter ordered the establishment of primary schools in connection with the monasteries, as well as technical schools in a few towns. To provide materials for instruction he caused suitable manuals to be translated, and when the question was raised by the Holy Synod whether the language into which the translation was made was to be the old Slavonic of the service-books or the language in common use, he decreed that it should be neither. It was to be the language used in his diplomatic chancery, and by this decree he gave Russia what is now written by the people of his native land. To make reading easier he revised the old Cyrillic alphabet, reduced the number of letters, simplified their forms, and got a Dutchman to cast new founts of type.

Peter was probably most successful in developing the commercial and industrial side of Russian life. Under his direction factories, foundries, and mines were opened under Russian management, agriculture was stimulated, establishments for breeding horses were set up, the vine was introduced into some provinces, the forests were protected, and, to facilitate intercourse and the transit of goods, he devised a network of canals.

It must not be supposed that any of these reforms were meant to secure Peter's personal ends. In his eyes they were only means to an end, and that was the service of his country. He was absolutely unselfish, and he was ready to accept any one who would help him to achieve his purpose, with complete indifference to his helper's position or pedigree.

Mentschikov, who became his Chancellor, began life as a pastry-cook's boy. He was a man of unbounded ability, but he never learned to read, and he could only sign his name. Shafirov, who became Vice-Chancellor, was a broker whom Peter took out of a shop in Moscow. Devier, the Chief of the Police, was a Portuguese Jew whom Peter found on a Dutch ship serving as a cabin-boy. Jagoujinski, who became director of the great ironworks at Tula, was a serf working as a blacksmith. Besides these, there were others of similarly obscure origin, not excluding even a negro.

Catherine, Peter's second wife, is the most illustrious of them all. She was born a serf somewhere in Livonia. She appeared first as a domestic servant in the house of the Lutheran pastor of Marienburg. When the town was taken by the Russians in 1702 she became the mistress of a Russian officer. From him she passed to General Scheremetev, and from him to Mentschikov, in whose house Peter found her. She was quite illiterate, but she had abundance of common sense, and she fascinated the Tsar so that he married her privately in 1706, and in 1712 repeated the ceremony in public. In 1718 she received the title of Tsarina, and in 1720 her coronation took place. She was in many respects an admirable consort to her husband. Her equable temperament was not disturbed by his explosiveness, and she had a strange power of subduing him even in his volcanic rages. She never interfered in politics, she sought nothing for herself, and she tolerated her husband's excesses and infidelities philosophically. She bore him twelve children, all of whom, except Anne and Elisabeth, died in infancy.

It cannot be said that Peter's reforms were popular. They were introduced by autocratic decrees, they disturbed every vested interest, and they introduced changes to which the slow-going mentality of the people could not adjust itself. So great was the opposition he encountered that even his tremendous energy failed to carry his projects to complete success. Conservatives in politics united with reactionaries in religion, and when they did not venture on open hostility they retarded the wheels of progress by the deadweight of their inertia. The leaders of the opposition were the clergy and those who were associated with the Old Believers, and it was with them that he came into conflict. Peter himself had no interest in religious controversy, and if the Old Believers had been wise enough to keep their politics apart from their religion he would have left them unmolested to the end of his days. In 1700 he said that if they worked in his forges and paid his taxes they could pray in any way they liked. But when he found that they would neither work in his forges nor pay his taxes his mood changed. The decrees issued by Sophia were put into force once more, and for years he harassed and flogged and tortured them without mercy. As he failed to break down their opposition he came to a compromise in 1712, promising to stop the persecution on condition that they paid double taxes and wore a dress that made them look ridiculous. Ten years later he endeavoured to stop the propagation of their opinions by silencing their teachers, and with the view of suppressing their peculiar form of worship he forbade runaway priests or Bezpopovtsi elders to conduct religious services. His moderation did as little as his severity to check the growth of the movement, and the Old Believers became a power which the Church could not ignore.

To some extent they took their revenge by circulating strange stories about their oppressor. They said he was no true-born Russian. He was a changeling. The true Tsar had been killed on his tour in the West and an impostor had usurped his place. Some of them had a more sinister explanation. They said he was the incarnation of the power of evil—in fact, he was Antichrist, a being with whom they dare not come to terms. They turned everything against him. His order to shave the beard was taken to prove his desire to destroy in man the image of God, for did not the holy ikons always depict God with a beard. The order to take a census of the people before drawing up the taxation registers was preliminary to enrolling them in the army of Antichrist. The change of the first day of the year from September to January was a sign that the years of our Lord were to be remembered no more, and that the years of Satan were to begin. The smoking of tobacco, which Peter practised and encouraged, was held to be condemned by Scripture because that which goeth out of the mouth defiles a man.

This widespread discontent required nothing more than a point round which it could crystallise to make it dangerous. Unfortunately such a point was found in Peter's son Alexis. Alexis was unlike his father in everything, and his antagonism to Peter's policy was fostered by his confessor, the protopop Yakov Ignatiev, who familiarised Alexis with the idea of bringing the reforms to a standstill after Peter's death. In 1711 Alexis was married greatly against his will to Sophia Charlotte of Wolfenbuttel. The young couple began life well enough, but three weeks after the wedding Peter ordered Alexis away to Poland and kept him on the move for a twelvemonth. His young wife was practically abandoned, and as no provision had been made for her maintenance she was reduced to such poverty that she had to borrow money from Mentschikov. Natalia, her first child, was born in July 1714. In October 1715, in giving birth to a son, who became Peter II., she died.

On the day of her funeral Peter sent Alexis a stern letter, threatening that if he did not turn from his evil ways he would be cut off like a cancerous swelling. To his father's chagrin he replied that he would accept disinheritance gladly, for his own desire was to live quietly. Peter retorted that if he would not serve the State he must become a monk. Alexis replied that he had no objections to become a monk. This made Peter even more angry, and on 26th August 1716 he ordered Alexis to join him in his Pomeranian Army. In place of doing so, Alexis took to flight. Peter's agents found him in Naples, and it was only after they produced letters from Peter promising pardon for all his faults and permission to marry his mistress, and to live on his own estates, that he consented to return to Moscow.[1]

On 3rd February 1716 he appeared before his father, who overwhelmed him with abuse, and declared that

[1] Palmer, vi. 1218.

pardon would be granted only on condition that he gave
the names of his associates. A set of entangling questions
was then placed before him, and, with the warning that
the slightest failure or mistake would cost him his life,
he was commanded to answer them in writing. On
13th June he was brought before the Metropolitan, the
archbishop, and several bishops. In their presence Peter
charged him with conspiracy and rebellion, and asked of
what punishment he was worthy. They asked for proof
of his guilt. Torture was then applied to his servants, his
confessor, his uncle, and himself, but nothing could be
elicited. All that he himself admitted was a desire for his
father's death in the hope that he might succeed to the
vacant throne. On the 24th June he was condemned.
The clergy who had been consulted with regard to the
nature of his punishment presented a memorial in which
they balanced the severity of the Old Testament against
the clemency of the New, and concluded that Peter might
act as he thought fit. On the 26th of the same month
Peter, accompanied by a few friends, entered the prison
in which Alexis was confined, and when they left it a
few hours afterwards the unhappy prince was dead. The
report became current that he had been knouted to death,
and that the first blows had been struck by Peter's own
hand. This may or may not have been the case, but in
the whole business Peter's conduct was unpardonable.
Alexis may or may not have been right in wishing that his
father's reforms would come to a standstill. He may or
may not have been justified in thinking that the welfare
of Russia would be reached along other lines than those
which Peter was following. It is certain that no proof of
treasonable conspiracy against his father's policy or his
father's life was ever produced, and even if it had been, a
spark of paternal feeling would have made the last scenes
in the youth's life impossible. The stain on Peter's name
is indelible.

The reactionary spirit against which Peter was striving
was strongest in the Church, and for the Church and its
clergy Peter had the most profound contempt. In March

1690 the Patriarch Joachim died and was succeeded by Adrian, a feeble old man, who was Metropolitan of Kazan. Joachim made a will in which he besought the Tsar to abide in the Orthodox faith, to defend the traditions of the Fathers, to forbid heretics to preach or to build churches on Russian soil, or to contract marriage with Russian subjects, or to hold command in the army, navy, or civil service, or to introduce foreign fashions in dress. In other words, he condemned Peter's whole policy and practice, and asked him to reverse it.[1]

Adrian's first pastoral address was constructed on the same lines, and in a sermon preached before one of Peter's campaigns he followed it up by denouncing the use of tobacco and the practice of shaving the beard.

Peter was not slow to show his anger. He not only refused to walk in procession on Palm Sunday holding the bridle of the Patriarch's mule, he forbade the procession itself and replaced it by another. From the most drunken of his companions he chose his old tutor Zotoff, created him mock Patriarch, surrounded him with mock clergy, filled them all with liquor, and sent them staggering along the street. On his head Zotoff carried a mitre surmounted by a little naked Bacchus. His crozier was adorned with figures of Venus and Cupid, his attendants carried bowls of wine and brandy, lighted tobacco leaves were used as incense, and in the performance of a mock ritual Zotoff used crossed tobacco-pipes. Adrian replied to the insult by shutting himself up in his palace and allowing the business of the Church to go to pieces. He died on 16th October 1700, and with him the line of Patriarchs came to an end.

Peter had already resolved to treat the Church as he treated other departments of State, and to replace the Patriarch by a college or board of management. But he felt he must allow the people time to become familiar with the idea of a Church without a Patriarch before its headless condition was constitutionally fixed. In a search for a man who would keep the chair in existence without actually filling it he found Stephen Yavorsky.

[1] Palmer, vi. 1551.

Yavorsky was a native of Volhynia, who caught Peter's attention in 1700 by a sermon he preached in Moscow. Peter made him Bishop of Riazan, but Yavorsky had scarcely reached his See when he was summoned to Petrograd to become guardian of the patriarchal chair. After entering on office he tried to raise the Moscow academy and other schools from the low condition into which they had fallen by introducing teachers who were for the most part Jesuits. They gave instruction in Latin, mathematics, and branches of Western learning, and attracted many pupils. Dositheus of Jerusalem was intensely annoyed by this policy, and wrote Yavorsky a furious letter. He also wrote in similar terms to Peter, who paid no attention to the communication, and went on filling the schools with the best teachers he could find and appointing to the bishoprics as they became vacant men who were pledged to support his reforms.

In 1713 Yavorsky wrote a treatise against the Old Believers, in which he tried to show that Moscow was not the apocalyptic Babylon, and that Peter was neither Antichrist nor the forerunner of Antichrist. Unfortunately his zeal in his master's defence cooled when he found there was no intention of appointing another Patriarch, and that the interference of the civil courts in the Church's affairs was increasing. On 17th March 1712 he preached against some of the fiscal regulations, and in 1714 he held a Synod against those who went over to Lutheranism, and he executed one who did so. In defence of his position he wrote a book called *The Rock of the Faith*, which Peter did not allow him to publish. He converted Peter's annoyance into alienation by showing his sympathy with Alexis, and in 1718 he was brought to Petrograd and put under surveillance.[1]

Peter found a man much more to his mind in a Little Russian named Theophanes Prokopovitch, who became rector of the academy in Kiev in 1712 and Bishop of Pskov in 1716. When Peter returned from his second foreign tour, Prokopovitch was entrusted with the task of replying

[1] Palmer, vi. 1596.

to the Doctors of the Sorbonne, who had approached Peter with regard to the union of the Eastern and Western Churches. Yavorsky had drafted a reply that nothing could be done because of the vacancy in the Russian Patriarchate. Peter naturally set this draft aside. The draft prepared by Prokopovitch in June 1718 formulates the reply which in substance has been given to all later proposals regarding reunion. It says that the Russian bishops alone cannot settle the matter, for many peoples not included in Russia combine to make up the Eastern Church. The four Eastern Patriarchs would need to be consulted, and a full representation of the whole Eastern Church would need to be secured. Sectional action would be valueless.

So far as Peter himself was concerned the reply was a piece of insincerity. He had no scruple about sectional action when it suited him to have none. In 1723 he ordered the Russian bishops to treat in a sympathetic spirit proposals for union made by certain English churchmen.

The design of reducing the Church to the level of the other departments of State at last took practical shape. The draft embodying Peter's ideas, which was prepared by Prokopovitch, opens with a series of reasons intended to show that the rule of a college is more advantageous than that of a single individual. It was submitted to Peter in February 1720. After making a few changes on it he laid it before six bishops and three archimandrites who happened to be in Petrograd. Then it was laid before a special meeting of the Senate and signed. Two copies were made. One was deposited in the Imperial archives, the other was sent round the eparchies to receive signatures.[1] Then on 25th January 1721 Peter instituted the Holy Synod by a special decree. He appointed the membership to be one president, two vice-presidents, four councillors, and four assessors, with a secretary. The oath which the members of the Holy Synod were compelled to take before entering on their office was word for word the same as that taken by members of the Senate in similar circumstances, the

[1] Palmer, vi. 1639.

only difference being that where " Senate " occurs in the one, " Synod " occurs in the other.   In Peter's opinion the Senate and the Synod stood on the same level.

On the 16th September 1721 there issued from the press a series of regulations by which the members of the Synod are directed in their respective offices.   The first defines the nature of the Holy Synod and expounds the reasons for its creation.   The second defines the affairs that are to come within its jurisdiction.   Under the first are affairs common to the whole Church and to the orders in it, and to all classes of men.   Under the second are the affairs pertaining to particular orders—bishops, priests, deacons, monks, schoolmasters, scholars, etc.   To these an appendix was added in April 1722 regulating the admission to the monastic life and the dress and deportment of priests, monks, and nuns.

If anything were needed to prove Peter's total ignorance of the nature of the Church as a spiritual organism deriving its life and power from Jesus Christ and governing itself in accordance with His revealed will, the proof is found in the last section of the regulations by which the members of the Holy Synod are directed in their respective offices : " As to the extent of their power, His Imperial Majesty has been graciously pleased by his sovereign authority to grant such a power to the spiritual college as is expressly declared in His Majesty's edict printed in the beginning of these regulations." [1]   There is no other Church in Christendom which has bowed its neck so meekly to the yoke of the civil power.

At first the Tsar was represented in the Synod by Yavorsky, its president.   After Yavorsky's death the office became permanently vacant, and on 11th May 1722 Peter issued another decree that a man of resolution chosen from among his officers was to be attached to the Synod with the title of Procurator in the same way as a Procurator was attached to the other colleges.   He was to act as the Tsar's eye and ear, watching how the Synod performed its duties, restraining it when it transgressed the

[1] Consett, p. 124.

limits assigned to it, and reporting to the Tsar everything worthy of imperial attention. In theory the Procurator was not a member of the Synod. He sat at a table by himself while the Synod sat at another, but in fact the Procurator was the Synod's lord and master. He alone, as the representative of the Tsar, arranged its business. Its decisions had to be endorsed by him if they were to receive the Tsar's approval, and so long as the autocracy lasted it was a mere tool in the Tsar's hands.[1]

The Synod was therefore not a venturesome body, neither was it a representative body. Under the autocracy the Church courts were all nominated bodies, and none of them was allowed to function at its own discretion. The civil government marked out the area of each diocese, appointed to it a bishop, surrounded him with a committee which acted as his consistory, but it took no account of the wishes of the members of the Church in these proceedings. In the same way the Synod was created by the Tsar, its powers were defined by the Tsar, the number of its members was fixed by the Tsar, and in the discharge of its functions it was held accountable to the Tsar.

Peter, however, thought it necessary to give the Synod some sort of ecclesiastical standing. Therefore, on 30th September 1721, he wrote to the Patriarch of Constantinople intimating that he had followed the example of the pious rulers of the Old Testament by reforming the Church, and that he had created the Holy Synod as a High Court of judgment to exercise all the functions formerly exercised by the Patriarch. He said he had instructed it to rule in accordance with the dogmas of the Orthodox Church, which were to be considered fundamental and unchallengeable, and that the members of the Synod had sworn to maintain them. He added : " We rely on your Holiness as the chief bishop of the Holy Catholic Eastern Church to approve of the institution, and at once to inform the Patriarchs of Alexandria, Antioch, and Jerusalem of the matter."

The letter was really a command, and the Patriarch of Constantinople did not hurry his reply to it. After two

[1] Palmer, vi. 1650.

years' silence he sent a letter, not to Peter, but to the Holy Synod itself, in which he confirmed what Peter had done. " The Synod is," said he, " and is to be named our Brother in Christ by all pious and Orthodox Christians, both clergy and laity, rulers and subjects, and by all official persons and dignitaries, and it has authority to do and to perform all that is done and performed by the four Apostolic and Most Holy Patriarchal thrones." The letter was dated 23rd September 1723.

Of all the colleges which Peter founded the Holy Synod is the only one which has survived to the present day. In subsequent reigns a few changes were made in it, but they were essentially trivial, and they were determined more by the temperament and policy of successive Tsars and Pro-curators than by the initiative of its own members. As a rule it has been opposed to change. It has stereotyped the forms in which religious life expresses itself to such an extent that the spirit has gone out of them. It has exalted immobility to the rank of a first principle, and it has been cruelly intolerant of dissent. It has looked on every new movement in Church and State with alarm, and has joined its forces with those of the civil power to stifle the spirit of liberty and free thought in blood.

Peter's attack on the Church's rights of self-govern-ment went hand in hand with an attack on its wealth, and its wealth was great enough to excite the cupidity of an autocrat who was desperately in need of money. The monks were numerous, and in Peter's opinion they were no better than parasites. In a ukaz of 21st January 1721 he said : " As it is now impossible to lead back the monks to the duties of their calling we must think of some other way to make them pleasing to God and useful to the State. We are the more bound to do this since their manner of life at present is only a cloak. They are the cause of the scorn and reproach which is brought on our religion, and, besides, they are dangerous to the State because they are for the most part an idle and useless crowd who have brought into the monastery only the love of ease and indolence. The greater part of them are peasants who,

far from renouncing the pleasures of the world, which they
never had, really entered the monastery to procure these
and to escape the secular duties which their laziness made
irksome. If you ask what use they are, one can only
answer absolutely none either to God or man."

At an early date in his reign Peter found an opportunity
of starting the process of confiscation. Nine days after
the death of the Patriarch Adrian one of Peter's advisers
named Kourbatoff suggested that the property of the clergy
should be brought under imperial administration, and the
boyar Mushkin Pushkin was set over the monastery court
with powers which practically placed the Church's property
at the disposal of the Crown.

In 1722 Peter caused a census of the monks to be taken,
and found that the various establishments contained
not less than 14,534 men and 10,673 women. Many of
these had no more right to be called religious than if they
had been guests in an hotel. They constituted a floating
population which drifted from one monastery to another
enjoying the benefits of travel and the pleasures of change,
and living lives that were frequently characterised by moral
laxity. Peter also ordered a register of the property of the
monasteries to be compiled, and found it to be enormous.
They owned nearly a million serfs. The Troitska Lavra
alone possessed 92,000 serfs, besides fisheries, mills, fields,
and forests without number. The archimandrites who
ruled these establishments wore diamond buckles in their
shoes, and their robes and other appointments were on
the same scale of magnificence.

This was more than Peter could tolerate. He ordered
all those who were not regularly tonsured and enrolled
to be cleared out of the convents and nunneries, and he
laid down regulations which made entrance to the monastic
life more difficult. No man was to be allowed to become
a monk till he was thirty years of age. He was not to be
admitted if he were a soldier who had deserted his regiment,
or if he were a peasant who failed to produce a letter of
recommendation from his owner, or if he had a wife alive,
or other dependants left unprovided for, or if he could not

show proof of the consent of his parents. No woman was to be accepted as a nun below the age of fifty, and if at any time after that age she desired to leave the monastic life for any reason she was to be allowed to do so. In both cases there was to be a period of probation which in the case of men was fixed at three years, and the rules governing the behaviour of professed nuns were specially strict.

Under Pushkin's superintendence some of the monasteries were closed, others were united, and the attractions of the monastic life were reduced to zero. In order to employ the monks usefully, they were compelled to take under their care invalid soldiers and the aged poor, and to relieve their minds of secular distractions Peter took the expenditure of their revenues into his own hand. Out of these he gave each monk the meagre annual allowance of ten roubles of money, ten measures of corn, and a quantity of fuel. The balance was consigned to the coffers of the State.

These reforms were much needed, and although the monks were infuriated they did not dare to make open opposition. Besides, the piety of the faithful could not be restrained, and wealth of many kinds continued to flow towards them.

In spite of his interest in the efficiency of the Church as a branch of the civil service, Peter's personal conduct was a prolonged insult both to morality and to religion. He was habitually a drunkard and a libertine. He not only threw the reins on the neck of his own lusts, he encouraged others to do the same. At an early period he created what he called the Council or Conclave of the Most Drunken, and he kept it going till his death. At intervals he revised its statutes, and the changes all tended to greater ribaldry and profanity. The members of the Conclave were selected from the most dissolute of his associates, and along with them were enrolled, against their will, some of the most honourable men in the Empire. The proceedings at their meetings baffled description. The first president was the sot Zotoff, his cardinals were men like himself. They met in an apartment called the Hall of the

Consistory, and its only furniture was wine-casks. At the end of the room on a pile of barrels, bottles, and glasses was the throne of the Knez Papa, and as his cardinals defiled before him one by one they had to swallow a glass of brandy. After more liquor was consumed a procession was formed, headed by the Knez Papa, seated on a wine-butt drawn by oxen. It took its uncertain way to a hall lined on each side with narrow beds, and after the members lay down they were forbidden to rise till the conclave was over. During the three days it lasted they were plied with drink, and stimulated to all sorts of filthiness. The condition of the place speedily became sickening, but Peter reeled from bed to bed in wild hilarity, noting down anything specially ribald or blasphemous, and deriving the keenest pleasure from the degradation of his associates. In 1714, at the marriage of Zotoff, who was then an old man of eighty-four, and again at the election of his successor, the proceedings, all carefully arranged by Peter himself, reached the limit of disgusting debauchery.[1]

It is impossible to escape the conclusion that for Peter moral considerations did not exist. He had ignored them so long that at last he became incapable of recognising them. Of religion, in so far as it implies the fear of God, the love of the Saviour, and the effort to live a holy life, Peter had none. His zeal for the interest of his country was both real and intense, but it rose no higher than concern for its material welfare, and his efforts to secure this were to some extent frustrated by his impetuosity. The Church was no more than a machine which he saw might be useful, so he put it into the best working order and kept it under his own control. He made it his humble servant, and he so terrorised it that it made no protest against his outrageous behaviour, and even addressed him with obsequious flattery. The orations delivered by prominent churchmen were justified by the political benefits he endeavoured to confer on his country ; in so far as they referred to his character, they prove nothing but the orator's servility.

[1] Waliszewski, *Peter*, p. 160.

CHAPTER XIX

FROM CATHERINE I. TO CATHERINE II.

TOWARDS the end of his reign, Peter began to be concerned about the succession to his throne. He intended to nominate Catherine, his wife, as his heir, and to pave the way for this he had her publicly crowned in Moscow on 17th May 1724. Catherine was, however, caught by her husband in compromising circumstances, and although she was not repudiated she fell out of favour, and her formal nomination never took place. The instructions which Peter tried to give on his death-bed in 1725 were completely unintelligible. Catherine's friends took instant advantage of the situation, and a few hours after the breath was out of Peter's body she was publicly declared to be Tsarina.

So far as she understood Peter's reforms she sympathised with them, but she was easy-going in her temperament, and she relaxed the strain of the previous twenty years. The nobles and others whom Peter had compelled to serve in what they considered bitter bondage were delighted at the change, and began to feel that the good old days were returning. She died on 17th May 1727 after a career impossible in any other European country, in which she passed from the lowest depths of obscurity to the highest pinnacle of power and fame.

Shortly before her death she chose as her successor the son of Alexis, and he ascended the throne as Peter II. He was only a youth, and for a time was completely in the power of Mentschikov. He liberated himself by a dramatic blow and sent the powerful noble and his family to Siberia. He then fell under the control of the Dolgoroukis, and he was on the point of overthrowing them likewise when he died of smallpox on 30th January 1730.

The intrigues which followed resulted in the election of Anne, Duchess of Courland, daughter of Peter the Great's elder brother, Ivan. She had had a hard life. Her husband died soon after her marriage, and she suffered much from the jealousy of her neighbours and from poverty. When she came to the throne she took her revenge, and with the aid of her favourite Biron, the son of a groom, whom she created Duke of Courland, she pursued her enemies with implacable ferocity. At the same time she surrounded herself with Germans, whose tyranny and cruelty created the conviction that the sooner they were got rid of the better. Discontent was universal, but Biron's spies were everywhere, and a whisper against any one was followed by arrest, torture, imprisonment, or death.

Heretics and dissenters had to endure severe sufferings. In 1730 she ordered the Holy Synod to take more vigorous measures to rid the land of heresy, and in 1731 she issued a ukaz that all dealers in magic should be burned alive, and all who consulted them should be flogged to death.

Anne died in 1740 at the age of forty-seven. She had chosen as her successor Ivan, the two-month-old son of her niece, the daughter of Peter's half-brother Ivan V., and she had appointed Biron as Regent. For thirteen months the infant was known as Ivan VI.; then a palace revolution sent Biron to Siberia, consigned the youthful Tsar to the fortress of Schlusselburg, and seated on the throne Elisabeth, daughter of Peter the Great. Elisabeth, who was about thirty-two years of age, was indolent, frivolous, and licentious. Her personal conduct overstepped the bounds of decency, but she was intensely patriotic. She expelled the Germans from the Court, and took the side of Austria against Frederick the Great. She displayed an interest in literature, and in her reign there appeared the first great Russian writer, Lomonosoff. With her approval the first Russian University, that of Moscow, was founded in 1758. She also devoted some attention to religion. She built churches and went on pilgrimages. She dismissed civilians from the Court which managed

13

the Church's property and replaced them by clergy, and she salved her conscience for her own irregularities by continuing the persecution of heretics and dissenters. She died on 25th December 1761.

The succession to the throne was already secured. In February 1742 Elisabeth sent for Peter, the son of her sister Anne, and announced that she had chosen him to occupy the throne after her decease. He was a youth of dull intellect, vulgar manners, and dissipated habits. At the age of seventeen he was married to Sophie Anhalt-Zerbst, a charming girl of sixteen, who took the name Catherine on her conversion to Orthodoxy. Catherine was as clever as her husband was stupid, as cultured as he was ignorant, and the marriage was a failure from the first. A breach opened between husband and wife, and after nine years of disappointment the birth of a son, whose paternity was extremely doubtful, did nothing to close it. Parties began to form, one round Peter, German and reactionary, another round Catherine, Russian and progressive. A deadly struggle was only a question of time.

The first act of Peter III. was to show his intense German sympathies by announcing his accession to the throne to his idol, Frederick the Great, and to end the war with Prussia by renouncing all the advantages which Russia had gained. Victory was really within his grasp, and the mortification of the Russian Generals was intense. In pursuance of his Germanising policy he roused the army to indignation by stripping it of its national dress and clothing the regiments in German uniforms, by imposing on it a German discipline and by creating a German regiment. He put the finishing touch to his unpopularity by confiscating most of the wealth that still remained to the monasteries, and by subjecting the monks to absurd regulations regarding their dress and their beards. He also abolished certain fast and feast days, and showed disrespect to venerable ikons.

Catherine, on the other hand, was doing all she could to wipe out the memory of her German origin and to identify herself with the Russian people. She mastered the Russian language, she conformed to Russian customs, she surrounded herself with Russian courtiers, and she visited Orthodox Churches, and she displayed herself prominently at the great religious services. She became, in fact, the ruler on which Russia set its heart.

The opportunity of placing her on the throne came unexpectedly. There was a rumour that Peter meant to divorce her and disinherit her son. Her friends therefore resolved to remove him from the throne, and when he was amusing himself at Oranienbaum a group of Catherine's supporters visited him and compelled him to abdicate. A few days afterwards, at the village of Ropscha, he died suddenly. The official account attributed his death to colic ; a more accurate statement is that he was strangled by Catherine's favourite, Alexis Orlov.

In pursuance of her design of ingratiating herself with her Russian subjects, Catherine justified the hostility of the Orthodox Church towards the religion of the West. In the manifesto which she issued on 2nd July 1762 in connection with her coronation she said : " Of all the dangers into which Peter III. brought Russia none was so great as that of the complete ruin of the Greek religion, whose doctrines were being rooted out in such a way that one had to ask whether the old faith of Russia was not being replaced by one that is new."

On the occasion of her coronation Setchenov, Metropolitan of Petrograd, delivered an oration in her presence in which he repeated similar sentiments even more vehemently. He said : " What disgrace was put upon us by the infatuation of Peter III. With horror we looked forward to the time when our holy, priestly garments would be stripped off us, when our hair would be shorn, and our venerable beards shaved off, and clothes cut after the fashion of those worn by preachers in Prussia and Holstein would be forced on us. Then another catechism, the Lutheran, would have been put into our hands if Peter had not been fortunately and adroitly carried off to prison. Count Butterlin, Field-Marshal Count Rasomowski, the hetman of the Ukraine, Count Von Panin, our ambassador in Sweden, have discharged their duty magnificently, and our Russian Guard have presented the prince with a catechism of their own fashioning. They ask from him no confession of faith further than his signature to his own abdication, and I swear to you, my brethren, that I never read his name with greater pleasure than when it appeared on that document." It is surely surprising that Catherine tolerated such language regarding her husband.

She was now seated on the throne, but there was a rival in existence in the person of Ivan VI., who had already spent weary years in captivity and had become an imbecile. Personally, he was of no consequence, but as he might have become a rallying-point for disaffection it was desirable that he should disappear. What happened in his prison is unknown. What is certain, is that a few weeks after Catherine's accession he died suddenly.

Catherine's reign constitutes an era in which the nobles reached the height of their power and splendour, while the serfs were plunged deeper into misery. The former rejoiced in their release from the drudgery of public service, the latter groaned under the heavy yoke of their owners' idleness and extravagance. Following Catherine's lead, the upper classes began to adopt Western fashions in dress and deportment. They cultivated an acquaintance with Western literature, especially with the philosophy of the French Encyclopædists and with the writings of Voltaire and Rousseau, and they spoke the French language in preference to their mother-tongue. Catherine's Court was at first a delightful place to live in to those who did not care to look below the surface.

Catherine began her reign with a high purpose of making Russia at least as well governed as any other nation in the world. For the accomplishment of this purpose she resolved that first of all there must be a new codification of the laws, and in the middle of 1667 she summoned a great Council to undertake the work. She herself had given much attention to the matter in hand. She had drawn up a series of instructions in 526 paragraphs, half of them summarising what she had gathered from

Montesquieu and the other half copied almost verbatim from a treatise on Crime and Punishment by Beccaria. At first she took the Council very seriously, and had bright visions of what it was to accomplish, but the vision faded. The majority of the members had no real knowledge of what they were meant to do, and when some of them began to ask inconvenient questions about the serfs, she lost conceit in it altogether and left it to itself. When the war with Turkey broke out in the end of the year she brought its sessions to an end on the pretext that the members would be more useful elsewhere.

Her next endeavour was to improve the organisation of the administration. For this purpose she devised a symmetrical system which on paper was admirable. In place of ten unwieldy " governments " into which Peter had divided his Empire, she created fifty, each with its provincial capital and governors. These fifty governments were again divided into districts with the necessary district officials. In both cases the principle of division was not area but population. There was, however, a link missing between these Councils and the Imperial Courts of Justice. The Councils thus became a law unto themselves, and as they were filled with nobles and with the dependants of nobles, the lower classes of all sorts were at their mercy, and oppression became more rife than it ever had been.

Another subject that engaged her attention was education, and in 1764 there appeared a general regulation for the education of children of both sexes. It ought to be noted that Catherine had her eye on both sexes. In the same year, as a sample of the manner in which she wished her ideas to be carried out, she founded the Smolny Institute for the daughters of nobles and the higher classes on the model of the Institute at St. Cyr founded by Madame de Maintenon. From that time to the Revolution the Smolny Institute was one of the most select educational establishments in the Empire.

She also appointed a commission which reported in favour of a scheme providing one school for every 200 families, but there was no money to erect the buildings, no teachers to give instructions, and no text-books to put into the pupils' hands.   Casting about for help she invited her friend, Baron Grimm, to become Director-General of Education, but he thought it safer to advise her from a distance.   She also sent letters to Oxford, to Turin, and to various parts of Germany.   In 1786 the Emperor of Austria sent her Jankowitcz de Marievo, a Serb by birth, who was said to be one of the best educationists in the world.   Under his directions training-schools for teachers were begun in various centres, and from these a thin network of schools was slowly drawn across the country.   The instruction given was frankly secular, and was inspired by the ideals of the Encyclopædists and others whom the Orthodox clergy held to be the spawn of Satan.   It did nothing to support Orthodoxy.   On the contrary, it did not a little to under-mine it by introducing the scholars to ideals which the clergy thought were subversive of religion.   Catherine therefore had a heavy battle to fight, and her project did not meet with the success which it deserved.

In these years Catherine took great pleasure in posing as a patroness of learning and of the Arts and Sciences. She attracted learned men to her Court, and conducted a voluminous correspondence with others.   She herself was an authoress of some repute.   She started a journal called *Motley*.   She permitted the establishment of printing-presses and the publication of books.   Poets began to appear, novels began to circulate, magazines and newspapers multiplied with rapidity, theatres were opened, dramas were written, Catherine herself wrote satirical comedies, and the profession of acquaintance with literature became fashionable.   An Academy of Belles Lettres was founded, and Princess Dashkov, Catherine's bosom friend, became president of the Academy of Sciences.   The princess also composed a dictionary of the Russian language, wrote Memoirs, and edited a review.

But when Catherine found that other magazines were published more radical than her own, and that the news-papers were exposing the corruption and abuses of her administration, her attitude towards the freedom of the

Press changed.   When she heard of the French Revolution she became reactionary, the liberty of the Press was suspended, the propaganda in favour of reform was stopped, and its advocates were silenced.   But the ferment of thought which was beginning was not stopped.   It was only driven out of sight.

Simultaneously with this movement among the cultured classes there arose a more alarming movement among the serfs.   These included 94 per cent. of the whole population. All of them were steeped in ignorance and superstition, all of them lived in a dull round of exhausting toil and ceaseless misery.   The serf had no rights which his master was bound to respect.   At his master's pleasure he might be sent to work in the house, the forest, the field, or the factory.   He might be married to any woman whom his master chose.   He and his family might be sold as a unit or individually like cattle.   He might be punished in any way that seemed good, even though he died in agony, and against his owner's brutality there was neither check nor redress.[1]

At an early period this state of matters engaged Catherine's attention, and, inspired by humane ideals, she resolved to reform it.   In 1766 she created the Free Economic Society and instructed it to study the agrarian problem.   In 1776 she offered a prize of a thousand ducats for the best answer to the question how the serfs could be set free without damaging the interests of their owners. She herself sketched a scheme for the benefit of the serfs on ecclesiastical lands which had been confiscated to the State.   It is also said that in 1784 she prepared a decree under which the children of serfs born after 1785 were to be considered free, but she did not publish it.

There is no doubt that at first Catherine sincerely desired to mitigate the hardships of the serfs' lot, but all the landowners were against her.   The General Council, representing many vested interests, was against her.   Besides, she owed her throne to great nobles who owned many serfs, and she did not care to offend them.   As time went on,

[1] Kornilov, p. 125.

and as politics engaged more of her attention, and as her own sensuality blunted her moral sense, she formed the habit of rewarding her favourites and others for their shameful service by giving them grants of crown lands and of the serfs attached to these, till she had reduced 800,000 peasants who had a limited freedom to the rank of serfs who had none.   In her closing days she allowed herself to be persuaded that no landowner in the world was so tender-hearted as a Russian landowner, and no servant was so well off as a Russian serf.   Cases of dreadful cruelty were frequently brought to her notice, but she closed her eyes to them.

The serfs, on the other hand, came to the conclusion that any change must be an improvement, and outbreaks of discontent took place incessantly, until in 1773 there was a great revolt under Pugatchev.   This man was really an ignorant peasant who gave himself out to be Peter III., Catherine's husband, miraculously preserved from his murderers, and therefore the true heir to the throne.   By promising free land to all who joined him, and by authoris-ing his followers to kill the landowners and seize their property, he gathered an immense multitude and swept through the country, laying everything waste before him. When Catherine heard of mansions in flames, and cities being taken, and whole provinces lying at Pugatchev's feet, she set a price of 500,000 roubles on his head and sent an army against him.   After fierce fighting the rebellion was crushed.   Pugatchev was captured and brought to Moscow, where his hands and feet were cut off, and his body was quartered while he was still alive.   Thereafter the right of appeal to the throne, which had been the serfs' last defence against oppression, was taken away, and the common law of Great Russia was extended over the Ukraine, thereby reducing the free peasants of that region to the hopeless bondage in which their brethren groaned. So deep-seated was the terror which this rebellion produced in Catherine's mind that, in her later years, she allowed no reference to emancipation to be made in her hearing, and she encouraged reactionary measures which made the serfs' lot worse than ever before.

Catherine's relation to the Church was determined by her moral character. A woman such as she was had no real interest in it as an organisation existing for spiritual ends. To her it appeared as a corporation which exploited the superstitious fears of the people, and expropriated wealth which ought to belong to the State. In spite of the restrictions imposed by her predecessors, that wealth had steadily increased, until it included the most fertile arable lands, the most valuable forests, and the most productive fisheries in every part of the country, and in addition the clergy possessed nearly a million of serfs. Catherine looked on these vast accumulations with an envious eye, and she carried the policy of Peter the Great a step further forward. He placed ecclesiastical property under the control of the monastic court, which managed it under the supervision of the Holy Synod. Peter III. proposed to confiscate the property. In 1764 Catherine translated the proposal into action by seizing the whole of the monastic lands and revenues, with a few trivial exceptions. She justified herself in a scornful speech which she addressed to an assembly of bishops and arch-bishops in January 1763 : "Were I to ask you, my lords, who you are, you would say the followers of the Apostles who were commanded by God to despise riches and who had therefore to be poor. If they were otherwise they contradicted the Gospel which they preached. I need not draw your attention, my lords, to the fact that the duties of the bishops of the Primitive Church were limited to the spiritual interests of believers, and that their kingdom was not of this world, since it was that of truth. I often heard this from your own lips. How then can you keep such vast wealth ? You possess such properties that your power is equal to that of kings, and you have more serfs under your jurisdiction than the subjects of many princes in Europe. Your Order, which is founded for study, meditation, and prayer, gives you enlightenment which I cannot expect from other men. I am, therefore, astonished that you do not see that the vast properties you hold are simply unlawful arrogations of the property of the State, which, if you wish to act loyally, you must give up. You declare yourselves to be my most faithful subjects. Surrender to the Crown what belongs to it." No one dared to open his lips, except Arsenius, Metropolitan of Rostov, who, relying on the support of his brethren in the Ukraine, published a protest in March 1763 declaring it was sinful to take property which had been dedicated to Holy Church and apply it to secular uses. He was promptly seized and imprisoned in Solovetski, from which he was transferred to Revel, where he died in 1772. Entrance to the monasteries was again made more difficult.

Catherine was the nominal head of the Orthodox Church, but she had no attachment to it because it was Orthodox. From her point of view, one section of the Church was as good as any other. Her conversion from Lutheranism to Orthodoxy before her marriage gave her no mental struggle. If sufficient inducement had been offered she would have embraced Catholicism with equal tranquillity. She saw no urgent need for persecuting dissenters, and in place of driving the Old Believers out of Russia she set herself to attract them back by relaxing the restrictions imposed on them. However, when they began to build churches the Holy Synod appealed against their presumption to the Senate, and when the Senate ordered the churches to be destroyed, Catherine did nothing to stop the destruction. If she was sometimes harsh towards the sectaries, it was not for reasons of religion. As soon as they lived peaceably, persecution ceased. So far did her toleration go, that in defiance of a remonstrance from the Holy Synod she authorised the construction of a number of mosques in the city of Kazan.

Her real indifference to the Orthodox Church appears in her behaviour towards that section of it which was found in Poland. Poland was in disorder. The power of the King was limited, the Diet was paralysed by the absurd liberum veto. The nobles were divided, petty potentates did what was right in their own eyes. On the western borders were Lutherans, whose sympathies were with Germany. On the east were members of the Orthodox

Church, whose sympathies were with Russia and Moscow. But the mass of the Polish people were fiercely Catholic, and they treated the Lutherans and the Orthodox with great harshness. The four Orthodox bishops were reduced to two, and the two to one, and the one was often put in peril of his life, while Orthodox people were persecuted to the limit of human endurance. George Kominski, their only bishop, therefore appeared at Catherine's coronation and besought her to interfere on behalf of her suffering co-religionists. As Russia was already on the outlook for a pretext for dealing with Poland, he was led to expect assistance, and after Augustus III. came to the throne Russian influence made itself felt to such an extent that a party of patriotic Poles formed a league to secure a strong central government. They also allied themselves with the Jesuits, and with their help succeeded in getting all dissenters from Catholicism disqualified for public office. When Augustus died in 1763, Russian emissaries created further confusion ; then, in 1764, in concert with Prussia, it set on the Polish throne Stanislaus Poniatowski, one of Catherine's favourites. When the Diet met in 1765 Kominski pled for equal civil rights and for liberty of conscience for the Orthodox members of the Polish State. When he repeated his appeal in the Diet of 1767 the rage of the Catholics knew no bounds. Then the Russian ambassador, as the champion of liberty, seized some of the Catholic leaders, dispatched them to Siberia, marched Russian troops into the country, and quartered some of them in Warsaw. Under compulsion the Diet then accepted the Russian Protectorate, and granted the civil and religious rights which it had up to that time refused. The patriotic Poles then declared war. Turkey did the same, and Russia, in alarm, agreed to a suggestion of Frederick the Great that Prussia, Austria, and Russia should divide Poland between them. The first partition took place in 1772, the second took place in 1793, the final partition took place in 1795, and after it Poland ceased to exist.

The Orthodox Poles now thought that their troubles

were over. Russia was Orthodox, and under its shield they were safe. They were soon undeceived. They were a feeble folk, a minority, whereas the Catholic Uniates were numerous and dangerous. Catherine therefore threw the Orthodox overboard and gave the Catholics a free hand to carry on their propaganda and continue their persecutions, while obstacles of all sorts were placed in the way of those who in terror had professed Catholicism and now desired to abjure it. When the obstacles were removed in 1794, not less than two millions returned with a rush to the fold of the Orthodox Church. The popular delight in Russia was great, but Catherine's participation in it was insincere. She had accomplished her political purpose, and the position of the Orthodox in Poland ceased to interest her.

In Russia itself, under the cold blight which emanated from her Court, the Orthodox Church sank to a low level of moral impotence. The profession of liberalism, culture, and progress was a mere glitter playing on the surface of a cesspool of corruption. The glitter was most dazzling in the highest circles of society, and there the corruption was most profound. Catherine herself, with her shameless succession of favourites, all of whom had an acknowledged position, set an example which her courtiers usually followed. Practically every noble had his mistress, and every lady her lover, and even if only a fraction of the tales told about them is true, enough is left to prove that libertinage, profligacy, and other deadly sins had ceased to be thought worthy of notice, and still less worthy of reproach. Platon, who became Archbishop of Moscow in 1775, was a learned man and an eloquent preacher, and a capable ecclesiastic who secured Catherine's goodwill by supporting her policy with regard to the Church, but in 1786, when she appointed Pamphilov, one of the secular clergy, and therefore a married man, to the office of Bishop, Platon protested vigorously against this breach of ancient custom and contended that the honour should be reserved for a monk. Nevertheless, in the graver matter of the breach of the moral law, which was notorious and universal, neither he nor any of the clergy had anything to say. He has acquired distinction as a theologian by his catechism, and as an historian by his history of the Russian Church. He would have earned a nobler name if he had followed the example of John the Baptist, who rebuked Herod and his paramour to their face. Even in the days of Ivan the Terrible more than one monk took his life in his hand and denounced his sovereign's sin. In the milder reign of Catherine the only thing that stirred the higher clergy to public remonstrance was the loss of their property and the fear of losing their privileges.

CHAPTER XX

PAUL

CATHERINE died on the 6th November 1796 and was succeeded by her son Paul, who was at that date a man of forty-two. In his childhood Catherine displayed no maternal affection towards him, and as years went on their relations were characterised by antipathy. Paul held that his mother had stolen the throne from him and had deliberately excluded him from public life. He was a Grand Duke, but he was not allowed to appear in the royal Council. He was an Admiral of the Fleet, but he was not allowed to go on board a ship. He was a General, but he was forbidden to take part in military manœuvres. All he could do was to travel once or twice in foreign lands and drill a regiment of soldiers in the grounds of the palace at Gatchina. Worst of all, he had to endure the slights which his mother's courtiers heaped upon him.

Filled with joy at having reached the throne, after weary years of waiting, Paul began by showering benefits all around him. He gave away about forty thousand pounds in money, and lands that were far more valuable. He distributed military decorations indiscriminately. He released those who had been imprisoned by the secret police, and pardoned all criminals except murderers. He brought back from exile such men as Novikov and Radistchev, and he released Kosciusko and other Poles who had languished in dungeons since the close of the war for Polish independence.

When this fit of exuberance was over he let loose the resentment which had been gathering in his mind against his mother and her regime. He exhumed his father's body from the Church of St. Alexander Nevski, where it had been huddled underground, and laid it to rest with great pomp in the fortress of SS. Peter and Paul, and in the procession from the one place to the other, with bitter irony, he compelled Count Alexis Orlov, one of his father's murderers, to walk bareheaded behind the coffin of his victim carrying the imperial crown. He dug up the bones of Potemkin, his mother's most notorious favourite, and flung them into a ditch. He expelled the Princess Dashkov, his mother's confidante, from Petrograd, and forbade her to remain longer than three days in any one place. He afterwards confined her to her estates. He drove Zoubov, the favourite at the time of his mother's death, over the frontiers into Livonia. From the register of 1702 he expunged all the records relating to the *coup d'état* which had set his mother on the throne. He also issued a decree to the effect that the will of the reigning sovereign should no longer decide who was to be the next occupant of the throne, and declaring that in all time coming the heir should be the eldest surviving prince of the Royal Family. This was one of the few really sensible things he ever did. It was probably prompted by the knowledge that Catherine intended to set his claim aside and to nominate as her successor his son Alexander.

Thereafter he began what he fondly imagined was a series of reforms. His general principle was that of reversing everything his mother had done. She had a leaning to France, to French philosophy and culture. He had no interest in culture. All his leanings were to Germany, and his idol was Frederick the Great. He began his reforms with the army, and everything he did roused the spirit of disaffection. He insulted the Field-Marshals and Generals who had conducted victorious campaigns by sending them to learn their business from German tutors. He nearly ruined his officers by compelling them to provide at their own expense new uniforms of the pattern which his capricious fancy suggested to him. He exasperated the private soldiers by stripping them of their simple and comfortable dress and buttoning them up in coats and gaiters that were usually too tight for them, as well as by plastering their hair with a mixture of grease and powder that made cleanliness impossible.

He worried them with evolutions that had no relation to warfare, and if he found anything, even a button, out of its place he visited the offender with punishment that was often cruel and sometimes implied death. On more than one occasion when he lost his temper he commanded a regiment to march straight away to Siberia, and on parade days the officers had a carriage or a sledge ready and loaded with their baggage lest at a moment's notice they should be sent into exile. During his reign he banished to Siberia no less than twelve thousand officers and soldiers for failing to carry out accurately his ridiculous regulations. When the famous General Souvarov expressed the general sentiment in a bitter witticism, he too was disgraced and banished.

After the same fashion he dealt with the Civil Service. He made a clean sweep of his mother's ministers and appointed in their place men whose acquaintance he had made at Gatchina. On the ground of inefficiency, his mother had closed the colleges founded by Peter and had substituted ministers directly responsible to herself. Paul re-established the colleges and reduced them to impotence by subjecting them to a committee of which he himself was the head. His mother had set up a system of provincial self-government. Paul abolished it in favour of a bureaucracy whose members were appointed at Petrograd or Moscow. He likewise destroyed the elective system in the chief towns and replaced the magistrates by officials chosen by the central government. But he did not carry any of these measures into complete working order. He stopped short in the transition stage and left the old and the new hanging, as it were, in the air.

In his general conduct one mistake followed another. He set the nobles against him by withdrawing the right of presenting remonstrances to the sovereign, by loading them with arrears of taxation, and above all by rescinding their immunity from corporal punishment. At the same time he irritated the common people. He did some things which ought to have secured their goodwill, as when he revoked the levy of ten serfs per thousand as conscription and when he suppressed the tax on wheat and reduced the salt tax, and forbade the selling of serfs away from the lands which they cultivated, and allowed serfs on government lands to substitute a money payment for the labour they were expected to give, and especially when he allowed them a small measure of local self-government. These things were supposed to pave the way for emancipation, but emancipation was not in Paul's programme. He held that serfdom was essential to the prosperity of the State, and that private landowners with unlimited powers over the serfs were the best guardians of public order. Therefore, when the serfs petitioned them to right their wrongs he commanded those who carried the petition to be flogged publicly as much as their masters wished. When agrarian disorders broke out he crushed them with violence, and in four years' time reduced 530,000 free peasants to hopeless bondage by assigning them with the Crown lands on which they lived to private ownership. His reign was short, but it was long enough to kindle the flames of discontent in every rank of society.

As Catherine, like Peter the Great, recognised the advantage of intercourse with the rest of Europe she not only invited foreigners to settle in Russia but encouraged young Russians to travel abroad. Paul reversed this. He recalled the travellers and forbade all foreigners except ambassadors and similar officials to cross the Russian frontiers. He forbade the wearing of clothes cut after foreign fashion. He forbade the importation of foreign books on any subject, even on music, and he restricted the activity of the printing-press.

As part of her policy, Catherine entered into alliance with foreign powers. Paul sent a letter to his mother's allies intimating that while he had a friendly disposition towards them, he would not join them in military operations anywhere or at any time, for his reign was to begin an era of peace. But it was not long till he was drawn into the vortex of European politics by his ridiculous procedure with regard to Malta. Intercourse between Russia and the Knights of Malta began in the seventeenth century

14

and was kept up briskly under Catherine. In January 1797 Paul agreed to maintain a Grand Priory of the Knights in Petrograd in exchange for certain lands in Volhynia. He was thereafter offered and accepted the Protectorate of the Order. There were already two Protectors—the Emperor of Germany and the King of the two Sicilies—but they made no objections to the creation of a third. In June 1798, when Napoleon was on his way to Egypt, Malta surrendered to him. He expelled half of the Knights he found there, and some of them went to Petrograd. The Priory in Petrograd denounced the surrender and offered the post of Grand-Master to Paul. He accepted it. Now the Knights were a Catholic Order, and as their Grand-Master Paul presented to the world the amazing spectacle of the head of the Orthodox Church occupying a position of subordination to the Pope. Paul himself felt there was something here which required correction. He therefore created a Grand Priory of Orthodox Knights, and sent out invitations to foreign princes inviting them to take an example of loyalty and honour from it, and to enter into communication with it. It is believed he cherished the quixotic hope of uniting not only all the Knights but all the great powers under himself for the purpose of securing the peace of the world.

As Napoleon was still holding Malta, Paul formed an alliance against him with England, Austria, Turkey, and Naples. England captured Malta and held on to it. This annoyed Paul intensely. He therefore formed a new alliance with Prussia, Sweden, and Denmark against England, and with Prussia against Austria. At the same time he threw himself into the arms of England's enemy, France. Napoleon skilfully flattered him and suggested the employment of Russian troops against the English possessions in India. Paul dispatched several regiments of Cossacks eastwards across the barren steppes with a double supply of horses, but no provender. Before they reached the frontiers half of them were dead. Fortunately for the survivors, Paul's reign came to a sudden end, and they were recalled.

The institution which suffered least from Paul's activity was the Church. He himself, after an eccentric fashion, was a religious man, and with respect to forms of religion differing from his own he was tolerant to an unusual degree. Among the first to benefit by this was the Old Believers. When Paul was a youth his instructor in religion was Platon, who, in 1775, was made Archbishop of Moscow. He became Metropolitan in 1787, and when Paul came to the throne he used Platon as a Counsellor. Many of the Old Believers were said to be willing to return to the State Church if the Holy Synod would raise the curse laid on the use of two fingers by the great Synod of Moscow in 1667, and give them a bishop who should consecrate the priests they required after the ancient rite, and allow the services of the Church to be conducted after the old order, and give them a supply of holy oil, and refrain from asking them to shave their beards or wear European clothes. With the exception of the second, these conditions were agreed to, and in 1800, with Platon's consent, a decree was published which it was hoped would pave the way for the return of the wanderers to the fold. But the Old Believers feared a trap, and they received the decree without enthusiasm. Their fears were afterwards justified; nevertheless, many took advantage of the terms offered them, and to-day the Edinovertsi, as they are called, have about two hundred and fifty churches and nearly one million members.

In this connection it should be noticed that Paul took no forcible measures to convert those who belonged to other communions. On the contrary, he endeavoured to secure that every man practised the religion he professed. He caused the Catholics to produce certificates that they had been to confession and had received absolution. In his reign, therefore, the Catholic Church enjoyed greater favour than ever before. But it was not allowed to forget that he claimed to rule it as an autocrat. In this he followed the example of his mother. In 1769 Catherine on her own initiative created the office of Archbishop for those churches of White Russia which were at that time in her Empire, and she decreed that this Archbishop should be responsible not to Rome but to the Russian Minister of Justice. In 1773, again on her own initiative, she appointed as head of the Catholic Church in Russia a canon of Vilna named Siestrencewicz, designating him Bishop of White Russia and fixing his episcopal seat at Mohilev. She also gave him full power over all the Romish clergy, regular and secular alike. Once more, for the purpose of showing her complete independence of Rome, when Pope Clement IV. abolished the Jesuit Order, Catherine continued to recognize it, and allowed its members to carry on as before. Presuming on her favour, they repudiated their allegiance to Siestrencewicz and appointed a vicar of their own. This was more than Catherine could stand, and she not only raised Siestrencewicz to the dignity of Archbishop, but confirmed his jurisdiction over all the Catholic orders in Russia, Jesuits included. She also forbade appeals from his decisions to any authority outside her Empire, and decreed that all Bulls and letters from the Pope should be submitted in the first place to her Council, which would decide whether or not they were to be published.

At the beginning of his reign Paul conferred on Siestrencewicz several tokens of his favour. He gave him the Order of St. Andrew and the title of Metropolitan, obtained for him a Cardinal's hat, and made him Commander of the Grand Cross of St. John of Jerusalem. Siestrencewicz took advantage of this to try to secure further favours for his Church, but Paul had no intention of allowing the control of the Romish clergy to slip out of his Imperial hands. Catherine had decreed that before a Papal Nuncio entered Russia he must first state what he was sent to say and do, and must receive formal permission to cross the frontier. But in 1798 Litto, Archbishop of Thebes, entered Petrograd without permission, announced himself as Papal Legate, and proceeded to interfere with the arrangement of the Catholic dioceses which had just been settled by Paul's government. Litto next began to liberate the Jesuits from their vow of obedience to Siestrencewicz. Paul ordered him to desist. Litto protested, and refused to ordain a monk whom Paul had appointed to the See of Kamiencz, whereupon he was ordered to leave Russia within twenty-four hours.

The Jesuits, however, found another champion in an Austrian monk named Gruber. He was an able and cunning man, with some reputation as a scientist. He arrived in Petrograd nominally on educational business, and was quickly introduced to the Tsar. It was not long till he had free access to the Imperial Cabinet, and he used his persuasive powers with such effect that he gained for the Jesuits the Catholic Church of Petrograd with all its endowments. He also obtained for them the estates which had been confiscated when their order was abolished in Poland in 1773. Further, by dint of incessant complaint he undermined the position of Siestrencewicz, so that the prelate was forbidden to appear in Court, the decoration of the Order of the Knights of Malta was taken away from him, and on 14th November 1800 he was expelled from his office altogether. After that it was easy for the Jesuits to spread their organisation over the Empire. With Paul's aid they even planted outposts in Turkey. In Russia itself they captured the higher classes by schools which attracted large numbers of pupils and in which they made many converts. They even rose so high in favour that at the request of the Russian Government Pope Pius VII. published a brief cancelling the Bull of Pope Clement IV. in so far as it applied to Jesuits in Russia, re-established them as one of the permitted orders, and allowed them to continue all their former propaganda. Before the brief and the accompanying letter from the Pope reached Russia, Paul was dead, and the Bull was put into operation in the reign of Alexander I., not by the General of the Order, Carew, who had also died, but by Gruber himself, who succeeded him.

In another direction in Paul's reign the position of the Romish Church was strengthened. The Jesuits persuaded him to give them unlimited authority over the Uniates, and they stirred up the Catholic landowners to persecute not only the Uniates but also the Orthodox on their estates in order to force them into the Romish Church. There was, however, such an outcry that the Russian Government ordered the persecution to cease. This stopped the policy of violence, but it was easy for the Jesuits to exert pressure in more subtle ways, and under it the Uniates weakened.

All this was highly offensive to the Orthodox. They felt it intolerable that the head of the Orthodox Church should give such encouragement to its enemies. It was a betrayal of Orthodoxy, and not of Orthodoxy only but of Russia as well, for it was always the Catholic powers that Russia had most reason to fear. Paul, however, took no account of popular resentment and went on to outrage Orthodox sensibilities in other directions. On the assumption that the clergy were on the same level as officers of the army and the navy, he included them in the table of ranks, assigning to each individual the civil rank suggested by his service to the State. He also proposed to confer on the clergy the decorations given to other officials, and it was in vain that the Metropolitan Platon besought him on his knees not to insist on acceptance of the Order of St. Andrew. Paul was inflexible, and Platon had to yield.

In the same fashion he dealt with the appointment of clergy to Church offices. To the intense indignation of the monks he decreed that one-half of the ecclesiastical dignities from the rank of bishop upwards should be reserved for married priests. This was a tremendous violation of ancient custom, and it meant a serious blow to the monks' privileges, but Paul considered that it gave poor priests the chance of rising to dignity and comfort of which the ancient system deprived them, and he braved the monks' displeasure. At the same time, for the benefit of the priests who had to remain in poor parishes, he decreed that each of the parish churches in the country and some parish churches in towns should each have a glebe attached to it, and that this glebe should be cultivated for the priests' benefit by the community or congregation which he served. Then he spoiled the effect of what he had done by ordering that the sons of parish priests who did not enter their father's profession should be conscripted into the army.

From first to last Paul's policy knew neither continuity nor consistency. It was determined by his moods, his self-conceit, and his vanity, and no one knew what he would do next. His mind was ill-balanced to begin with, and the exercise of autocratic power disordered it to the verge of insanity. He kept every one about him in a state of nervous tension, and nothing pleased him so much as the thought that he could make his subjects tremble. As his reign went on his really rational moments became fewer, and they appeared at longer intervals. Even those who were most devoted to his interests became suspected of disloyalty, and thousands who were innocent of all fault were dispatched to Siberia. Paul's second wife, Maria Feodorovna, was both beautiful and accomplished, and she bore him ten children. Nevertheless, he neglected her for mistresses who were vulgar and ugly, and he outraged decency by bringing them into his wife's palace. As he lost his mental self-control he began, without the slightest justification, to believe that Maria was as unfaithful to him as he was to her, and he planned to separate her from her sons, and shut them all up in prison. This brought matters to a climax. Count Pahlen, Count Panin, Count Zoubov, General Benningsen, and others formed a conspiracy to get rid of him. His son and heir, Alexander, was induced to join them on the solemn assurance that nothing more than deposition was meant. On the night of 23rd March 1801 a small band of them entered the palace. An altercation, then a violent struggle ensued, and in the course of it Paul was stabbed and strangled to death. When Alexander heard the news he was overcome with horror and grief, and for a long time refused to be consoled. But Russia heaved a sigh of relief.

CHAPTER XXI

ALEXANDER I.

ALEXANDER I., who now ascended the throne, was born in December 1777. Immediately after his birth his grandmother, Catherine II., took him under her special care. She engaged his nurses, composed fairy-tales for his amusement, devised a plan for his education, secured as his tutor the Swiss La Harpe, and in his sixteenth year married him to Princess Louise of Baden, a charming girl almost his own age. Believing that Paul, his father, was unfit to govern, she resolved to proclaim him heir to the throne, but death interfered before she carried out this intention. During Paul's reign Alexander was grieved and shocked by his father's folly, but when he received the crown from hands that were red with his father's blood, his youthful brightness disappeared. A tendency to melancholy took its place, and at the first opportunity he banished to their estates most of those who were concerned in his father's death. It was only a sense of duty that constrained him to accept his onerous responsibilities, and he began to cherish the hope that some day he would be able to abdicate.

He began his reign by promising to rule after the laws and heart of his grandmother, and the people, forgetting the misgovernment of which she had been guilty, cherished the hope of an era of liberty and peace. Even the serfs refrained from the rebellions which were usual at such a time.

His first measures were full of wisdom. He released multitudes who were languishing in prison and exile. He restored their charters to nobles and to cities. He relaxed the tariff on imports, and encouraged trading relations with England and France. He cancelled the prohibition of foreign books and private printing-presses. He appointed a permanent Council of twelve members to advise him in political affairs, and on 5th June 1801 ordered it to report on the functions it should discharge in the State. This raised the hope that he would give Russia some sort of constitutional government, but Alexander had no such intention. An autocrat he was, and an autocrat he meant to remain. He also set up a commission to revise the existing laws, and appointed a Committee to investigate the internal administration of the Empire, and to suggest reforms. On the basis of its report he decreed in December 1802 that the colleges still existing should be dissolved and reconstituted, as the ministries of the Army, the Navy, and Foreign Affairs, and that four new ministries should be created—those of the Interior, of Finance, of Education, and of Justice. To these he added the Ministry of Commerce. As the highest administrative and judicial body he created the Senate, whose powers were to be limited only by his will, and at first he authorised it to express its opinion whether his decrees were in accordance with existing laws and whether they could be carried out. But when the Senate exercised the authority he had given it, he was both surprised and mortified by its criticism, and told it sharply to confine its attention to decrees which had been issued in the past, and to take no cognizance of those which might be issued in the future.

The serfs also came in for a share of his attention, and plans for the alleviation for their hard lot followed one another in quick succession, until in 1818 he ordered Arakcheiev to devise a scheme for their liberation in some way that would not burden the landowners, and that would not imply compulsion. Arakcheiev eventually proposed that five million roubles should be set aside to compensate those who were willing to let their serfs go free, and that each serf so liberated should be assigned five acres of land for his subsistence. In the existing state of Russia it was impossible to provide the money required, and the whole result of the scheme was to give the serfs a glimpse of a terrestrial paradise and then to drive them back to the wilderness. Their discontent increased, and local rebellions became incessant.

At an early age Alexander convinced himself that he had

a talent for diplomacy, and constituted himself his own Foreign Minister. His policy was governed partly by consideration for the material interests of Russia, partly by the idealisms which he had imbibed from La Harpe, and partly by his personal likes and dislikes. For the purpose of securing peace, he endeavoured to keep Russia free from entanglement in European politics, until Napoleon's policy of aggression alarmed him and made him resolve to thwart it. With this intention he met the King of Prussia at Memel in 1802. Then when Napoleon proclaimed himself Emperor and made it plain that he meant to conquer Europe, a Russian envoy was sent to England to propose a League of Nations whose business should be to secure peace by international arbitration. The League was formed, and England and Russia, Sweden and Austria, became members of it. Napoleon, on his side, took instant action to break it up. On 2nd December 1805 he struck Austria a terrific blow at Austerlitz, and on the 26th December compelled it to accept his terms of peace at Pressburg. In 1806 another coalition was formed with Prussia in the place of Austria. On 16th October of that year he struck Prussia an equally terrific blow at Jena, entered Berlin in triumph, issued from it his famous decrees against British commerce, marched through Poland, and, by his victory at Eylau, on 8th February 1807 compelled the Russians to retire behind their own frontier. After the battle of Friedland, 13th June 1807, in which he was again victorious, he met Alexander on a raft in the river Niemen and arranged a treaty which was afterwards signed at Tilsit on 7th July. By this treaty Russia promised to close her ports to British vessels and to send an order to England that English opposition to Napoleon must cease. From 1808 to 1812 the provisions of the treaty were carried out with increasing difficulty and reluctance, for every year meant increasing commercial loss to Russia, and when Alexander discovered from the terms of a secret treaty which came into his hands that Napoleon was determined to destroy the political importance of Russia at the first opportunity, a rupture became inevitable, and at length war broke out,

In March 1812 an immense French army entered Poland, crossed the Niemen on 24th June, and advanced into Russia through a tract of country which its inhabitants had stripped of food, forage, and shelter before they took to flight. After the battle of Borodino, 7th September 1812, in which the French and the Russians lost almost equal numbers, Moscow was entered on 14th September. Two days later the city took fire. The story of the retreat is well known. It began too late, and the French troops were exposed to the rigours of an exceptionally severe winter. Starving, blinded by snowstorms, benumbed by a temperature far below zero and a bitter wind, and harassed day and night by the Russians, who made raids on them like wolves on a flock of sheep, the wretched fugitives struggled homewards. On 18th December all that was left of them recrossed the Niemen, and Russia was free.

Flushed with victory, Alexander could not content himself with the deliverance of his own people from whom he considered the enemy of mankind. He resolved to deliver Europe. For this purpose he formed an alliance with Prussia, and Austria joined in. Napoleon gathered another army, met his enemies at Dresden on 26th August, and then at Leipzig on 16th October 1813, where, after a battle lasting three days, he was defeated with immense slaughter. On 31st March 1814 the allies entered Paris in triumph. On 11th April Napoleon abdicated. In November a Congress met at Vienna, and among other things it handed over to Russia the greater part of the Duchy of Warsaw. This was designated the Kingdom of Poland, and Alexander gave it a constitution. But on 1st March 1815, while the Congress was still sitting, Napoleon left Elba, arrived at Fontainebleau in the end of the month, and gathered round himself another great army. On 18th June 1815 he was finally crushed by the British troops at Waterloo.

These tremendous events made a deep impression on Alexander. When his army was in retreat and his enemies were advancing he turned for consolation to his neglected Bible and to prayer. After the French had disappeared across the frontier he said : " Through the fires of Moscow my soul has been enlightened, and God's judgments have filled my heart with a warm glow of faith such as I have never felt before. It was then that I learned to know God as He is revealed in the Holy Scriptures, and as soon as I understood and knew His will and His law I resolved to consecrate myself and my government to Him for the furtherance of His glory. From that time I became a different man."

Just when his mind was in this state of exaltation an agent of the British and Foreign Bible Society, the Rev. Dr. John Paterson of Edinburgh, who had gone to Russia to develop the Society's work, made the acquaintance of Prince Alexander Golitzin, the Minister of Public Worship. Through his mediation a memorial was presented to the Tsar, describing the nature of the Bible Society, detailing its regulations and laws, and asking permission to establish a branch of it for the benefit of Russian subjects belonging to other than Orthodox confessions. On 6th December 1812 he gave the permission requested by writing in the memorial as follows : " So be it, Alexander." [1] A committee was formed, with Golitzin as president, and on 11th January 1813 a public meeting was held. It was attended by " about forty of the first men of the Empire, nearly all the Ministers of State, the leading men of the Holy Synod, the Metropolitans of Petrograd and Novgorod, the Chief of the Russian Clergy, the Roman Catholic Metropolitan, and members of all religious denominations in Petrograd. The rules of the Society were read, and the Imperial ukaz permitting it to be established It was then declared to be formed, and Golitzin was appointed its first president." [2] On 28th January a subscription list was opened, and ten thousand roubles were collected. Alexander was asked to become patron. He refused, but requested his name to be enrolled among the ordinary members, and he not only sent a donation of twenty-five thousand roubles, but promised an annual subscription of ten thousand roubles more. With such influential support the work of the Society went on smoothly, and a

---

[1] Paterson, p. 188,   [2] *Ibid.*, p. 191.

branch was opened in Moscow. In the following six years no fewer than 173 auxiliaries were founded, most of them in Russia, but some in distant regions such as Georgia and Siberia. By special decree the version of the Bible prepared by the Society was appointed to be read in all seminaries and schools. It was also read to spontaneous gatherings in the village churches and private houses, and practically everywhere.[1]

At this time the Russian people were craving for more spiritual light and leading than the Orthodox Church seemed able to give. Parish priests were always ignorant, and often drunken. The services they conducted neither enlightened the understanding nor touched the conscience. Copies of the Scriptures were few, and such as were to be had were in the Old Slavonic, so that when a cheap version in vernacular Russian was offered for sale, it was hailed with delight. Prince Golitzin wrote to Lord Teignmouth, President of the Bible Society : " Entire governments, whole provinces, raise their voices to our committee, and entreat us to satisfy the hunger of millions of our countrymen. . . . All support our Society. . . . Even peasants give us of their poverty."

The effect produced by the popular study of the Scriptures was remarkable. The intelligence of the readers was awakened. Their sobriety, their industry, and their value to the State all alike increased, but they began to ask questions which the priests could not answer, to hold meetings which had no connection with canonical services, and to display a startling independence of thought and judgment. A campaign of misrepresentation was therefore begun, and the political unrest of the times gave it success which it did not deserve.

While the Bible Society was thus creating a ferment in the religious world, a similar ferment was beginning in other circles. The Russian officers who visited Germany and France not only saw in these countries forms of social intercourse with which they were unfamiliar, but also came into touch with systems of government which left

[1] Paterson, p. 199.

some room for the expression of the people's will. Following the example set them in these countries, they formed clubs. Some of these were educational, some literary, some political—all were more or less revolutionary. Their membership was confined to nobles of the highest rank, generals and distinguished officers, and some of the more cultured and prominent civilians. Their aim may be broadly stated as the establishment of a measure of constitutional government. They differed, however, as to the process by which this could be effected. Some relied on peaceful argument to persuade the people to effect the necessary changes. Others were prepared, as soon as possible, to set up a Republic by violence, even against the popular will.

The spirit which they fostered soon became manifest. In 1820 the Simeonovski regiment mutinied against the brutality of its commander. The Polish Diet rejected the Bills submitted to it in Warsaw, and there was a revolution in Naples. These things alarmed Alexander, and his alarm was increased by the discovery that secret societies of a fanatical type were multiplying in his own dominions. His mood, therefore, changed. He became convinced that the democratic ideals of his youth were impracticable, that the movements for reform must be crushed if the State was to be saved, and that the monarchs of Europe must stand shoulder to shoulder in self-defence. At the same time his goodwill to the Bible Society was undermined partly by the Jesuits and partly by the Orthodox clergy. The Jesuits, through such agents and friends in the Court as the Countess Golitzin, wife of the Procurator of the Holy Synod, the Countess Rostopchin, wife of the Governor of Moscow, the Countess Tolstoy, wife of the Imperial Marshal, and many more, represented that while all secret societies were bad the Bible Society was the worst of all, for it destroyed the foundations on which Russia's prosperity was built. Alexander began to doubt whether the circulation of the Scriptures was the beneficial thing he expected it to be. On the other hand, the Orthodox clergy harassed the Tsar with complaints of the injury which the reading of the Bible was doing to the State Church, inasmuch as whole villages were leaving it and going over to the heretics and dissenters. When Golitzin tried to quiet Alexander's fears, an outcry was raised against him so loud and insistent that Alexander ordered him to retire from the presidency of the Society on the ground that he had too much to do. He obeyed, and in April 1824 his place was taken by Seraphim, Metropolitan of Petrograd.

In the days when the Society was enjoying the sunshine of Imperial favour Seraphim supported it with great zeal, and in Moscow as late as 1820 delivered an oration in which he denounced a triple woe on the man who hindered the circulation of the Scriptures or forbade the common people to read the Word of God in their own tongue. But when the clouds gathered and the cold wind of imperial suspicion began to blow, the burden of Seraphim's eloquence changed, and in 1825 he delivered another oration condemning the idea of allowing all and sundry to read the Scriptures without the consent or guidance of the Church. By his management the work of the Society was hampered and slowed down. After the death of Alexander I. it came to a standstill. In August 1826 the Tsar Nicholas I. placed it under the Holy Synod, by whose cold hand it was quickly strangled. At the date of its extinction it had 289 auxiliaries and it had circulated 600,000 copies of the Scriptures in forty-five languages.

The operations of the Jesuits against the Bible Society were, however, only one of their many activities. At Court they had a powerful champion in the French émigré, Count de Maistre, and an astute leader in Gruber, both of whom were admitted into the highest circles. At the same time they captured the goodwill of the Intelligentia by opening schools with excellent staffs of teachers, and they naturally used these schools for propaganda work among their pupils. On the strength of a promise that they would improve agriculture, they were allowed to enter Siberia, but when they proposed to send out missionaries to the tribes living on the east of the Ural Mountains they were told that the Orthodox Church itself would send men to teach these tribes the arts of civilisation.

On the whole, their success led to their undoing. When Golitzin found that not only his wife and his nephew but many others of high rank had joined the Church of Rome, he became frightened, and laid the whole situation before Alexander. Alexander was no longer in the mood to tolerate them. As an autocrat he was annoyed by their renunciation of his authority. As head of the Orthodox Church he felt bound to defend it against its enemies. Therefore, on 10th December 1815, he banished them from Petrograd. Four years later they were banished from Russia and forbidden to return, as their presence had become hurtful to the prosperity of the State. The lands which they owned were scandalously mismanaged, and their serfs were grievously oppressed. They weakened the attachment of the Empire to the Tsar by their intrigues in White Russia, and when Napoleon crossed the frontiers they openly espoused his cause in the hope that his triumph over the Russian Army would pave the way for their victory over the Orthodox Church.

From this time onward the temper of the Russian Church began to show a decided change. It became definitely intolerant. In previous reigns no special hostility was shown to foreign religions. It was assumed that no man would change his religion any more than he would change his nationality, and Lutherans, Catholics, Calvinists, and Orthodox lived peaceably side by side. But the Russian clergy began to feel that in face of the dangers which were assailing their Church from heretics and dissenters on the one hand and from the Jesuits on the other, this easy-going policy could not be continued, and as Alexander set himself to extinguish the flame of political discontent which was flickering here and there among his subjects, the Orthodox Church followed his example and adopted a policy of religious persecution.

Alexander's disappointment at the failure of the schemes he started for the good of his people was intensified by the fate which overtook the scheme which he floated for the benefit of Europe. His personal resolution to live a Christian life was immensely strengthened by the Baroness Julie von Krudener, whom he first met at Heilbron, and afterwards at Heidelberg and Paris. In the interviews he granted to her she addressed him not as a sovereign or a soldier, but as a sinner, and pressed him to accept the salvation offered him in Jesus Christ. He was deeply touched, and, later on, even when questions of importance were under discussion, he would withdraw from the circle of statesmen and shut himself up in his private apartments for the study of the Scriptures and for prayer.

After the Convention of Paris, by which the Allies bound themselves to exclude Napoleon and his family for ever from the French throne, he proposed what was called the Holy Alliance. His openly avowed purpose was to make the law of Christ supreme in the government of Europe. Those who joined the Allies undertook to rule their subjects according to the precepts of the Christian religion, to look on their peoples as sections of one great Christian brotherhood, to remain in Christian fellowship with each other, and to assist each other at all times and in all places. The statesmen, who had to consider problems from the practical point of view, had no patience with Alexander's pious proposals and pledges. Lord Castlereagh characterised the scheme as a piece of sublime mysticism and nonsense. Metternich called it a sonorous nothing. But Alexander persuaded the King of Prussia and the Emperor of Germany to join him in it, and it was ratified in September 1815 in Paris. As the King of England had to consult his parliament before committing himself, he stood aloof.

Unfortunately the political principles held by the monarchs who formed the alliance did not commend themselves to their people. The monarchs stood for the divine right of kings and for unlimited autocracy. The peoples demanded some form of self-government and a constitution in which their rights were recognised and defined. At that time a compromise between the two was impossible, and in proportion as the people's demands became more insistent the monarchs' resolutions to refuse them became more determined. In other words, their policy ceased to aim at the good of the people, as the people interpreted that phrase, and became dynastic, selfish, and tyrannical. At the same time, the interests of Christianity dropped out of sight and the monarchs devoted their efforts not so much to the establishment of righteousness and peace as to securing the stability of their thrones and retaining their hereditary privileges. In these circumstances Alexander gradually declined from his idealisms and sank to the level of an ordinary reactionary. All his life he had discharged the duties of his exalted station with little pleasure, and as one disappointment followed another a deeper melancholy settled on his spirit, and made him at last look forward to death as a messenger of mercy.

In his closing days, the Tsarina, from whom he had been long alienated and separated, was reconciled to him, and as she had fallen into delicate health the royal pair journeyed to the Crimea in the hope that the change would restore her strength. At Taganrog, Alexander himself was seized with a violent fever, and on 1st December 1825 he passed away. In spite of his faults and failures he deserves to take rank as one of the few truly Christian sovereigns who have sat on the Russian throne.

In his case, however, as in the case of some others, there is a persistent belief that the officially reported day and place of his death was not the real one. It is admitted that a man very like him died at Taganrog and that his body was buried at Petrograd. The curious thing is that twelve years later there appeared in a tiny village of Siberia, on the edge of an endless forest, a strange old man who never disclosed his antecedents. He lived in almost perfect solitude, visited on rare occasions by a few friends evidently of the highest rank. He had a gentle face and a sweet smile, but he had also the bearing of a soldier, and some of his bodily attitudes and gestures were identical with those of the deceased monarch. He died in 1859, and there is a widespread conviction among the peasantry that the saintly hermit who called himself Theodor Kouzmitch was really the Tsar Alexander I.

CHAPTER XXII

NICHOLAS I.

ON the death of Alexander the law of inheritance transferred the Crown to his brother Constantine. Constantine, however, refused to accept it, and although for three weeks Nicholas urged him to do so, he remained firm, and at last with great reluctance Nicholas allowed himself to be proclaimed Alexander's successor.

During this interregnum the revolutionists believed that the hour had come to strike a blow for liberty, and they organised a mutiny of the guards, which broke out in St. Isaac's Square on 26th December. The mutiny had no popular support. Its leaders were officers for the most part, and so little did the soldiers know what they were shouting for that many of them thought that " Constitutia " was the name of Constantine's wife. Nicholas, however, took it seriously, and following up a vigorous investigation, in which he himself took part, five of the leading Decembrists were hanged. One of these was the brilliant young poet Ryleeff. Of the rest, thirty-one were sentenced to hard labour for life in Siberia. One of these was the novelist Bestuzheff. The remainder were imprisoned or degraded, and the common soldiers who had taken part in the revolt were sent to Georgia, where they quickly fell in the war with Persia. The main result of the rising was that Nicholas started on a policy of repression which he pursued to the end of his life.

In his interviews with the Decembrists he learned that the people had reason for discontent, and after his coronation, which took place in Moscow in October 1826, he appointed a commission to find out what was actually required.[1] In his report Borovkov the secretary said;

[1] Kornilov, p. 235.

" It is necessary to grant clear, positive laws, to establish justice through swift court proceedings, to raise the moral standard of the clergy, to support the nobility which has deteriorated and become completely ruined, to establish commerce and industry on secure foundations, to direct education in accordance with the status of the pupils, to improve the condition of agriculture, to abolish the humiliating sale of men, to rebuild the navy, to encourage private persons to go to sea—in short, to rectify the innumerable disorders and abuses." Choosing from this list what seemed most urgent, Nicholas set himself to initiate reforms, and he had no hesitation in believing that he could carry them through. " I shall be surprised," he said, " if any of my subjects dares to act counter to my will, once that will has been made known."

He was by nature a martinet, and he began by putting all the servants of the State into uniform. If he had had his way he would have arranged all his subjects in groups like regiments, and would have brought them under military discipline. Uniformity and obedience to supreme authority were the passion of his life.

In order to regulate the people's conduct more effectively he arranged for a codification of the laws. Previous codes were out of date and confusion was universal. " There is no law in Russia," said Puschkin ; " the law is nailed to a stake and that stake wears a crown." Nicholas therefore entrusted to Speranski and a small committee the gigantic task of reducing the legal chaos to order. After infinite labour they produced a complete system, and it was published in 1833.

In 1826, for the purpose of nipping disloyalty and rebellion in the bud, Nicholas created the famous Secret Police, the third section in the Chancery. Their instructions were to gather all possible information about political parties, to keep in touch with all persons under surveillance, to reduce to impotence all persons suspected of being harmful to the State, and to report directly to the Tsar everything it might be useful for him to know. The officers were strictly charged to carry no distinguishing mark, to do their work silently, and to remain as far as possible unknown even to each other. It was not long till they covered the country and till every one began to distrust his neighbour.

Fearing that education might foster the spirit of restlessness, Nicholas endeavoured to arrange it in such a way that the various classes of the people would remain in the position in which Providence had placed them without desiring to rise above it. In May 1827 he decreed that the children of peasants might attend primary schools but nothing higher. In 1828 he reserved the secondary schools for the children of officials and gentry. In 1833 he found a minister to his mind in Uvarov, who said on assuming office that his aim was to construct dams to stop the flow of new ideas into Russia, and who declared he would die happy if he could retard the educational development of the country by fifty years. In the report on the University of Moscow, in which he denounced the pernicious influence of Western thought, he said : " I firmly believe that we shall be able to avoid these mistakes, and shall succeed in capturing the minds of the youth and bringing them to the point where a regulated, fundamental education must merge together with a deep conviction and warm belief in the true Russian conservative principles of Orthodoxy, Autocracy, and Nationality, which constitute the last anchor of our salvation and the surest pledge of the strength and majesty of our country."

For the purpose of creating these educational dams from 1835 onward the independence of the Universities was restricted, the number of students was limited, and subjects likely to provoke discussion were cut out of the curriculum. Students were forbidden to attend foreign seats of learning, but at Speranski's earnest request an exception was made in favour of those who went to study law. After 1848 the restrictions became more severe. A rigorous censorship of all printed matter was established. Authors of new books had to submit their MSS. and get approval before publication, and newspapers had to send an MS. copy of their contents before they were allowed to appear.

Nevertheless, the intellectual activity of Russia was not entirely suppressed. Along certain lines it burst forth with great vigour. Poems, dramas, novels, and historical works were published. Some of the brightest stars in Russian literature shone in this period, but their work in the eyes of the censor was void of offence. If revolutionary teaching had been suspected, the authors could not have escaped punishment. Nevertheless, such teaching was sometimes there. A line in a poem, a sentence or two in a novel, an episode in a play, were enough to suggest a world of thought to those who could understand. But the prevailing mood in Russia became one of sadness. Liberty had almost ceased to exist. There seemed to be no escape from ever-present tyranny, and the future looked blacker than the past. Over and over again we hear the note of hopelessness, and even of despair.

The problem of the serfs was now urgent. Special commissions considered what should be done but came to no conclusions, until in 1834 Speranski laid down the principle that the landowner had no legal claim on the person of his serfs, but only on the serf's labour, and that while he was right to demand one-half of the serf's time he was bound to give the serf enough land to provide for his family and to pay his taxes. In 1848 landowners were permitted to liberate their serfs and give them the use of land at a rent. The serfs refused to pay any rent, for they assumed their allotments were their own property. In 1847 communities of serfs were allowed to buy themselves out of serfdom along with the land they cultivated, if the estate to which they belonged were being sold for debt. Neither did this please them. They said they were asked to buy what was their own, and like its predecessors, the measure was practically useless. It only drew attention to the subject of emancipation, and incited the serfs to increased restlessness. In 1848 the French Revolution broke out, and Nicholas set himself with grim energy to stamp out the revolutionary spirit in his own dominions. It was, however, impossible to do this, so that while there was an appearance of peace on the surface of society there was a movement underneath which, like steam in a boiler, was becoming dangerous because the safety-valve of public discussion was tied down.

The foreign policy of Nicholas was controlled by the same principles as those which governed his home administration. He was everywhere the defender of the rights of reigning monarchs and the enemy of democracy. Besides, as Russia had been the bulwark of Christianity against the Tartars he was, in his own opinion, its protector against the Turks. There was need for protection. In the Balkans, for example, the Orthodox Christians of Greece were sorely harassed by the Turks. Nicholas hated Greeks, but as they were Orthodox he could not close his ears to their cry for help, and in 1827, in alliance with England and France, the Turkish Fleet was sunk at Navarino. In 1828 he threatened Constantinople and forced the Sultan to sign a treaty promising to stop the persecution of Christians, to recognise the independence of Greece, to open the Dardanelles to merchant vessels, and to pay an indemnity. His success not only brought Russia great prestige as a military power, but confirmed his resolution to play the part he had adopted.

In 1830 France repudiated the divine right of kings, deposed Charles X., and gave the crown to Louis Philippe. The spirit of revolt spread to the Netherlands, where Nicholas' sister Anne was Queen, and when Belgium seceded from Holland and formed itself into an independent kingdom, Nicholas was both incensed and alarmed. He was, in fact, on the point of sending an army through Prussia to the Rhine to maintain Absolutist and Legitimist principles when his Ministers assured him that the national finances would not stand the strain. He then turned his attention to the revolutionists in his own realms, and specially to those in Poland.

When he came to the throne there was widespread discontent in the provinces where his brother Constantine was governor. In 1830 the Poles attacked the Russian palace in Warsaw and compelled Constantine to fly for his life. In January 1831 the Diet declared Poland a republic, self-governing and free. Russian troops were at once poured in. By the end of October the country lay at Nicholas' feet, and he set himself to crush it once and for all. He abolished the Diet and all electoral institutions. He wiped out the ancient Polish territorial divisions and substituted governments on the Russian model. He turned the civil administration into a bureaucracy, dependent on Petrograd. He incorporated the Polish regiments in the Russian Army. He forbade the use of the Polish language and the Polish system of weights and measures. He confiscated the estates of Polish landowners and sold them to Russians. He caused thousands of prominent Poles to be shot or hanged. He degraded the middle classes to the rank of Russian serfs. He caused Polish children under sixteen years of age to be separated from their parents and sent to distant parts of Russia. He tore 45,000 Polish men from their families, marched them into the Caucasus, and planted them in its most unhealthy districts. In short, he did everything he could think of to destroy Poland as a nation and break its spirit.

The Catholic Church in its Uniate form was the national Church of Poland, and as it had played a great part in sustaining the spirit of independence it came in for a special share of suffering. In order to reduce it to impotence, Nicholas forbade the celebration of Mass, except on Sundays and great Church festivals. He forbade priests or parents to teach children the Romish Catechism. He forbade the baptism of infants by any but Orthodox priests, and claimed these infants for the Orthodox Church. Uniate places of worship were pulled down or closed. Uniate priests were expelled from their parishes, and the members of their congregations were driven to Orthodox services by soldiers armed with the knout and the bayonet. Uniate monks and nuns were subjected to horrible tortures to compel them to accept Orthodoxy. The nuns of Minsk, who were more than usually obdurate, were beaten, starved, tormented by thirst, exhausted by labours far beyond their strength, and when they resisted violation they were battered and trampled to death. They were tied up in sacks, only the head being left free, and with ropes round their necks were dragged behind boats in the waters of a lake till some of them were drowned. At last nature could bear no more, and in 1838 the leaders of the Uniates met at Polotsk and signed a petition to Nicholas, beseeching him to receive them and their people into the Orthodox fold. The petition was granted, and the Orthodox Russian clergy made great jubilations, ascribing this miraculous conversion to the manifest grace of God.

The action of the ruling powers towards those who antagonised the autocracy and towards those who were outside the Orthodox Church was to some extent approved by the Slavophils. These came together as a definite party about the middle of " the forties," and formulated principles which were to some extent in harmony with those of the bureaucracy and of the Holy Synod. They demanded complete freedom of speech and of creed, unrestricted liberty of self-government—personal, communal, and ecclesiastical—and on this account they were looked on with much disfavour and were made to suffer accordingly. But they held that the Russian State and the Orthodox Church had received a unique divine commission which gave them a claim on all true patriots and religious men. They maintained that no people on earth is so richly endowed by nature or so original as the Slavs, no institutions are so suited to a people's needs as the institutions of the Slavs. Therefore, nothing can be borrowed from foreign nations which would benefit the Slavs. Further, the function of the Slav race is to keep alive the knowledge of divine things. The Western nations have been led astray by reason and logic. Russia, on the other hand, by its humility, has not only saved its own soul, but has shown the way of salvation to others, and whereas in the West the Christian faith has been corrupted by Papal tyranny, and disintegrated by Protestant individualism, and emptied of its contents by rationalistic philosophy, the Orthodox Church of Russia has preserved it in its ancient purity. Besides, in the West class antagonises class. In Russia, however, society is organised in an orderly fashion under the Autocrat, and the Christian brotherhood of the people is made manifest by the communal institutions of peasant life. The business of Russia is, therefore, to liberate all Slavs from alien rule and to bring all Christians into the fold of Orthodoxy.

One of the principal Pan-Slavists was A. K. Khomiakoff. Theologically he maintained that the whole of the Church of Christ now existing upon earth is contained within the Orthodox Eastern Church, of which the Russian Church is part, and for this reason his writings have become textbooks in the Church seminaries. At first, however, because of his political opinions, they were proscribed and had to be printed abroad. On the other hand, V. S. Soloviev endeavoured to find out a philosophical basis upon which the doctrine of the East and the West could be brought into harmony. But as he displayed very distinct leanings towards Catholicism his efforts were doomed to failure from the beginning.[1]

Another spokesman on the same side was P. J. Chaadiev. He wrote a philosophical letter in French to a lady friend, and by some strange oversight on the part of the censor it was published in *The Telescope*. Chaadiev renounced Uvarov's formula in its entirety, and he did so in the name of religion. Russia, he said, had no originality. All its ideas were borrowed, and there was nothing to be proud of in its history. At first there were savage barbarities, then came rude superstition, then humiliating subjection to the Tartars, and after them to the Grand Dukes of Moscow. The Empire in its isolation was as devoid of religion as it was of civilisation. The Orthodox Church was, in his opinion, a decadent institution in which Christian truth was corrupted by superstition, and Christian practice was made difficult by ignorance and prejudice. The way of salvation was therefore to throw Orthodoxy overboard and to embrace Catholicism, for Catholicism was the real defender of Christian doctrine and the stimulating force behind all Christian progress.[2]

Against all these, others of the Intellectuals like

---

[1] Birkbeck, i. 222.   [2] Kornilov, i. 285.

Bielinsky maintained that while the Slavophils dreamt of a Russia prosperous and happy under the ægis of the autocratic Tsar and the Orthodox Church, these dreams could never become concrete realities until autocracy was replaced by complete self-government, and Christian faith by scientific materialism.

Opinions such as these, of course, gave great offence. Nicholas, after reading Chaadiev's letter, declared it to be the work of a madman. The clergy were furious, and the usual result followed. Chaadiev was officially declared to be insane, his publisher was exiled, and the censor endeavoured to secure that no copies of his work got into the people's hands. There were, however, many who sympathised with him, and their vigorous propaganda, conducted for the most part in secret, created excitement which the violence of the Government did nothing to allay. But this violence had little influence on the life of the common people. They were sunk in ignorance so deep that they knew nothing about the questions which agitated the educated classes. Like the fish at the bottom of the sea, they took no notice of the wheeling and screaming of the birds in the air.

In the meantime, the Orthodox Church was going on its way, busy with its own concerns. Soon after Nicholas came to the throne he brought Philaret out of his retirement and made him Metropolitan of Moscow, and it was not long till strife raged for the second time round his catechism. The Procurator of the Holy Synod was Protasov, whose education had been influenced by the Jesuits, and he attacked the catechism because it fell short of the sympathy with Latinism which appeared in the similar manual of Peter Mogila. The Synod therefore revised the catechism, but not as Protasov wished. On the contrary, they intensified its Orthodox peculiarities, with the result that, in 1842, Protasov got Philaret excluded from the Holy Synod and dismissed to his diocese. Philaret was in fact looked on with suspicion by the more conservative section of the Orthodox clergy, and his version of the acts of Cyril Lucar, Patriarch of Constantinople, heightened

the distrust with which he was regarded.   In 1631 Lucar
published what he called the Eastern Confession of the
Christian Faith, in which there was some distinctly Cal-
vinistic teaching.   This Confession was condemned first
by a Synod held at Jassy in 1642, and also by a Synod
held at Jerusalem in 1672 under the Presidency of Dositheus,
the Patriarch.   This Synod endeavoured to show that the
Confession was not written by Lucar ; that if it had been
he must have published it secretly ; and that, as a matter
of fact, it is not the Confession of the Eastern Church.
In 1838 Philaret published Lucar's work in a version in
which the Latinisms objected to did not appear.   Even
in this form it was never officially accepted, and, because
of his connection with it, Philaret remained to the end
of his life under a cloud.   He was often consulted in affairs
of State.   He is even said to have drafted the edict for the
emancipation of the serfs which was published in 1861,
and he pressed forward the work of translation with such
effect that, in the year after his death, and in spite of the
opposition of the Procurator, Tolstoy, a version of the
Scriptures in the vernacular was put into circulation.

As a counterblast to Chaadiev's letter, Nicholas published a decree in 1841 in which he announced that the
safeguarding of the Orthodox Church was one of the first
duties imposed on him by Providence, and gave warning
that he would take severe measures against all who sought
to injure it.   Heretics and dissenters were, in his opinion,
first cousins to revolutionaries, and both were to be dealt
with as traitors to the State.   Some of those who incurred
his displeasure in this connection, such as the Skoptsi
and the Khlysti, were leniently treated because, although
they were suspected of immoral practices, they attended
the services of the Orthodox Church, and also because
they had no scruples about bribing the police and the parish
priests.   Others were treated with severity, in spite of
the fact that they were in all respects good citizens.   For
example, the Old Believers were expelled from public
offices and forbidden to engage in trade or to become
merchants, except in a small way.   They were not allowed

to build new churches or to repair their old ones. Their marriages were declared to be invalid, and they were forced to get their children baptized by an Orthodox priest. Their taxes were doubled, and the police were instructed to see that their conduct kept within the limits prescribed to them.

If the regulations had been enforced, the continued existence of the Old Believers would have become difficult, if not impossible, but they found ways of making friends which need not be inquired into, and to a large extent they were left undisturbed. Sometimes, of course, the higher authorities interfered and put the provisions of the law into operation. Those who suffered as the result of this were looked on as martyrs, and their death did more to propagate the faith for which they gave their lives than all they could have done by argument and persuasion.

Among others to whom the attention of the Government was directed were the Molokani. The Molokani call themselves Spiritual Christians. They have received their nickname from the fact that they eat milk and the products of milk in Lent and on days which the Orthodox Church holds as fasts. They trace their history back to the time of Ivan IV. to a serf named Semenov, who received a Slavonic Bible from an English physician, his master, and to a Doctor of Moscow named Tveritinov who, in the reign of Peter the Great, rejected ikons and the ritual of the Church on the ground that God who is Spirit is to be worshipped not with ceremonial, but in spirit and in truth. In the reign of Catherine I. the Molokani took shape as a sect as the result of a split from the Doukhobors. When Pobirohin, the leader of the Doukhobors, began to teach that the incarnation of Christ was repeated in every individual, and that the light which was in Christ is found in every individual, his son-in-law, Uklain, maintained that the law of truth is found only in the Scriptures. After making many converts in private discussions, he appeared in public for the first time at Tambov. In spite of his immediate arrest, his teaching was widely accepted, and it was not long till, in the province of Tambov alone, he had more than five thousand disciples.

The Molokani based their doctrine upon Scripture as firmly as any Protestant. Their method of interpretation is, however, peculiar. On the ground that the letter killeth and that the Spirit alone gives life, they expound the text after what they call a spiritual fashion and evade the duty of obedience to the most positive precepts by explaining them away. They reject the divinity of Jesus, but they accept Him as a great prophet. They believe in His miracles and, after their own fashion, in His resurrection. They also believe in a life beyond the grave in which God forgives all sinners, and they look for the coming of a Messiah who will usher in an era of peace They reject the Sacraments as of no value, and their worship is confined to reading the Scriptures, singing hymns, offering extempore prayers, and listening to addresses by their elders. Their life is marked by sobriety, industry, and thrift. The marriage tie is formed by a public declaration before witnesses. Divorce is almost unknown. Lawsuits are rare, and they consider war forbidden by the principle of brotherhood. They are excellent citizens, and wherever they are left unmolested they become prosperous.

In spite of their practical godliness, and indeed to some extent because of it, they drew upon themselves the ill-will of their neighbours. The parish priests were annoyed because they ceased to pay the customary fees for official services. The lazy and drunken peasants took their pure lives as a rebuke, and the anger of the Government was roused by their refusal to perform military service. At first missionary priests were sent to bring them back to the Orthodox faith, but they were no match for the Molokani either in knowledge of the Scriptures or in power of argument, and they had to be withdrawn. In 1826 Nicholas took sterner measures with them. He issued a decree that both the Molokani and the Doukhobors should be given the choice of enlistment in the army or exile in Siberia. Those who were drafted into the army performed willingly the peaceful tasks allotted to them. but they refused absolutely to carry arms or to fire a shot.

The cruellest tortures failed to reduce them to obedience, and their uncomplaining endurance had such an effect on the other soldiers that the officers protested against receiving any more of them for fear of ruining discipline. In 1839, 1840, and 1841, in pursuance of the policy of weakening them, their settlements were broken up, and the members were scattered over the Caucasus. But Nicholas found that to scatter burning coals among combustible material is not the best way to extinguish a fire, and the uncomplaining meekness and the unmistakable nobility of character displayed by the Molokani not only won for them many converts but also many sympathisers who never joined their ranks.

Towards the end of his reign, Nicholas appointed a commission to discover the numbers of the dissenters and heretics, and to report what means might be taken to extirpate them from the Empire. To his dismay, and to that of the Orthodox clergy, it was proved that extirpation was impossible. In some provinces not less than half the population held schismatic doctrine. In others, whole towns and villages were in the same condition, and the total number was not less than eight millions.[1]

A distinction was then drawn between sects which were more and sects which were less pernicious. In the case of those who were less pernicious, such as the Popovtsi who had priests, the Government imprisoned the priests in the hope that their flocks would find their way back to the State Church. In many cases this hope was realised. In many more it was not, and the pastorless people joined some of the more fanatical sects. No mercy was shown them, and in proportion as the fury of the persecutors increased, the more unshakable became the conviction of the persecuted that the Government of Russia was in the hands of Satan. Their plain duty was, therefore, to resist to the death, and so steadily did they resist that towards the end of his reign Nicholas allowed his severity to relax. In point of fact, he was beaten by the fortitude and patience of his suffering subjects.

[1] Kornilov, i. 295.

" The number of trials and severe penalties inflicted
upon dissenters of all categories grew from year to year ;
according to official data, between 1847 and 1852 there
were over five hundred verdicts a year against them, and
the number of persons tried for belonging to the schism
during those five years was twenty-six thousand four
hundred and fifty-six." [1]

Following out the principle that, as head of the Russian
Church, he was the divinely appointed guardian of
Christians in other lands, Nicholas drifted into the Crimean
War. The ostensible cause of the war was a dispute about
the holy places in Jerusalem, in which the Orthodox Church
as represented by Russia, and the Catholic Church as
represented by France, took opposite sides. Behind this,
however, was the desire of Russia to establish itself as the
guardian of Orthodox believers in Turkish territory with a
view to the ultimate occupation of Constantinople. The
dispute with regard to the holy places was settled after
some difficulty, and as this removed the pretext for
interference, Nicholas went on to demand that the Sultan
should sign a convention acknowledging the Protectorate
of Russia. The Sultan refused. The Russian ambassador
then delivered a message to the effect that Russia would
take all measures necessary to accomplish its purpose.
In October 1853 war was declared. In March 1854 France
and England intimated their belief in the justice of Turkey's
cause and joined her as allies. Austria and Prussia stood
aloof, but pledged themselves to assist each other in case
of attack.

The war which followed was waged for the most part
round Sevastopol. All through it the corruption, incompetence, and mismanagement of the bureaucracy was
beyond description, and Nicholas was forced to recognise
that the administration of his Empire was rotten. He
himself toiled to arm and equip his troops, to supply their
needs, and relieve their sufferings, until, worn out with
fatigue and anxiety, he was seized with pneumonia and
died on 2nd March 1855. Among his last words were a

[1] Kornilov, i. 297.

protest that his aim was to protect the Orthodox Greek
Church in the Turkish Empire and was not to extend his
dominions at Turkey's expense.

If it had been possible for one man to control the thought
and life of a great people, Nicholas I. would have controlled
it.   He had an iron will, he knew exactly what he wanted,
and he had the Holy Synod and the Orthodox clergy on
the one hand, and the army and the police on the other,
ready to use their tremendous power for the purpose of
crushing religious dissent and political disloyalty.   Even
with their assistance the task was beyond him.   If he had
allowed free discussion of the ideas that were fermenting
in his people's mind the result might have been a peaceful
development of the nation's life towards a higher level of
prosperity and power than it had ever reached, and his
own position as constitutional monarch, and that of his
successors, might have been established beyond fear of
attack, but when he fastened down the safety-valve by the
restrictions he imposed on free speech and on the Press, he
made the disruptive pressure of the new ideas all the more
dangerous.   He left the fabric of the autocracy strained
at every point, and his policy, carried to its logical issue by
those who came after him, inevitably produced a devastating
explosion.

CHAPTER XXIII

ALEXANDER II.

ALEXANDER II., who now came to the throne, found a tremendous task awaiting him. The first thing to be done was to end the war, for the country could fight no longer, and after the fall of Sevastopol peace was signed in March 1856.

In his policy regarding internal affairs Alexander was disposed to follow his father. The popular belief in his liberal sympathies was entirely mistaken. By instinct as well as by training, he had no respect for constitutionalism, but he saw that in many directions reform was imperative, and he was ready to carry it through on the distinct understanding that it sprang from his imperial initiative and was directed by his imperial will. He relaxed the censorship of the Press, and removed the restrictions imposed on universities and the prohibition of foreign travel. Then he concentrated his attention on the serfs. In a speech to the nobles assembled in Moscow in March 1856 he said : " It is better to begin the abolition of serfdom from above than wait till it begins to abolish itself from below." His audience was taken aback, but Alexander had made up his mind that the abolition he suggested must take place.

He waited to let the serf owners take the first step. When they refused to move he sent a communication to the gentry of Lithuania, who seemed less unsympathetic than the others, intimating that their rights over the bodies of their serfs were to cease to exist, but that their rights over the land would continue in force, except over the sections of land on which the serfs' houses stood, and over the allotments which the serfs cultivated. These were to remain in the serfs' possession on condition of payment of rent. The communication met with a mixed reception. The landowners in the Black Soil regions of the centre and south were willing to free their serfs because they could no longer afford to feed and house them, and because they saw in landless and needy multitudes of men and women a supply of cheap labour which could be exploited indefinitely. Those in the districts north of Moscow, which were less fertile, were willing to give up their barren lands on condition that they kept their serfs, for their revenues were derived from what the serfs earned either in the field or the forest, or in the foundries and factories. Money was necessary to keep up their dignity, and to wring it from the serfs was the only way of getting it they knew of.

After protracted discussion it was determined that the serfs should be set free—but not completely; that the owners should be allowed to keep their land—but not the whole of it. They were to surrender the land which the serfs cultivated, and the serfs were to pay by instalments for the land which in this way was assigned to them. This Act of emancipation was published on 3rd March 1861.

The serfs hailed the Act with rejoicing, but as nothing had been done to make them familiar with its provisions, they were speedily filled with surprise and disappointment. It did not give them what they wanted, and it imposed conditions which they resented. They assumed that the land belonged to them originally, and that it was now to be restored to them. It was useless to tell them they might each have an allotment if they paid for it. They contended that the land belonged to them to begin with, that it had been taken from them by violence, and it ought to be handed back unconditionally. Besides, the sections assigned to them were too small to live on. In former days that did not matter, because the landowner fed them and paid their taxes, but now they had to feed their families and pay everything themselves, and they could not do it. They were really worse off in liberty than they had been in servitude. With the childlike confidence in the good intentions of the Tsar which characterised them till a recent date, the serfs assured themselves that the landowners were taking advantage of the Tsar's distance from his people to disregard his orders and to introduce fresh methods of tyranny. Therefore, while there were outbreaks against the landowners everywhere, there was no attack on the autocracy. In many districts soldiers were required to restore order, and bloodshed followed. At Bezdna more than one hundred casualties were reported. It is probable there were more, and similar figures might have been returned from other places.

The landowners were equally discontented. Many of them could do nothing to support themselves, and now that they had lost the produce of the serfs' labour they sank to the brink of poverty. Alexander tried to relieve their distress by retaining for them certain well-paid posts in the civil service. Those who secured these posts were fortunate. Those who did not secure them were often compelled to sell their remaining property, and in their descent down the road to ruin they fanned the flames of rebellion that were kindling round them.

The priests' sons formed another discontented class. Those who failed to obtain a parish had difficulty in finding occupation anywhere. Everything was closed against them, except poorly paid clerical work or work in a factory, and in every city shabby groups of them might be seen loitering in the public squares ready to do anything that would bring them in a rouble, and hoping against hope that some one would engage them to sing a Mass or do some other service for which a priest was required. Many of them sank to the most abject poverty, and vented their spite against society in various forms of crime.

In spite of iron discipline, the army also was restless. The higher posts were filled by men who had no qualifications except their birth. The rank and file were, for the most part, conscripts torn from their homes and enlisted for long periods, often for life. Along with these there were in the ranks political offenders who used their opportunities to carry on a propaganda which was none the less successful because it was secret. The stolid demeanour of the regiment on parade was no proof of its loyalty to the autocratic regime.

These and other centres of discontent had, however, no connection with each other, and on that account they did not alarm the Government. Besides, the discontent was not directed against the autocracy as a political system, it was directed against individuals who were held to be responsible for the sufferings under which the people groaned. In the case of the Intelligentsia, however, things were different. They maintained that the misery and injustice of the people were the direct outcome of autocracy, and that peace would be impossible until autocracy was replaced by constitutional government. They had, however, little influence. They were out of touch with the common people. They did not understand the actual problems which Russian statesmen had to face, and they spun theories out of a weird combination of natural science, materialism, and positivist philosophy which they assured themselves were the foundations of a new heaven and earth.

Many, if not all, of these theorists were young men and women in the universities. So long as they confined themselves to abstract discussion the Government took as little notice of them as if they had been blowing bubbles, but when they issued a proclamation in April 1862 to the effect that the Romanovs must expiate with their blood the wrongs of the people, action followed at once. The students' clubs were closed, newspapers and magazines which allowed revolutionary articles to appear were suppressed, and the editor of one of them, Tchernishevski, was exiled to Siberia. At the same time, police supervision of suspects was made rigorous and minute.

The revolutionists then pushed their theories further, and Nihilism was born. The term was dropped by Turgueniev in his novel, *Fathers and Sons*, and it was promptly employed to designate the theory that the institutions on which society is built must first be swept away, and then when nothing at all of them is left a better order will become possible. In the Nihilist State there is to be no constraint or compulsion of any kind.   As the bodies of the serfs had been emancipated from the tyranny of their masters, so the minds of men would be emancipated from the obligations imposed by morality and religion, and their social and economic life from law, tradition, and custom. Every one would be free to follow his own inclination, without regard to the dogmas or the ideals which regulate human life at present, and the result would be a State which had no need for police, because every one would live virtuously, or for priests, for there would be no more reverence for the superstitions on which the Church is founded.   These doctrines were preached especially by Pisarev, and they were enthusiastically accepted by the rising generation.

There was enough fanaticism in the revolutionaries to make them dangerous, and, with the view of ushering in the Nihilistic State, clubs were formed.   As a first practical step fires were started simultaneously in several districts of Petrograd.   By these the public were terrorised and the Government was alarmed.   It gave the police a free hand and arrested scores of students of both sexes.   Some were imprisoned, some were flogged with the knout, some sent to Siberia, others were executed.   The effect of this was quite different from what was expected, for the sufferings of these revolutionary dreamers roused the passion of their comrades to white-heat and turned many of the civilian population, who were previously unsympathetic with them, into rebels and conspirators.

In 1863 the Polish revolution broke out.   The Western powers left the insurgents to their fate.   Russia showed no mercy, and everywhere there was terror and tears. With this indication of what they might themselves expect, the revolutionists in Russia paused to consider their position.   While they were doing this, Alexander sapped the strength of their movement by various reforms which removed some of the abuses that were notorious.   In 1863 the universities were made autonomous, and in 1864 secondary schools, some of them classical, some technical, were opened.   The provision of elementary schools was left to the Zemstvos and other local authorities. In December 1864 a judicial system based on the practice of Western Europe was instituted. Under it justice was to be the same for all. Trial by jury was allowed, except in political cases. Men skilled in the law were made judges and were paid decent salaries, while petty offences were assigned to the jurisdiction of courts presided over by magistrates elected by the Zemstvos and Town Councils.

These reforms modified opposition to the Government policy, and encouraged the hope of a constitutional system to such an extent that the gentry of Moscow besought the Tsar in January 1865 to call a representative assembly which could express the mind of the people. Alexander told them bluntly that no such assembly was required, for he was fully aware of what was needed to perfect the organisation of the State, and he would act on his own initiative. He certainly had various projects before him, but what he would have done remains unknown, for at this juncture an incident occurred which cut his policy into two sections and changed him from an autocrat with some progressive ideas into a pitiless reactionary. Those who desired the downfall of the autocracy were not agreed as to the methods by which it was to be accomplished. Some placed their confidence in an appeal to reason and justice. Others had no patience with such a slow process. One of the latter was a youth of noble family named Karakasov who, against the urgent appeal of his associates, fired a pistol at the Tsar on 4th April 1866. The bullet missed its mark, but from that moment Alexander resolved to crush the spirit of revolt at any cost. On 3rd September 1866 Karakasov was hanged, and a long series of imprisonments, floggings, and banishments followed. Provincial governors received almost unlimited powers to deal with suspected persons. The Zemstvo schools and similar institutions were placed under inspectors, charged to see that instruction did not fall into bad hands, and in the universities the new Minister of Education decreed that the teaching of science should be superseded by the teaching of the classics. The result of this policy was that many students went abroad to Germany, to France, and elsewhere, and came into contact with the men whose writings had already done much to stimulate their political activity, imbibing from them materialistic and atheistic conceptions of human life.

In this connection two names may be mentioned—those of Bakunin and Herzen. Michael Bakunin, son of a noble family, was born in 1814. In 1841 he went to Berlin and became one of Hegel's disciples. In 1843 he went to Paris, and was infected by the socialism of St. Simon and Louis Blanc. In 1849 he was arrested in Dresden, claimed by Russia, and sent to Siberia, from which he escaped in 1851 and reached London. By this time he had thrown Hegelianism overboard and had set himself to seek truth and liberty in new forms of social life. In his judgment the way to liberty was to destroy everything that imposes restraint : " Man's task is," he says, " to liberate himself from all fetters in which his fellow-men seek to bind him. Belief in God is the chief of these, and every one who would be free must deny the existence and spurn the authority of a Divine Being. The existence of God implies the abdication of reason and justice ; it is the negation of human liberty, and of necessity ends in a slavery both theoretical and practical. The slave of God becomes the slave of the Church and of the State." The Church is an engine which brings men into bondage by means of superstitious terrors. The moral law is the means by which the Church retains in bondage men who have a right to gratify their appetites as unrestrainedly as the birds of the air or the beasts of the field. The State is likewise an organisation intended for oppression. It is the most complete, flagrant, and cynical negation of humanity, and the free development of personality requires that it should be abolished. For the same reason, individual States must cease to exist, and a great international brotherhood must be created. In that brotherhood every one must be allowed to do exactly as he pleases, and the result, says Bakunin, somewhat optimistically, will be universal righteousness and peace.

Alexander Herzen, who has been called the Voltaire of Russia, was born in Moscow in 1812. At the University he studied chemistry and the natural sciences. After several short experiences of exile he made the acquaintance of Hegelianism, Positivism, and Materialism, and the writings of the French socialists. He left Russia in 1847, spent some time in France and Italy, settled in London in 1852, remained there till 1867, and finally went to Paris, where he died in 1870. He was neither an individualist nor an anarchist like Bakunin. Hegel had taught him that the individual has relations to others from which he cannot extricate himself, and duties to others which he cannot evade. He had also learned that the State is an institution, binding its members into a unity which, while retaining its own individuality, ought to recognise the individuality of other States and form with them a great human confraternity in which each section is necessary to the welfare of the whole. Therefore, while he devoted his life to exposing the corruption and inefficiency of the autocratic regime, he did not demand that the State should be reduced to ruins before its reconstruction began. He wrote many books and treatises, and for several years edited from London a journal called *The Bell* (*Kolokol*), which, strange to say, was regularly laid by an unknown hand on the Tsar's study table, and was read with equal regularity by His Majesty.

As a materialist, and therefore also an atheist, Herzen had no room in his thought for religion or the Church, but there were times when he felt that the science of matter and force was unable to satisfy his desire for spiritual truth. He looked on the Church as an institution of great value to the Government, because it preached the duties of contentment and patience and soothed those who were suffering with hopes of better things in the life to come. In 1843 he spoke of Orthodoxy as in a condition of absolute arrest; nevertheless, in the weakness of the Church, he discovers a great negative advantage, namely this, that it has no influence on Russian life, while the life of Western Europe is permeated by Catholicism. For Herzen, therefore, Catholicism is Christianity *par excellence*, while Orthodoxy is no more than an evil possibility. Herzen, however, made an honourable exception in the case of the Old Believers, whom he regarded as the healthiest element in the nation. " We owe to them," he says, " the preservation of the national ideal, of national tradition, national manners and customs." [1]

Herzen's method of creating the new social order differed profoundly from that of the more ardent revolutionists. He held that the mass of the people, bound by tradition and accustomed to servitude for generations, could neither be liberated from their bondage nor made adequate to the responsibilities of freedom by a terroristic *coup d'état*. The true policy was to hasten slowly and teach the people how to liberate themselves. Propagandists were therefore required in all classes of society, and they would be more useful than assassins.

Herzen's cry, " To the people," was taken up and repeated by many powerful voices, and the youth of both sexes, especially the students, responded to it in large numbers. Disguised as physicians, teachers, clerks, day labourers, blacksmiths, foresters, midwives, and nurses, they spread themselves over the country. They taught the ignorant to read and write, they healed the sick, they relieved the misery of the poor, and all the time they preached that the condition of happiness and prosperity was the overthrow of the autocracy. They had, however, surprisingly little success. They belonged to a world from which the common people were shut out, and they never really got into the confidence of those among whom they laboured. The peasants in particular obstinately suspected them of evil designs, and sometimes denounced them to the police, for they were as yet in no mood to tolerate anything to the detriment of " The Little Father."

It was, in fact, the ignorance, the inertia, and the blind devotion of the common people which was the strongest bulwark of the autocracy and the Church. Against the incessant attacks on religion the Orthodox clergy failed

[1] Masaryk, i. 394.

to set up a satisfactory defence. As an intellectual force leavening the thought of the nation they ceased to count. The bishops had neither the scholarship nor the philosophic ability needed to expose the fallacies of the theories which had become fashionable. The monks in their convents lived a life of utter mental stagnation. The parish priests for the most part had to slave for their existence like serfs, and from sheer poverty were unable to take an interest in anything outside their ordinary routine. For the most part they were harassed by sordid cares. They were miserably paid, and for everything outside the regular Church services they had to drive hard bargains with their parishioners. Few of them had preaching gifts, and they were not encouraged to cultivate what gifts they had, still less were they expected to supervise the morals of their people. When free from official duty they worked in the fields, and too many of them spent their leisure time tippling in the taverns. They were not really worse than their neighbours, but their drunkenness was proverbial. When any one of them acquired a reputation for saintliness people flocked to him with pathetic eagerness for the blessings he was believed able to give. But this seldom happened, and in any case the parish priest was the last man in Russia who could meet a revolutionary propagandist in debate and defend the position which the revolutionist attacked. He could, however, denounce an adversary to the police, and if he suspected a parishioner of revolutionary sympathies he quickly found means to make that parishioner's life a burden.

When the Government discovered how rapidly the loyalty of the educated youth who were studying abroad was being disintegrated, it ordered them all to return to Russia before 1st January 1874. It was a foolish order, for those who returned began at once to inject into the current of the nation's thought the poisonous ideas by which they themselves had been corrupted. The Government therefore took a further step. In 1877 it arrested 770 of them and punished them so severely that many who escaped the hands of the police gave up their propaganda work in despair. The remainder became more frantically Terrorist, and on 14th January 1879, the day after the Tsar signed the death sentence which had been passed on 193 of them, Vera Sassulitch shot General Trepov, Chief of the Police in Petrograd, on the score of his cruelty to a political prisoner. She was tried in public, and from the point of view of the bureaucracy this was a mistake, for the revelations she made in court roused such a storm of popular indignation that, in spite of her admission of guilt, the jury acquitted her. A campaign of repression followed, and was met by a campaign of assassination. One prominent official was murdered after another, and on 14th April a youth named Soloviev fired a pistol at the Tsar himself near the Winter Palace. Martial law was at once proclaimed, the Secret Police were stirred to feverish activity, and arrests and executions were multiplied.

In the meantime, trouble was brewing in the Balkans, where the Turks were cruelly oppressing the Christians. In May 1876 the Bulgarian massacres shocked the con- science of Europe. In July, Serbia and Montenegro declared war. In May 1877 Russia did the same. In the campaign which followed, Russia slowly gained the upper hand, but the congress of powers at Berlin robbed her of the full fruit of her victory, and sent a wave of indignation over the country. The Ministry and the Tsar himself were fiercely blamed for the humiliation to which they had consented, and increasing numbers of the people began to demand some form of constitutional government. Alexander had secured a constitution for the Bulgarians which gave them inviolability of person, an independent judicial system, and liberty of the Press, and by means of newspapers which issued from presses which the police failed to discover, and by resolutions in various assemblies, the Russian people began to ask not only for the ad- vantages which Bulgaria enjoyed, but also for the abolition of the standing army, the division of the land among the serfs and the factory-workers, and the calling of a repre- sentative assembly.

As Alexander showed no sign of granting the popular

demands, a secret tribunal condemned him to death on 20th August 1879. One attempt after another was made on his life. On 1st December, as the imperial train was arriving at Moscow it was wrecked by a bomb. On 17th February 1880 the dining-room of the Winter Palace was blown to pieces a few moments before the imperial party entered it. Other acts of a similar description made it plain that something must be done in the interests of peace.

The Tsar was really not so unimpressionable as he seemed to be. He had already appointed a commission under Loris Melikov to find a way out of a position that was becoming intolerable. Melikov was a staunch upholder of autocracy, but he saw that to some extent the people must now be allowed to share the responsibilities of government. While he was firm in his dealing with those who broke the law, he extended the liberties of ordinary citizens, he allowed the district and provincial councils to ventilate their opinions freely, he improved the system of taxation and the legal status of the peasants, and he strongly urged the Tsar to assemble groups of competent public men to meet and formulate plans for the general welfare.

By these and other measures he undermined the hold of the Terrorists on popular sympathy, and in their exasperation they resolved to strike a blow which, in their opinion, would shake the autocracy to its foundation. Melikov was aware of this, and in order to secure the sympathies of the people still further in support of the Government, he persuaded Alexander to consider the draft of the definite political constitution. As he was supported by a majority of the Council of State, Alexander yielded to their arguments and sent a rescript to the Ministry of the Interior with an order to publish the document on 12th March 1881. All over Petrograd, however, the Terrorists were on the watch for him, and on the 13th March, when he was returning to the Winter Palace from an inspection of troops, his carriage was wrecked by a bomb. He escaped for the moment, then a second bomb burst at his feet and inflicted such ghastly injuries that he died two hours afterwards without regaining consciousness.

So great was the shock given to public feeling by this outrage that after the Tsar's death the people swung almost in a body to the side of the Government. The assassination of officials went on for a time, but the people were so hostile, the police were so vigilant, arrest was so certain, and punishment was so severe that those of the revolutionists who remained at liberty were disheartened. Some of them made their peace by recanting their opinions, others fled for safety to England, France, and Switzerland.

CHAPTER XXIV

ALEXANDER III.

ALEXANDER III. was even more of an autocrat than his father had been, but he had so much respect for his father's memory that he felt he ought to carry through the measure granting constitutional government which his father had agreed to. At the same time, it was out of harmony with his own instincts, and after some hesitation, which was finally dispelled by the arguments of his former tutor, Pobiedonostseff, he made up his mind and declared it in a manifesto issued on 29th April, in which he said : " In the midst of our great grief God's voice commands us to stand courageously at the helm of the Government, relying on the Divine Providence, and with faith in the power and truth of the autocracy which, for the benefit of the people, we are called on to strengthen and guard from encroachment." After the appearance of this manifesto Loris Melikov resigned his office.

At this crisis the revolutionists gave Alexander an opportunity of coming to terms with them, which he was ill-advised enough to reject. They sent him a letter in which they said : " Sire, you may rest assured that on the day on which the supreme power ceases to be autocratic, and on which you firmly decide to listen to what the conscience and the will of the people are dictating to you, on that day you will be able to clear the streets of the spies who are a dishonour to the Government, you will be able to leave your escorts in their barracks, and uproot the gallows which demoralise the people. When these conditions are realised, a peaceful conflict of ideas will take the place of the present violence, which we abhor even more than your servants, and which necessity and circumstances alone have forced us to use." Alexander's reply was to call to his side some of the most reactionary men in the country. Of these the most important and conspicuous was K. P. Pobiedonostseff. K. P. Pobiedonostseff was a brilliant lawyer, and he had a sincere desire for Russia's welfare, but he was narrow-minded, intolerant, and fanatically devoted to the support of autocracy and of the Orthodox Church. In 1880 he was made Procurator of the Holy Synod, and for twenty-three years thereafter, through the Synod on the one hand and the Tsar on the other, he became the really ultimate autocracy in the Empire. Both in Church and State his policy was reactionary, for he feared the progressive movements which had begun would result in nothing but disaster. With regard to democracy he said: "Among the falsest of political principles is the principle of the sovereignty of the people, the principle that all power issues from the people and is based upon the national will." [1] Parliament is not an institution for carrying out the national will. It serves for nothing but "the satisfaction of the personal ambition, vanity, and self-interest of its members. It is, indeed, one of the greatest illustrations of human delusion." [2] The Press does not represent the opinion of the people: "Any vagabond babbler, any tradesman, with his own money or the money of others, may found a newspaper and scatter broadcast calumny, slander, and lies. It is hard to conceive a despotism more pernicious than that which the Press exercises, and its vagaries must be restrained by the strong hand of authority." [3] "Trial by jury leads to the perversion of justice. It is both reckless and irrational to suppose that it can establish either the guilt or innocence of the accused. In the Law Courts casuistry is practised and crimes go unpunished." [4] The traditional connection between Church and State is essential to their existence. Separation would imply the destruction both of religion and of morality, and the only Church which the Russian State ought to recognise is the Orthodox Church. Its adherents may be ignorant, its clergy rude and lazy, but it, and it only, is the Church of Christ, and it is as far above Catholicism on the one hand as it is above

[1] *Reflections*, p. 32. [2] *Ibid.*, p. 35. [3] *Ibid.*, p. 62. [4] *Ibid.*, p. 60.

Protestantism on the other. Its duty is to keep itself free from entanglements with Churches abroad and to repress dissent and heresy at home.[1] When a man with opinions such as these became the guiding spirit of a new government it is evident that a desperate struggle with the forces of reform and progress was bound to ensue.

The struggle did not begin at once. After the resignation of Melikov, Ignatiev was appointed Minister of the Interior, and he continued to some extent Melikov's policy. This was intensely displeasing to Pobiedonostseff, and in May 1882 he was forced to resign. His place was filled by Count Dimitri Tolstoy, a reactionary after Pobiedonostseff's own heart. In 1884 he stripped the universities of their powers of self-government. In 1887 he reduced secondary education to the level of a class privilege by a circular in which he proclaimed, "that the children of coachmen, servants, cooks, laundresses, and small shopkeepers and like persons" should not aspire to rise above the position in which they were born. He also endeavoured to confiscate Zemstvo primary schools and transfer them to the clergy who, under Pobiedonostseff's directions, would soon have destroyed their efficiency. But the opposition he met with was so great, and the cost of carrying them on at the Government expense was so heavy, that he finally left them alone. Bunge, the Minister of Finance, succeeded in carrying into operation some measures prepared under Melikov's superintendence, such as a reduction of the redemption payment on allotments and the abolition of the poll tax, and the institution of a better system of tax collection, but in the long run he also had to retire.

Pobiedonostseff and Tolstoy found an ally in Pazukhin, a landowner in Simbirsk, who was made chief of the Chancery. He was a reactionary of the most extreme type. He believed that the emancipation of the serfs and the other reforms of the previous reign were a series of profound mistakes. They were, in fact, the cause of all the misery from which Russia was suffering. Their

---

[1] *Reflections*, p. 24.

influence had, therefore, to be counteracted, and the old system of class differences, class government, and class privileges had to be restored. Following out this policy, the self-governing power of the Zemstvos was attacked. In July 1889 the method of electing the members was seriously modified. In 1890 the number of peasant delegates was reduced, while that of the landowners was increased to such an extent that the meetings became for all practical purposes assemblies in which the landowners had everything their own way. The authority of the Mir was also reduced to the vanishing point. In every district a Government official was placed with irresponsible power both in respect of the local affairs which the Mir discussed and also with respect to the peasants as individuals. The peasants naturally regarded this as preliminary to the re-imposition of the yoke of serfdom, and the autocracy could have done nothing better calculated to stir their sympathies in favour of reform.[1]

During the reign of Alexander II. the Russian frontiers in Central Asia had been pushed forward by a series of campaigns in which, one after another, Chimkent (1864), Tashkent (1865), Khodzhent (1866), Samarkand and Bokhara (1868), Khiva (1873), and Geok-Tepe (1881) fell before the Russian arms. Under Alexander III. railways were pushed out from the base thus acquired, and England became justifiably alarmed for the safety of India. His interest in these and in the problems which they raised absorbed his energies to such an extent that Pobiedonostseff and Tolstoy, and the other reactionaries whom he had associated with them, had almost a free hand in internal affairs. So far as trade and commerce were concerned, Russia prospered under them. The value of imports and exports increased rapidly. Factories and works of all sorts were multiplied. There was remarkable expansion in the coal and iron industries, and thousands of miles of railway were constructed. One consequence of this was that the peasants from the country who drifted into the towns remained there and became a proletariat.

[1] Beazley, p. 474.

Year by year their numbers increased, and although decrees were passed regulating the hours and conditions of their labour, their lot was really intolerable. They toiled for long hours and for low wages in the most insanitary conditions. But what angered them most was that a strike was declared to be a criminal offence, and those who advocated strikes were severely punished. Except in so far as the Government regulations defended them, they were at the mercy of their masters, who exploited them most cruelly. As a natural consequence, in the towns in which they swarmed and struggled for a bare existence they became a hotbed and forcing-house for revolutionary ideas. So rapid was the growth of these ideas that, in the hope of turning the attention of the workers away from political problems, the bureaucracy encouraged the trade unions to agitate for social and economic reforms, and sent out secret agents to stimulate the agitation. Some of the workers did not see the aim of the bureaucracy in this respect. Others did, and a struggle arose between them. The moderate men desired to see a socialistic State established peaceably. The extremists, whose mentality had been changed by the revolutionary propaganda, maintained that anarchy was a preliminary to reconstruction. The extremists prevailed. In December 1886 Alexander Oulianov, elder brother of Lenin, whose real name was Vladimir Oulianov, issued a manifesto in which he says: " The sole method for the struggle is systematic terrorism. This terrorism will not be a form of vengeance or of despotic judgment, nor will it be an unconscious protest of despair. Neither will it be a more direct means of abolishing the existing economic order. It will be a provisional, self-conscious, and revolutionary struggle against the police of the despotism who have no ground to stand on." Nicholas Morisov also said: " We must bring knives, dynamite, bombs, and poison into play. By this action the authorities will be kept in fear, the general public will be continually excited and demoralised, and the prestige of the present authority will be shattered." [1]

[1] Antonelli, p. 13.

In these circumstances it seemed plain to Alexander and the bureaucracy generally that the only course open to them was one of repression, and they followed it with the utmost energy. Spies and secret police were planted in every circle of society. Domiciliary visits, usually by night, disturbed the peace of numberless households. Trial by jury ceased, and suspects were condemned in secret. Hundreds of men and women vanished without leaving a trace. Thousands were sent into exile by administrative order, and the number of those who were executed and of those who were thrown into the dungeons of Schlusselburg or SS. Peter and Paul, and left there to rot in silence and darkness, will never be known. The liberty of the Press was entirely suspended, and the existence of newspapers was made almost impossible by the prohibition of private advertisements and of retail sale. The result might have been expected. The revolutionaries used the knives and bombs of which they had spoken.

While this was going on in Russia a similar policy was being carried out in Poland, and Polish patriots and Uniate churchmen suffered equally. In the Baltic provinces also the Lutherans felt the weight of Pobiedonostseff's heavy hand. He could not tolerate discontent with the autocratic form of government, and just as little could he tolerate dissent from the Orthodox Church, and therefore those in Russia who dared to live outside its pale suffered the most grievous persecution.

Perhaps those who suffered most heavily were the Jews. There had been Jews in Russia from an early date, and they had always been looked on with some disfavour, but their sufferings up to this time were of small consequence compared with their torments after it. Catherine I. made no secret of her antipathy to them, and in this respect she was followed by Anne and Elisabeth, both of whom ordered the Jews to leave the country. Catherine II. modified the policy of her predecessors by inviting them to settle in South Russia under conditions which paved the way for the restriction of their liberties afterwards. After the first partition of Poland, when she found that the section of the dismembered country which fell to her share contained large numbers of Jews, she ordered them to reside in a definite area. In other words, she created the Russian Pale. In 1824 Alexander I. forbade any Jew to reside within fifty versts of the borders of the Pale. Under Nicholas I. the area of the Pale was fixed definitely. In Russia it included the fifteen provinces—Bessarabia, Tchernigov, Grodno, Kherson, Kiev, Kovno, Minsk, Mohilev, Podolia, Poltavia, Taurida, Vitebsk, Volhynia, Vilna, and Ekaterinoslav. To these might be added Courland as a sixteenth. If we include with these the ten Polish provinces which finally lost their independence, the total number is twenty-six. It might appear as if this enclosure, containing as it does 350,000 square miles, were large enough for all practical purposes. But appearance differs from reality. The right of residing wherever they chose was denied to the Jews. In the country they were compelled to gather together into communes separated from the communes of the Orthodox. Certain towns were assigned to them, and in these they had to live in specified areas, which rapidly became congested and degenerated into slums. Besides, the crowding together of large numbers of men and women seeking work created such fierce competition that wages were reduced to the lowest point, and the majority of the Jewish community lived in semi-starvation. The Government was quite aware of this, and Pobiedonostseff is credited with the prediction that in due time a third of the Jews would be converted, a third would emigrate, and the rest would die of hunger.[1]

The opening months of Alexander's reign were marked by what looked like an attempt to exterminate them. In the spring of 1881 an anti-Jewish agitation broke out in Germany. In the summer of the same year it spread to Russia, and riots were of frequent occurrence. As the police made no attempt to stop these, the rioters proceeded to murder the Jews, not only singly and in families, but wholesale. In at least forty towns there were scenes that

[1] Kornilov, ii. 284.

would have disgraced an inferno. Thousands were put to death for nothing more criminal than their Jewish faith. Thousands more were reduced to destitution, and of the six million Jews who were living in Russia at this time there was not one but had a trembling heart, a failing of the eyes, and sorrow of mind, for neither day nor night had he any assurance of his life.

These pogroms were followed by official restrictions which were both oppressive and humiliating. In May 1882 the Jews were expelled from the country districts and ordered to settle in certain towns where the Jewish quarters were already full to overflowing. The only exception permitted was that of Jewish agricultural colonies. The Jews were forbidden to hold mortgages or leases of real property outside towns or burghs ; or to act as attorneys in the management or disposal of such properties ; or to transact business on Sundays and on the principal Christian holidays. In 1887 the area of the Pale was reduced by cutting out of it Rostov on the Don and Taganrog. The Jews in these districts had to sell their property at a ruinous loss and travel into the regions in which they were permitted to live. In 1888 another edict ordered that every Jew must go back to the place in which he had been living in 1882, and those who had changed their abodes in obedience to the edict of 1887 had to uproot themselves once more and return, usually in abject poverty, to the places they had left.

Other regulations were added of a peculiarly offensive nature. Not only had the Jews to pay all the taxes imposed on Russian subjects, they had to pay special taxes imposed on themselves alone. For every animal or fowl they killed for food there was a special tax. For every pound of food thus provided there was another tax, and on the rent they received for houses, shops, stores, and so forth, there was a special tax. On every distillery which they owned or managed, on every brewery, glasswork, copper or iron foundry, tar, pitch, or tallow work, there was a special tax. There was even a tax on the candles which they bought for the long winter nights.

Their clothing was taxed. Every Jew had to pay five roubles a year for permission to wear a skull-cap. These taxes were collected by the most brutal methods, and when they appealed to the law courts they were made to feel that whoever might get justice the Jew was certain to get none.

In the same spirit the advantages of education were denied to them. In June 1885 the number of Jews to be admitted to the Technological Institute of Kharkov— one of the only two such institutions existing at that date —was limited to ten per cent. of the whole number. In March 1886 the admission of a Jew to the Veterinary College of Kharkov was absolutely forbidden. In December 1886 the number of Jewish students attending universities within the Pale was limited to ten per cent. of the whole number. In other universities it was to be five per cent. In Moscow and Petrograd it was to be three per cent. In 1887 these restrictions were applied to all gymnasia and grammar schools without exception. When the Jewish communities endeavoured to establish schools at their own expense they were told that the ordinary establishments within the Pale were quite adequate to the needs of the inhabitants, and if on entering any of these a scholar or student concealed the fact of his Jewish birth, he was punished as if he had committed a forgery.

Treatment such as this roused in the Jews a hatred of everything that is called Christian, and inflamed them with a desire for revenge. Some of them found a place in the fighting organisation of the revolutionists. Others of them made war on their oppressors in more subtle ways. By their cunning and business ability they entangled their dull-witted customers in financial obligations and ruined them without mercy. In every district in which they were allowed to settle they sucked the blood of the people like so many vampires, and made themselves hated and feared. Centuries of persecution have compelled them to be servile and patient, but their servility is often the mask of a deadly passion that is waiting for its opportunity. There is no country in the world in which the cup of sorrow has been made so full or so bitter as in Russia, and little did those who pressed it to Jewish lips think that in the days to come Jewish hands would press it to their own.

The policy of crushing those who refused to accept autocracy as a form of government, and of persecuting the Jews, went hand in hand with the policy of harassing those who dared to dissent from the Orthodox Church, and in all this Pobiedonostseff was the driving force. Naturally the Old Believers had to suffer. Others suffered along with them. Among these were the Stundists. The Stundists came into existence as a sect about 1865. They base their creed on the Scriptures and believe in the inspiration both of the Old and the New Testament. They place little value on the Old Testament, however, on the ground that it is concerned with an obsolete dispensation, and they concentrate on the teaching of Christ and His apostles. Whatsoever they find in that teaching they accept. Whatsoever they do not find they refuse. For this reason they refuse to observe the Church Fasts or to venerate ikons, or to perform the Orthodox ritual in divine worship, or to recognise the Orthodox hierarchy. Against it they maintain the spiritual priesthood of all believers. In general, their doctrines correspond with those of Lutheranism, with special emphasis on Justification by Faith.

In 1870 the Stundists were visited by some Baptists from Prussia. A religious revival began. It spread like wildfire, and in Petrograd it received great support from Lord Radstock and others. The moral transformation which it wrought in the lives of those who became Stundists was marvellous. Those who had been indolent, drunken, and vicious became sober, thrifty, and prosperous. They paid their taxes punctually, and upheld law and order. Of their loyalty to the State there could be no question. They prayed for the Tsar at every meeting, and even their persecutors have given them certificates of which they may be proud. The police superintendent of the Tarashtshanski district says in his report : " They are distinguished from the rest of the population by their uniformly high standard of morality, and in the villages in which they reside crime has practically disappeared. Owing to their sobriety their economical condition is incomparably better than that of the Orthodox population, and no comparison at all need be made between their respective intellectual levels, seeing that all Stundists can read and write. Their family life is in all respects exemplary, and their relations with each other are, in the best and broadest sense of the word, Christian." [1] If the Procurator of the Holy Synod and the higher clergy had not been blinded by religious prejudice, they would have encouraged a movement which produced such excellent results, but their passion for uniformity and their bigotry drove them in another direction.

In the first place, they tried to bring the Stundists back to Orthodoxy by argument. Books and pamphlets exposing Stundist errors were published. Journals inculcating Orthodox truth were circulated. Pamphlets and tracts were distributed. Bands of missionaries were sent out. But the Stundists were so well versed in the Scriptures that the missionaries had small success, and an archbishop expressed grave doubts as to the wisdom of any public discussions on religion. An Orthodox missioner, by name Terletski, who had been sent out by the Archbishop of Kiev, was so chagrined by his failure to win back even one Stundist that he declared the wandering sheep could be gathered into the Orthodox fold by nothing less than the following measures : That all Bible readings and prayer-meetings should be prohibited, that soldiers should be quartered in the huts of all who were suspected of Stundism to prevent such meetings being convened by night or in secret, and that all Stundist preachers should be condemned without trial to penal servitude in the mines of Siberia. [2]

At the same time slanderous reports were circulated in all directions. Ambrosius, Bishop of Kharkov, caused a

[1] Lanin, *Contemporary Review*, Jan. 1892.
[2] Conybeare, p. 249.

poem to be fixed to the door of every church in his diocese, of which the following verses will be a sufficient sample :

> " Roar, ye Church thunders,
>   Arise, ye cursers of the Holy Council,
>   Strike with eternal anathema
>   The progeny of the damned Stundist.
>
> The Stundist destroys the dogmas,
>   The Stundist rejects the tradition,
>   The Stundist scoffs at the ceremonies.
>   He is an apostate, the damned Stundist.
>
> He is stern and gloomy like a demon,
>   Shunning the sight of the faithful Orthodox.
>   He hides in dark haunts,
>   This enemy of God, the damned Stundist."

The police were set in motion against them, and in pointing out suspected persons, in tracking them to their hiding-places, and in inflaming popular passion against them the parish priests were most active, and in this miserable work they had, as they knew, the approval of their superiors as well as the assistance of the police. In 1891 a Council of the clergy met at Moscow, with Pobiedonostseff as President, and it implored the Government to adopt the following, or similar, regulations : That all offenders against Orthodoxy should be tried not by a jury, which was apt to acquit them, but by ecclesiastical judges ; that their passports should be marked with an entry declaring the owners to be Stundists, so that no employer should give them work, and that no landowner should allow them to rent or purchase land, and that no inn-keeper should give them shelter ; that the police should have power to drive them into Orthodox churches to hear sermons against their faith ; that all Stundist families should be broken up, the children being taken from their parents and handed over to strangers ; that any Stundist found reading the Bible or praying in company should be banished to Siberia ; and that any Stundist who read the Scriptures or preached in public should be sentenced to penal servitude in some remote part of the Empire.

Pobiedonostseff and the clergy were determined to exterminate the Stundists, and the methods they employed were ruinous fines, rigorous imprisonments, banishment to remote regions, and the racking tortures of incessant hardships. Those who were exiled were also denied the usual alleviations of a convict's miserable lot. At that time the most degraded criminal was allowed to take his wife and children with him to his place of banishment if they were willing to go. The Stundists were forbidden to do this. The wives were told they must stay behind with their children, and embrace Orthodoxy, or else go with their husbands and leave their children to any one who would receive them. Their mental anguish was more unendurable than any physical suffering, yet the Archbishop of Kharkov complained that the action of the civil authorities was lacking in wholesome severity.[1]

The irony of the situation is that from the reign of Nicholas I. to the end of the reign of Nicholas II. the Orthodox Church was lying in a state of spiritual torpor, and it was outside its fold that any real religious earnestness was to be found. With few exceptions the clergy had ceased to be worthy of respect and had ceased to be respected. In the time of Nicholas I. the Marquis de Castine said of them : " The Russian clergy have never been and never will be anything more than a militia dressed in a uniform somewhat different from that of the secular troops of the Empire."

The following quotation from a report given to the Grand Duke Constantine indicates how far they had fallen below the Christian ideal : " The people do not respect the clergy, but treat them with derision. In nearly all the popular stories the priest, his wife, or his labourer is held up to ridicule, and in all the proverbs and popular sayings where the clergy are mentioned, it is with contempt. The people shun the clergy, and have recourse to them not from the inner impulse of conscience but from necessity. And why do the people not respect the clergy ? Because they form a class apart, because they remain in the mere dead form of

[1] Lanin, *ut supra*.

ceremonial, and at the same time despise these forms even to blasphemy, because the clergy continually present examples of want of respect to religion, and transform the service of God into profitable trade. Can the people respect the clergy when they hear how one priest stole money from below the pillow of a dying man at the moment of confession, when they hear how he was publicly dragged out of a house of ill-fame, how another christened a cow, how another, while officiating at the Easter service, was dragged by the hair from the altar by the deacon? Is it possible to respect priests who spend their time in the liquor shop, who write fraudulent petitions, who fight with the cross in their hands, and abuse each other in bad language at the altar? How can they respect the clergy when they see everywhere among them simony, carelessness in performing religious rites, and disorder in the administration of the sacraments . . . or when they see that the consistories are guided in their decisions not by principles but by personal friendships and bribery."

The judgment of the Old Believers is to the same effect: " The official Church in Russia is dead, exhausted, under the thumb of les bureaucrats, subject to the Powers of the world, vending the heritage of Christ for a morsel of bread, with no faculty of self-reform from within and without the aid of the Government. In its relations with the police you behold it sacrifice sincerity and authority and enslave itself to Babylon. Russian Orthodox Christianity is wholly official, a mystic Byzantinism barely to be distinguished from pagan formalism. The Russian clergy preach to the people the indissoluble union of autocracy, Orthodoxy, and nationality, and deny the form of government to be a thing both human and mutable. This is why the clergy has made itself hated of an oppressed people, and has pardoned all and every act of violence. The Church has really transformed itself into a political institution, and its pastors, mere employees of the Government, by their conduct sow incredulity and atheism and slay faith in the people's heart. The faithful know that hierocratic despotism takes for its device the formula,

' I am the Church, the Church is I,' and, intolerant of such oppression, they abandon the temple." [1]

During Alexander's whole reign the country was seething with discontent, and every year added to the number of those who were ready to break out into open rebellion. They were not as yet under a single control, and on that account were not so formidable as they might have been, but Alexander and his Government could have done nothing more than they did to make them feel that the autocrat was their common enemy, and to unite their efforts to bring the autocratic system to the ground. As the Church was the ally and the agent of the autocracy, the educated classes looked at it with scorn, the revolutionists reviled and hated it. Only the ignorant masses of the people held to it, and it retained their allegiance by trading on their reverence for antiquity and their superstitious fears. It met the inarticulate desires of their religious nature, but it neither enlightened their understanding, touched their conscience, nor sanctified their lives. If they attended the services and paid the priest's fees, all was reckoned to be well.

[1] Conybeare, p. 256.

CHAPTER XXV

NICHOLAS II.

AFTER a lingering illness, Alexander III. died in October 1894, and was succeeded by his son, Nicholas II. During the first ten years of his reign he was under the influence of Pobiedonostseff, and at the end of it under that of his wife, a daughter of the Grand Duke of Hesse, and with these as his guides he took one step after another down the road which led the autocracy to the abyss.

He began by alienating all those who were endeavouring in a peaceful way to establish the right of the people to manage, at least to some extent, their own affairs. Using language put into his mouth by Pobiedonostseff, he said, in reply to a loyal address from Tver, that for some months there had been heard the voices of those who indulged in senseless dreams with regard to the participation of the Zemstvos in the direction of the internal affairs of the Empire. He therefore desired it to be known that, while he would devote his energy to the service of the people, he would also maintain the principle of autocracy as firmly as it had been maintained by his lamented father.

Popular feeling expressed itself in a remarkable letter to the Tsar dated Petrograd, 19th January 1895, but probably written abroad, in which Nicholas was asked if he realised the situation he had created. The writers declare their only wish was to inaugurate a closer union between the monarch and his people, to secure for the Zemstvos free access to the throne, to obtain the right of public meeting, and the assurance that the law would stand above the caprice of the administration. Finally, they bid him understand that he himself had destroyed the halo which for centuries had shone round the Russian monarch's head.

At the same time the conduct of the Tsarina angered another section of the people. Although she was of German birth, many deputations were sent to welcome her and to offer her costly gifts. When she entered the room where the deputies were assembled she did not even glance at the gifts, and after a few haughty words withdrew, leaving the deputies mortified by her disdain.

The coronation took place in Moscow on 26th May 1896. The occasion was celebrated with religious services and a display of barbaric magnificence, but it was also marked by great tragedy. When the people assembled on the Khodinsky Plain the barriers erected to regulate their movements were taken away by criminal mismanagement, and disorder instantly ensued. When it ceased, it was found that more than three thousand persons had been trampled to death or suffocated in the ditches by which the plain was surrounded. Nicholas personally could not be held responsible for the disaster, but if he felt any pity it was noticed that he showed none, and a general impression was created that he cared for the fate of those who had perished as little as if they had been flies.

Pobiedonostseff quickly established his hold on the Tsar, and not only persuaded him that he was called by divine favour to govern Russia as an autocrat, but also that he was charged to dispense the blessings of civilisation to barbaric nations, and to exercise an influence in Europe that would benefit all mankind. In Europe he created more than one serious situation, and in the Far East his policy led to the war with Japan. As the campaign went on the proofs of incompetence, mismanagement, and corruption which steadily accumulated strengthened the demand for reform which was making itself heard everywhere.

As the result of persistent propaganda the various classes of the Russian people now began to move into line for the final struggle with the bureaucracy. The first were the peasants. They showed their resentment against the conditions in which they were living by refusing to pay rent or taxes, by cutting down trees, by carrying off corn and cattle, and by burning hundreds of landowners' houses. Next came the factory workers and artisans. After the great famine, in which their struggle for existence became desperate, strikes broke out in all directions, and these had to be repressed by violence. In the hope that concentration on their social condition would divert their minds from political issues, the Government sent out secret agents with instructions to organise the workers and to incite them to more extensive demands. This line of action was a complete mistake, for the workers got completely out of hand, and the strikers largely became revolutionists.

The educated classes also went over wholesale to the side of revolution. In 1898 Bogoliepov, the Minister of Education, set himself to carry out the Holy Synod's orders to purge the universities of disaffection, and in 1899 he had many students flogged with the knout. As a protest, thirteen thousand of their comrades went on strike. In 1900 a meeting of a thousand students held at Kiev was surrounded by Cossacks, who seized 500 of them. Of these, 193 were sent to penal battalions in the army, and the rest were banished. Similar meetings were held at Petrograd, Moscow, and elsewhere, with similar consequences. Soon afterwards, Bogoliepov was assassinated, and working men showed their sympathy with the students by marching in procession down the streets shouting, " Down with autocracy."

The bureaucracy, knowing that its existence was now at stake, used all its power to destroy its enemies. Sipiagin was appointed Minister of the Interior in 1899, and in the thirteen months in which he held office there were sixty thousand arrests. He was killed by a bomb in 1902.

His successor was Count Plevhe, an extremely clever man, in whose veins there was a tinge both of Jewish and of German blood. He did his work with Jewish cunning and German thoroughness. He reduced the Zemstvos to practical impotence, and he perfected the system of espionage, applying it even in Court circles. He sent hundreds of revolutionists to execution, and thousands to banishment, but some of his agents played him false. They sold the revolutionists to the police, and they sold the police to the revolutionists. Of these, the most notorious was the engineer Azev, who, impelled solely by the desire of gain, sent dozens of revolutionists to death, and with equal indifference planned and secured the assassination of the Grand Duke Sergius, the attempted assassination of the Grand Duke Vladimir, of Trepov, Governor-General of Petrograd, of Kleyguels, Governor-General of Kiev, of General Minn, of the Prime Minister Stolypin, and he even planned three attempts on the life of the Tsar himself. His crowning achievement was the assassination of his paymaster, Plevhe, on 15th July, when he was driving through the streets of Petrograd.[1]

In 1905 an incident occurred which finally determined the attitude of the mass of the people not only to the autocratic system but also to the autocratic Tsar. Four workmen were dismissed from the Putilov foundry. Their comrades came out on strike. Men from other foundries and factories joined them, and, led by George Gapon, a Government secret agent, and accompanied by their wives and children, marched to the Winter Palace to see the Tsar and ask him to redress their grievances. They had no doubt of his power, and just as little of his willingness. But the Tsar, who knew they were coming, had already disappeared, and after the multitude had been told that he was not in Petrograd it was ordered to disperse. It refused. Even when warned of the consequence it still refused, and the soldiers were ordered to fire. Volley succeeded volley till 3500 dead and wounded were lying on the snow. The excitement over Russia was intense, and Bloody Sunday, as it was called, destroyed the last illusion in the people's mind that the Tsar could be trusted to right their wrongs. The stimulus to the revolutionary movement was tremendous. In ten provinces whole villages rose in revolt. In the towns and cities professional men and others of every occupation held meetings of protest. The students made demonstrations and the universities

[1] Alexinski, p. 190.

18

were closed. Strikes took place in districts as far apart as the Caucasus and the Baltic provinces. On the other hand, the Government used every weapon of repression and tyranny. In revenge, many prominent officials were assassinated. On 17th February the Grand Duke Sergius was blown to pieces by a bomb in the Kremlin, and on 3rd March the autocracy made a show of surrender. Nicholas announced his intention of calling an assembly elected by the people to participate in the work of legislation. On 3rd August he redeemed his promise in a way that roused the people to universal madness. In the same sentence in which he summoned the Duma, he intimated that it would have no more than consultative powers. The disappointment of the people became rage. One strike followed another with great rapidity, and on 7th October the whole nation went on strike for a fortnight. Nicholas then capitulated, dismissed Pobiedonostseff, and issued a manifesto promising inviolability of person and conscience with the right of free speech and public meeting, and extending the franchise of the Duma to classes which up till that time were denied civil rights. He also promised that no law would come into force without the Duma's consent.

The promise of constitutional government was hailed with joy, but the bureaucracy resolved to mingle the people's joy with tears. They found a pretext ready to hand. Some Jews among the revolutionists made the foolish boast that the Tsar's manifesto regarding the Duma was their work, and behaved so insolently as to annoy the native-born Russians. An anti-Jewish crusade was at once organised, and as it was directed from Petrograd there can be no doubt that the ministry approved of it. Their instruments were the Black Hundreds, men of the criminal classes, who were always ready for riot and bloodshed, and their special attention was directed to the Intelligentsia, the students, and the Jews. Pogroms were started in more than three hundred towns simultaneously, and, sometimes encouraged by the police, the Black Hundreds attacked Jewish houses, smashed the furniture, carried off valuables, and murdered those who resisted them. In Odessa there was a massacre lasting for four days in which there were nearly two thousand victims. At Kiev, at Kishenev, at Kalarasch, at Marienskaia, and a multitude of other places similar horrors were perpetrated.

With these scenes of terror as a background the Duma met for the first time on 10th May 1906. Furious discussions culminated in a deadlock, and the Duma was dissolved by a *coup d'état* on 8th July. Those of the deputies who escaped arrest fled to Finland, and from Viborg called to the people not to pay taxes or furnish recruits for the army. The revolutionists called on the workers to defend the popular cause by arms, but the people were worn out with excitement and terrified by the brutality of the police, and the bureaucracy quickly regained its former power.

A second Duma met in March 1907, and although its numbers were elected on a franchise which was manipulated in the interests of the bureaucracy, it was more hostile than the first had been. Stolypin then seized thirty-seven of its members on a charge of conspiracy, sent them to Eastern Siberia, and dissolved the Duma in June. The franchise was again manipulated in such a way that all but landowners, financiers, and wealthy merchants were excluded from the electoral roll, and the third Duma met in December 1907. It was more submissive to the Government than its two predecessors, but it resisted the extension of the Zemstvo system to the Western provinces, where Russians were in the minority, and another deadlock ensued. Stolypin ended it by ordering both chambers to suspend their sittings for four days. During that period he put the obnoxious proposal on the statute-book as an emergency measure decreed by the will of the Tsar. When the Duma reassembled it faced an accomplished fact. The people had by this time ceased to take much interest in the Duma, considering it part of the bureaucratic machine, and the composition and conduct of the fourth Duma did something to justify their opinion.

In the meantime, the revolutionists increased their

activity, carrying on a vigorous propaganda in every circle of society, and striking down many prominent officials. The task of maintaining even a show of order was not easy, but Stolypin did what he could. On the one hand he arranged that landless peasants should, without much difficulty, become small landowners, who had everything to lose from political disturbance. In this way he hoped to increase the stability of the social order. On the other hand, he multiplied the number of spies, secret police, and others, till every one went in fear of his neighbour. He enlarged the power of officials to such a degree that every magistrate, from the governor of a province down to a village constable, was made practically a despot with no restraint on his caprice or brutality.

" In the two years 1905–6, when he was strangling the revolutionary movement, in addition to those sentenced to death by the law courts, a great number perished without any trial. Not less than 26,000 persons were murdered in this way by the army and police, while 31,000 were wounded. But these figures do not include the notorious ' punitive detachments.' These on the Baltic provinces alone killed 1500 to 2000 of the inhabitants." The number of those sent to prison was 181,000. The number banished to Siberia was so great that it could not be estimated. The state of matters was no better in succeeding years. In 1908 the police seized 7016 persons and handed them to the military tribunals. Of these, 1340 were condemned to death, and this process of " pacification " went on until, on 1st September 1911, Stolypin was assassinated in presence of the Tsar in the theatre at Kiev. His successor in office continued his policy of brutality and bloodshed with pitiless severity. The revolutionists also continued their activity. Strikes of great magnitude broke out in Petrograd, Moscow, Riga, Baku, and many other places. The whole country became disorganised, ruin stared it in the face, and then came the Great War.

The result of all this appeared in a general breakdown of physical health and of the moral sense. Neurasthenia became amazingly common among the workers and the peasants. Those in a higher social station began to live for the pleasure of the day. " Let us eat and drink," they said, " for to-morrow we die." Physical love became the object of a special cult, and a wave of pornography swept across Russian literature. Others gave way to despair and ended their misery by suicide. " Between 1905 and 1909 there were in Russia more than forty-five thousand suicides, and the years when the reaction was at its apogee, the years 1908 and 1909, were the most fatal. In Petrograd in 1904, 427 suicides were reported ; in 1905, 354 ; in 1906, 532 ; in 1907, 716 ; in 1908, 1408 ; in 1909, 1438. In Odessa there were 256 suicides in 1905 and 642 in 1908 ; in Moscow 174 in 1906 and 614 in 1908."

Here is a sentence from a letter written before death by a young student of twenty years in Odessa : " To live as I would now is impossible, and live as it is possible I cannot. . . . I cannot witness atrocities and suffering, cannot hear the complaints and the sobs of the oppressed, and at the same time feel my impotence to solace, however little, this horror that is life. And I am going out of life, for there is nothing to live for." [1]

All through the reign of Nicholas II. religious persecution went hand in hand with political tyranny, and among those who suffered were the Doukhobors. They are said to have existed as a sect in the time of Catherine II., but they came into prominence at the end of the eighteenth century. Paul persecuted them. Alexander I. allowed them to settle at Milky Waters near the Sea of Azov. There they dwelt till 1824 and became prosperous, and then they came into collision with the Government on the question of military service. They objected on principle to bear arms. Russia, however, had no room for conscientious objectors, and in 1841–2 they were banished to the inhospitable region known as the Wet Mountains of Georgia. In 1864 their leader, Peter Kalmikof, nominated as his successor his wife, who associated with herself a young man named Peter Varigin. In 1887 Varigin was

[1] Alexinski, p. 292.

banished to Lapland, and afterwards to a more inaccessible spot called Obdorsk in Northern Siberia. From both these at intervals he wrote letters, some of them good sense, others to his adherents more questionable, urging them not to hold private property, not to bear arms, not to impose servitude on horses or cattle, not to till the ground, but to live on what it produced itself, not to work, but to follow the example of Christ and His apostles, who depended on charity, and not to wear clothing, but to go naked wherever the climate permitted it.

In 1893 three of his disciples made the acquaintance of Count Leo Tolstoy, and persuaded him that they and their master were suffering for their fidelity to the teaching of Christ. The doctrines they hold are certainly not those accepted by the Christian Church. They assert that the Holy Trinity is a Being beyond comprehension, the Father is light, the Son is life, the Holy Spirit is peace. This Trinity is affirmed in man, the Father by memory, the Son by reason, the Spirit by will. The Divinity of Jesus Christ as shown in the Old Testament is said to be nothing more than wisdom revealed in nature. In the New Testament he is represented as piety and purity incarnate. He is Son of God in the same sense as all men are sons of God. He is born, preaches, suffers, dies, and rises again spiritually in the heart of each believer. Salvation depends on the inward word which enlightens all who receive it, and reveals Christ in the depth of our souls. He in whom Christ lives is a priest unto himself and needs no other. True worship is in spirit, ritual is useless, and the Sacraments are an offence to God, who desires not signs but realities.

Tolstoy was naturally overjoyed to find a community living in accordance with his favourite principle, Resist not evil, and free from the disruptive tendencies which had blown to pieces the communities which he himself had founded. In his ignorance of the real position he made himself their champion. As the result of an agitation over their treatment, which he roused both in Europe and America, orders were given in 1898 that the Doukhobors were to be allowed to leave Russia on condition that they travelled at their own expense, that those who had been called for military service should serve out their term, and that if any of them returned they should be banished to Siberia. In 1899 over 7300 of them started for Canada. They took their peculiar principles with them and gave much trouble to the Canadian authorities.[1]

Of all the millions in Russia, however, the man most obnoxious to the Holy Synod was Count Leo Tolstoy. It would have given the Synod much satisfaction to deal with him, and not less satisfaction to the bureaucracy, but he had a European reputation, and they were afraid. Nevertheless, they went as far as they dared. In February 1892 Tolstoy wrote an article denouncing the indifference of the Government to the suffering of the people in the Great Famine. It was published in the *Moscow Gazette*, and at once it raised a storm. The reactionaries both in Church and State loudly demanded that he should be shut up in a monastery, and it was only by a fervent appeal addressed directly to the Tsar by one of his aunts, who was a lady at Court, that his safety was secured. As the attempt to imprison him had failed, the Holy Synod endeavoured to discredit him by issuing from their official press a book which looked like a companion to one which Tolstoy himself had published. Its contents gave prominence to the opinion of Father John of Kronstadt that Tolstoy was mad. In 1900, when Tolstoy was seriously ill, the Holy Synod sent out instructions that no masses or prayers for his benefit would be allowed unless he gave proof of his repentance. On 22nd May 1901 it formally excommunicated him on the ground that, " under the seduction of his intellectual pride he had insolently risen against the Lord, and had publicly repudiated the Orthodox Mother Church, and had devoted his talents to the dissemination of teachings repugnant to Christ and the Church, and to destroying the Orthodox faith, which had been confirmed by the universe and by which Holy Russia had been made strong."

Tolstoy replied that he had repudiated the Church and

[1] Maude, p. 37.

its Sacraments and was resolved in life and death to have nothing to do with its ministers, not because he had risen up against the Lord, but because he desired with all his strength to serve Him. To this he added a short positive statement of the fundamentals of his creed.[1]

In 1902; on the occasion of another illness, the Holy Synod gave instructions that if death supervened an Orthodox priest should instantly enter the house and come out again saying that at the last moment Tolstoy had expressed a wish to be restored to the Church's fellowship and had received the Last Sacrament before he expired.

In 1908, when he reached his eightieth birthday, the Holy Synod again denounced him as a dangerous heretic, and a Congress held at Moscow in July ordered the parish priests to warn the people against taking part in the demonstration to be held in Tolstoy's honour on the 28th August, and to arrange counter-demonstrations in which he was held up to execration.

On 7th November 1910 Tolstoy died at Astopovo. All over Russia and in Europe and America there were many public expressions of respect and sorrow, but the Holy Synod refused him burial rights and forbade the Orthodox clergy to hold any memorial service in any Orthodox church in the Russian Empire.

The spirit of intolerance which was manifested within the Empire was manifested in an equally aggravated form in Finland on the one hand and in Armenia on the other. At the beginning of the nineteenth century Alexander I. gave Finland a Special Act of Assurance, in which he guaranteed that the religion, laws, customs, and constitution of the Grand Duchy should remain inviolable. Alexander II. confirmed these pledges. Alexander III. did the same for a time, until his desire to unify the empire got the upper hand. Then he reduced the status of Finland to that of a Russian province. Nicholas II. went further. In 1894 he caused the Finnish Army to be reorganised under Russian officers on the Russian model. At the same time the Finnish soldiers were compelled to take the Oath

[1] Maude, *Tolstoy*, ii. 579.

of Allegiance to the Tsar. Russian was made the official language in every department of public business, and the national postage and coinage were suppressed. Protest followed protest. Nicholas refused to receive them. Thousands emigrated. Those who remained seethed with excitement, and General Bobrikov was sent to deal with them. He used his power so brutally that in 1903 he was assassinated. In 1905 there was a national strike which lasted for six days. Nicholas then cancelled all the encroachments which had taken place since 1909, but by degrees they were reintroduced and Finland became more disturbed than before.

The experience of Armenia was even more intolerable. In the eyes of Pobiedonostseff and the Holy Synod the existence of the Armenian Church as an independent organisation was an offence, and they resolved to ruin it. On the Turkish side of the frontier the troops of the Sultan were massacring all they could lay their hands on, and two thousand were butchered in Constantinople in one day. On the Russian side, by the orders of the Holy Synod, Prince Golitzin, Governor-General of the Caucasus, confiscated the whole property of the Armenian Church on Russian territory, its buildings, its lands, its endowments, and charitable funds to the total value of about fifteen million pounds sterling. The indignation of the Armenians at this barefaced act of robbery completely destroyed their lingering loyalty to the Russian throne.

All through the reign of Nicholas II. up to 1905 the Old Believers suffered grievous disabilities and much persecution. In spite of it, however, their numbers increased, and their consciousness that they were by no means a despicable body led them to demand better conditions than either Church or State was granting to them. For example, they asked that, in official documents, they should no more be designated by the offensive term Raskolniki (schismatics), but should be called Old Believers or Old Ritualists ; that they should have the right to possess their own churches and to open elementary schools for their own children ; that students who were Old

Believers should not be compelled to listen to lectures against their creed ; that their church registers should be considered legal documents ; that their clergy should be exempt from military service ; and that their children should be registered as Old Believers, although the parents under compulsion had been registered as Orthodox.[1]

Under pressure of the popular feeling the Senate intimated in December 1904 that the laws against them would be revised, and in April 1905 they were placed on something like a level with the members of the Orthodox Church. At the same time, an imperial decree divided those outside the Orthodox Church into three classes : (1) the Old Believers, who differed from the Orthodox Church only on points of ritual ; (2) sectaries, such as the Molokani, Doukhobors, Stundists, Tolstoyans, etc. ; (3) pernicious sects, such as the Khlysti and the Skoptsi.

These concessions instantly filled the Orthodox clergy with alarm, lest the members of their flocks should leave them and join the Old Believers, and they raised such an outcry that another decree was issued threatening imprisonment to any one who in any way persuaded an Orthodox believer to pervert to some other faith.

The actual temper of the Orthodox clergy towards all who dared to differ from them or to live in communion with some other ecclesiastical organisation was expressed in 1908 in a proclamation issued by Antonius, Metropolitan of Petrograd. In it he said : " The Orthodox Church is a divine institution. We teach that salvation can be obtained only while remaining in communion with the Orthodox Church. . . . We agree that it is possible, though abiding outwardly in the Church, to be a weak member of the Orthodox Church, but it is certain that a man who separates himself from the Orthodox Church separates himself from Christ. . . . Therefore when the Orthodox Church speaks of the enemies of the Church, its meaning is plain. Enemies of the Church are all those who profess any other religion or who deny that the Orthodox Church is the only true channel of the grace of Christ. . . ,

[1] Conybeare, p. 237,

To leave the Orthodox Church and to be at enmity with her is the greatest sin. For it there can be no justification. No failure of the clergy can serve as an excuse for apostasy. Such failure must be fought against while still remaining in the Church, but if any in fighting against the evils existing in the Church falls away from the Church himself, he only proves that he is far worse than those he has been trying to convict of sin."

After 1905, however, the Church completely lost its hold of the educated classes, and in the last days of the autocratic regime, one of the most prominent figures was unfortunately that of a man who brought religion into contempt. When the Great War broke out it quickly became evident that the destinies of Russia were in the hands of a self-seeking and corrupt camarilla which was sheltered by the throne, and that the Tsarina herself was not free from blame. She was sincerely devoted to the interests of Russia, and she was passionately attached to her husband. At the same time, she was a fanatical supporter of the autocracy, and, little as she knew it, she was like wax in the hand of the infamous Rasputin.

Rasputin was brought to her notice in a curious way. He was by birth a Moujik. He became a drunkard, a thief, a jail-bird, and, although married, immoral to a degree. About the age of thirty-five he resolved to become a Staretz, *i.e.* a wanderer or tramp who makes a special profession of religion. By pilgrimages and fervent prayers and austerities, which, however, did not prevent him from organising strange meetings characterised by hysterical fanaticism and immorality, he acquired the reputation of a holy man and gathered many disciples. The Tsarina had already borne her husband four daughters, but she was anxious to have a son, and she and her husband visited many shrines to implore the intercession of the saints towards this end. In the summer of 1903, after a prolonged vigil in the monastery of Sarov, Rasputin had the audacity to prophesy that in a year's time she would have her desire gratified. It happened as he said. An heir to the throne was born. The child was sickly from the first, but he was the apple of his mother's eye. The Tsarina heard of Rasputin's prediction from one of her favourites, and through this favourite he was introduced to the imperial circle. In a short time he completely dominated the Tsarina, made her believe he was her true friend, and persuaded her that her child's health and his safety were bound up together. This was an adroit move on his part, for he had already made himself hated and feared. The Tsarina, however, saw no fault in him, accepted all he said as a divine oracle, and acted both in domestic and public affairs exactly as he advised. Nothing could convince her of his political incompetence or of his degraded moral character, and those who were most anxious to avert the dangers which were threatening the country were the most eager to get rid of him. It was a relief and a deliverance when on 17th December 1916 he was assassinated.

In all Russia the autocracy had no longer any friends, and the imperial family was standing alone. When the war broke out there was a short rally round the throne, but when one disaster followed upon another the revolutionary forces which were working to ruin the discipline of the army and to disintegrate the social order gained the upper hand. Nicholas became a political nonentity, one of the most pathetic figures in modern history, blind to the signs of the times, misled and deceived by his Ministers, overborne by the more powerful personality of his wife and sometimes reduced to despair by her hysterics ; he remained autocrat in name, but he had no more power to control the course of events than if he had been a chip in a great torrent that is plunging into the abyss.

In February 1917 he was compelled to abdicate at Pskov, and on the night of 16th July 1918, along with his wife, his son, his four daughters, and a few faithful servants, he was brutally done to death in the cellar of the Epatievsky House in Ekaterinburg by a Jew named Yurovsky. From that moment the autocracy and the dynasty of the Romanovs ceased to exist.

CHAPTER XXVI

LENIN

THE revolution had triumphed. The Duma ceased to exist. The provisional government under Kerenski was overthrown, and Russia became a republic with neither President nor Parliament in any sense known to Western Europe. The highest authority is now the All Russian Congress of Soviets. It meets twice a year, and in the intervals its functions are delegated to an executive committee, of which Lenin was the first chief. Local government is in the hands of local Soviets with local congresses and executive committees.

Lenin was not, to begin with, the all-powerful leader he became. He was poor and obscure, and supported himself by writing for the revolutionary Press. His name was really Vladimir Oulianoff, and he was born in 1870, the son of an hereditary nobleman in the province of Simbirsk. He studied law in the University of Kazan, then went to Petrograd, where the execution of his brother on a charge of political conspiracy led him to form an iron resolution to destroy the autocracy by any means that offered itself. He then became a wanderer. When the Great War broke out he returned to Russia, seeing in the disturbed state of the country a magnificent opportunity for the propagation of his opinions, and the Germans are said to have made his passage through their country swift and easy on the understanding that he would endeavour to ruin the discipline of the Russian Army.

His most prominent colleague was a full-blooded Jew named Trotsky, a man of fiery energy and extraordinary eloquence. After the Revolution of 1905 he was banished to Siberia, from which he escaped. Until 1917 he wandered from one European city to another and took a prominent part in the Russian Social Democratic Movement. The outbreak of the Great War found him in America, from which he returned to Russia, where he carried on an utterly unscrupulous struggle for power, and finally became chairman of the Petrograd Soviet.   In this position, along with Lenin, he disorganised the defence of the country, and with him concluded the Treaty of Brest Litovsk which laid Russia at Germany's feet.

As the position of the Bolshevists was insecure they organised the Red Guard, and by a decree of 27th April 1918 developed it into the Red Army.   Military service was made compulsory on all males from eighteen to forty years of age, outside the circle of the bourgeoisie, the proletariat alone being allowed to possess arms.   Training lasts for five weeks, and at least twelve hours a week is given to it.   It now forms a force against which nothing in Russia can stand.

The aim of Lenin and the Bolshevists is easily understood.   It is the complete destruction of capitalism, and the destruction of the Christian Church.   Their place is to be taken by a communistic system, and a militant atheism. In the attempt to reach this end they have shed and are still shedding rivers of blood.   They have never numbered more than a small minority of the Russian people.   According to the statistics formulated by the Communistic Congress of May 1919, less than one-half of one per cent. of Russia is communist.   All the rest of the people, more than a hundred and fifty millions in all, are outside the communistic ranks, but they cannot move.   They are held down and terrorised by the Red Army.   Wherever disaffection breaks out soldiers are sent in overwhelming force, and when they retire they leave behind them smoking ruins, streaming blood, and a people paralysed by fear.

Whenever they came into power the Bolshevists started a thoroughgoing system of nationalisation based on the most gigantic process of robbery which the world has seen.

By a decree of 15th December 1917 all the private trading banks were declared to be the property of the State.   All coined gold was seized outright.   All the silver, jewels, objects of value, and securities lying in safe deposit

vaults were transferred to the State bank, but if any
lessee of boxes did not attend the opening of the vaults
within three days of a summons he was held to have surrendered his possessions, and no claim for compensation
was acknowledged. A fortnight later the great Putilov
foundries were nationalised. Thereafter the industries of
coal, iron, metallurgy, and transport of all sorts were
nationalised likewise. " By the end of 1918 the following
industries were completely nationalised — mining, oil,
rubber, electro-technics, sugar, water transportation. The
following were partly nationalised—metallurgy, textiles,
chemicals, etc. At the present time practically all the
important industrial enterprises are the nationalised
property of the State. Some small ones still continue to
run on a non-nationalistic basis, but their work and existence are precarious at the best, as all the supplies of fuel
and raw material are held by the Government." [1]

The land was nationalised by the fifth All Russian
Congress of Soviets at its sitting on 10th July 1918. The
peasants, believing that at last their desires had been granted
and that their rights of possession were secured, hailed
the decree with joy and, without waiting for legal permission, settled down on the portions they had selected.
It was not long until they found they had totally mis-
interpreted the situation. They were told that, as there
was no private property in land, they were not the owners
but only the occupiers of their farms, and that their produce
belonged not to them as private individuals but to the
State. They were, therefore, compelled to surrender
their crops to officers appointed by the State, and to accept
prices fixed by the State's authority. As these prices
were always low, their indignation equalled their surprise,
and they withheld their grain. The Bolshevists then
commandeered it wherever they found it. The peasants
have replied by growing no more than they need for their
own use, by hiding what they have harvested, and by
letting most of the land go out of cultivation. Some of
them have abandoned their farms and become brigands.

[1] Pasvolski, p. 38.

The Bolshevists have seized their parents, wives, and children as hostages, to be shot at the first movement of the runaways. Regions which a few years ago were scenes of plenty are now a silent and savage desolation.

The nationalising policy has also been applied to housing. In the large cities and towns many houses have been burned, many more have fallen into ruin, and the best of those that remain have been commandeered for the accommodation of the innumerable departments of State which have been set up. These houses are by no means sufficient to accommodate all who need them. A decree of 28th October 1918 has therefore empowered municipalities to seize all unoccupied buildings and to install in them citizens who have no houses or who live in unhealthy quarters. A beginning was made with public institutions. Soon afterwards the power was exercised to humiliate and terrify the bourgeoisie. Their apartments were filled with filthy and degraded men and women, who were instructed that they had a right to all the house contained. The owners were set aside and house soviets took their place. These sometimes include stable-boys and servant-girls. More often they consisted of groups of the inmates, who tyrannised over the rest and seized for themselves everything to which they took a fancy. Those who complained were denounced to the revolutionary tribunal. Overcrowding, dirt, and the lack of sanitation have made these houses hotbeds of disease.

The Press of Russia has also been nationalised. Every magazine and journal, every newspaper office and advertising agency, every printing-press has been confiscated, and no article, no leader, no report of a meeting is allowed to appear without the permission of the censor. " Full freedom of the Press," says Tchitcherin, " is only permissible after counter-revolutionary conspiracies which are stirred up from abroad have ceased." What the Russian newspapers print, and practically all the news which comes to Western Europe, is simply what the Bolshevists wish the world to believe.

To give their proceedings the appearance of legality

the ordinary law courts have been abolished, and others of a Bolshevist pattern have been set up. The officials connected with these are not selected because of their familiarity with legal principles or precedents. It is enough that they have secured the favour of the Bolshevist leaders and that their decisions are guided by the revolutionary conscience. Alongside these local courts there are others. On 17th December 1917 revolutionary tribunals with unlimited powers were established to deal with all who opposed the revolution or were suspected of doing so. These are crowned by the All Russian Extraordinary Commission for Combating Counter-Revolution. This tribunal gathers into itself all that was worst in the Star Chamber of England, the Inquisition of Spain, and the Council of Blood of the Netherlands. Its first president was Uritiski, a hunchback, who seemed to revenge himself for his deformity by hating all mankind. He did his cruel work for the love of it, and revelled in the agony of his victims. He and his commission were not obliged to report all the executions they ordered, but their organ, popularly known as the *Hangman's Journal*, in the official report for February 1920 registers the death of 6185 persons in 1918, of 3456 in 1919—a total of 9641 in Moscow and Petrograd alone. To these must be added a vast number of persons put to death all over the country. For example, in December 1920, after the defeat of Wrangel, 13,000 persons were executed in the Crimea alone. The Bolshevist leaders made no attempt to check this butchery. On the contrary, they have encouraged it. In April 1918 Lenin complained : " Our rule is too mild, and frequently resembles jam rather than iron." Trotsky said : " You are perturbed by the mild terror we are using against our class enemies. Know that a month hence this terror will take a more dreadful form."

In order to reduce the bourgeoisie to political impotence, Article IV. chapter xiii. of the Constitution of the Russian Socialist Federal Soviet Republic enacts that no one shall have a right to vote who employs hired labour for profit, who receives an income without working for it, who is a

19

merchant, a trader, a broker, a monk, a priest, or an ecclesiastic of any sort, or who was an agent of the former Tsarist police.

The attack on political rights was followed by an attack on personal liberty. The bourgeoisie were conscripted wholesale and deliberately set to tasks for which they were not fitted. Property owners were gathered into concentration camps and sent out in gangs to labour in public works. University professors, lawyers, manufacturers, and others like them had to do the work of navvies in draining the marshes and paving the roads. They had also to act as scavengers on the streets, to scrub barrack floors, and to clean out public latrines. Ladies of the upper classes were told off to cut firewood and kill locusts, the latter occupation consisting chiefly in the digging of trenches, into which the locusts were swept to be burned. The idea was evidently to humiliate the victims rather than to get the work done, and the Bolshevist newspapers openly rejoiced that they had been brought so low.

From the attack on liberty there was a rapid transition to an attack on life. The Bolshevists declare that no one above the rank of the proletariat has a right even to exist, and in many places a systematic attempt has been made to get the bourgeoisie exterminated. For this purpose special courts were set up, and in these, as in the similar courts of the French Revolution, trial was usually followed by a sentence of death. The process of the courts was often too slow for the bloodthirstiness of the mob. In Sevastopol, for example, the inhabitants of two of the most bourgeoisie streets were deliberately murdered. In Simferopol between two and three hundred of the bourgeoisie perished in the same way. At Yalta between eighty and a hundred were thrown into the sea. At Upatoria, Bolshevist sailors crammed the local bourgeoisie into a barge and sank it. In the first week of March 1918 there were similar horrors at Kiev, Rostov on the Don, Novotcherkask, and other places. Even the children were not spared. At Rostov on the Don it was in vain that the mothers made an agonised appeal for their little ones. The massacre of the babes of Bethlehem was repeated on a larger scale. The soldiers of the Red Army took all who were brought to them, stripped them naked, shot them dead, threw their bodies over an embankment, and scattered stable manure to cover the blood. It is impossible to describe what took place at Odessa. The scenes there could not have been more awful if they had been created by fiends from hell.

The Bolshevist policy of ruining capitalism has been carried out with complete success, but the happy days which were promised after its disappearance have not yet arrived. Misery is universal and ruin is staring millions in the face.

The resolution to destroy capitalism is accompanied by the resolution to destroy the Church. " We have got rid of the Tsar," said a young man in Odessa. " We shall now get rid of God." In so far as the Bolshevists have a philosophical theory, that theory is materialistic. They recognise the physical side of life, they take no account of the side which is moral and spiritual. They hold that man is an animal, essentially the same as other animals, that there is nothing sacred in his personality, and that any value he has consists in his value to the State. Morality is a system of conventions which may be set aside without blame whenever the interest of the State demands it. Right and wrong are words to which there are no corresponding realities. Anything is right which can be imposed on the weak by one who is stronger.

In conformity with these principles the Bolshevists endeavour to set human relations on a basis from which the spiritual element is shut out. This appears in their treatment of marriage. They have decreed that marriages consecrated by a religious ceremony will not be recognised as valid, and their issue will not be considered legitimate. If there is to be a marriage ceremony it must be a civil one, and even that is not essential. If the parties who propose to unite with each other consider any public proceedings necessary they may make a declaration before a civil official, and that will be enough. When either of them wishes to terminate the union all that is required is to intimate the termination to the civil court.   The idea of union for life is denounced as bondage which no one should be called on to endure.   Marriage, therefore, is to last just as long as the persons married are satisfied with it.   This practically means a reversion to the casual relationships of the jungle or the farmyard.

The point is further illustrated by a decree issued at Vladimir on lines similar to those issued at Lugo, Kolpin, and other places and published in the Izvestia.   According to this decree every girl who has reached the age of eighteen years is to be considered the property of the State, and she must register at the Bureau of Free Love in the Commissariat of Surveillance.   Thereafter she has the right to choose a co-habitant husband from men between the ages of nineteen and fifty.   The consent of the man is not necessary, and protest against being chosen is not to be listened to.   In the same way the right to choose from among girls who have reached the age of eighteen is given to men.   It is not necessary to suppose that decrees of this sort were issued everywhere, nor is it necessary to suppose that they were put into force where they were issued.   The fact that they could be drawn up throws a lurid light on the mentality and moral disposition which lie behind them.[1]

As might have been expected, the tie between parents and children is looked on lightly.   Children are to be treated as children of the State.   After birth they are to be taken into institutions into which their parents cannot enter, and in these they are to be fed, clothed, and educated at the public expense, and trained as communists.   The position of children in these institutions is lamentable from every point of view.   They are dragged up in the most harmful physical environment, and nothing is done to inculcate principles of honour, truthfulness, or honesty, or to develop their moral sense.   On the contrary, boys and girls are herded together till they are sixteen or seventeen years of age, and the result is indescribable.   According to the Bolshevist theory this is of no importance.

[1] *New Europe*, 31st Oct. 1918.

Just at this point Bolshevism meets with an obstacle grounded not only in the teaching of the Church, but also in the instincts of the human heart. The Christian tradition of centuries still constrains men and women to desire the blessing of the Church when they plight their troth to each other. Russian parents still love their children and refuse to let them go to strangers. The Bolshevists therefore employ violence. Those who are suspected of wishing to be married by the priest are intimidated, and when the wedding service is going on gangs of ruffians sometimes force their way into the church, and the wedding-party considers itself fortunate if all its members escape with their lives.

Distinctly Christian institutions are definitely assailed. On account of the association of the Lord's Day with the Lord's Resurrection, an attempt has been made to exclude it from the calendar. There is no objection to a weekly day of rest, but that day must not be the day of the week which has been consecrated by Christian usage. In the spring of 1918 orders were issued that on the last Lord's Day in April factories and shops of all kinds were to carry on as usual. Tuesday, 1st May, was declared to take its place as the Festival of the Holy Revolution, and business houses, shops, and factories of all descriptions were forbidden to carry on operations. In place of divine worship there were to be public revellings.[1]

The greatest of all Church festivals in Russia is Easter, and it is celebrated with a devotion and enthusiasm which Westerners, and specially Protestants, can scarcely understand. The churches are crowded to suffocation by multitudes who wait patiently during the long ritual until the welcome words, " Christ is risen." Then they salute each other and return home with joyful hearts and beaming faces. Easter is therefore peculiarly obnoxious to the Bolshevists, and they have done everything in their power to prevent its observance, but they have failed.

The isolated parish churches give the Bolshevists abundant scope for their activity, and in many places the

[1] *London Times*, 9th Dec. 1919.

services have been brought to a standstill. Some churches have been closed by direct order, others remain closed because the priests have been murdered. In others, which are still open, the walls are covered with posters and cartoons, sometimes clever, usually blasphemous, and no attempt dare be made to take them down. In some cases the ikons have been torn to pieces, harlots have been clothed in the vestments of the clergy and exhibited to uproarious congregations of rioters. Demagogues standing in front of the ikonostasis have delivered harangues whose leading features were ribaldry and obscenity, and the most solemn act of worship has been held up to derision by the performance of a Devil's Mass.

In the hope of striking a deadly blow at the Church it was formally disestablished by a decree of 23rd January 1918, and by the same decree all its property was confiscated. In fact, the property of all religious associations was confiscated, and if churches or objects dedicated to religious observance are to be used for acts of worship, permission to use them must be given previously by the local or central authorities. All the administrative functions of the Orthodox Church have now ceased. Formerly it exercised an extensive criminal jurisdiction over the clergy, and a civil jurisdiction relating to the validity and dissolution of marriage (which up to that date had been considered valid and legal only if it had received the blessing of the Church), and also with regard to the registration of births, marriages, and deaths. All these are now transferred to the Soviet authorities.

Immediately after the publication of this decree an attack was made on the Nevski Lavra, which is to Petrograd more than what St. Peter's is to Rome or Westminster Abbey to London. Within its vast extent it contains twelve churches and several chapels. Among its treasures were the Imperial Regalia, the wall of solid silver presented by the Tsarina Elisabeth, the candelabra of silver presented by Alexander I., and countless other gifts. A detachment of the Red Guard forced an entrance and began to make an inventory of the contents. The abbot resisted, and was

instantly seized. A great procession of clergy followed
by a crowd paraded the streets protesting against the
sacrilege, and similar scenes have been witnessed all over
Russia in the years that have followed.

Next came the murder of the clergy. The bloody work
was the spontaneous outcome of the passions of the mob,
but it was encouraged by those in authority, and Orthodox,
Lutherans, Catholics, and Reformed were all done to
death with impartial brutality. In Dorpat there was an
orgy of slaughter. The venerable Platon was seized and
dragged from his bed at midnight, then barefoot and clad
in his night apparel he and seventeen others were driven
into the cellars of his house and hacked to pieces with
axes. In the monastery near Kotlass the prior and all
the monks were shot. In Perm the bishop who had preached
against the Bolshevists had his eyes torn out and his
cheeks cut off. He was then marched through the streets,
and was finally killed. His ghastly fate created such
indignation that Vassili, Archbishop of Tchernigov, went
to Moscow to lodge a protest. He would have had a better
fate if he had gone into a tiger's den. He and his two
companions were cut to pieces. Archbishop Feofan was
subjected to an awful experience of refined torture, then
in a dying condition he was dipped through a hole in the
frozen surface of the river Kama, and drowned. At
Voronej the Bolshevist occupation was accompanied by
exceptional atrocities. The clergy and all the members
of their families were murdered, and the archbishop was
hanged in his own church on the altar gates. Prince
Troubetskoi says he is acquainted with provinces where
the number of priests murdered amounts to 10 per cent.
of the whole. Some had their eyes torn out, some had
their tongues cut out of their throats, some were crucified.
On the occasion of Tchitcherin's statement at Genoa
that complete religious freedom reigns in Russia the
Council of the Russian Church published a declaration
recording the Bolshevist execution of 28 bishops and
1215 priests.[1]

[1] *Hibbert Journal*, 1920.

The Soviet Government has been cynical enough to publish the official figures of executions in Russia since November 1917. The list includes 6775 schoolmasters and teachers, 8800 physicians, 54,650 officers, 260,000 privates, 10,500 police officers, 48,500 police soldiers, 12,950 landowners, 355,250 intellectuals, 192,350 workmen, and 815,100 peasants. The total list amounts to 1,766,118.

In a letter to the Archbishop of Canterbury received 12th February 1919, Sylvester, Archbishop of Omsk, says : "Having seized supreme power in Russia in 1917 the Maximalists [i.e. the Bolshevists] proceeded to destroy not only the cultivated classes of society, but have also swept away religion itself, the representatives of the Churches, and the religious monuments venerated by all. The Kremlin Cathedrals of Moscow and those in Yaroslavl and Simferopol have been sacked, and many churches have been defiled. The historical sacristies, as well as the famous libraries of the Patriarchs of Moscow and Petrograd, have been pillaged. Vladimir, Metropolitan of Kiev, about twenty bishops, and hundreds of priests have been murdered. Before killing them the Bolshevists cut off their limbs, and some of their victims were buried alive. Religious processions followed by masses of the people at Petrograd, Toula, Kharkov, and Soligalitch were fired upon. . . . Nuns are violated, women are made common property, licence and the lowest passions are rampant. One sees everywhere death, misery, and famine. . . . Only in Siberia and the region of the Ural Mountains where the Bolshevists have been expelled is the existence of the religious and civil population protected under the ægis of law and order."[1]

These atrocities have, however, failed to accomplish what was expected. So far from destroying the Church, the blows which it has endured have roused it to new vigour. It is inevitable that in this time of persecution many should fall away, and that many more should conceal their faith in fear of the consequences of open confession, but there are multitudes who refuse to be daunted.

[1] *The Christian East*, March 1920, p. 9.

Calamity has called out their courage, danger is making
them defiant, and they are forming centres round which
others stand firm.

In fact, in one important respect the policy of the
Bolshevists has been a stimulus to the Church's life. Its
connection with the State was a hindrance to its liberty
and growth from the first. Few perceived this, until in
the dreary period from the reign of Nicholas I. onwards,
ardent souls began to fret under the bondage in which they
were held, and the year which saw the opening of the first
Duma saw also the beginning of an attempt to loosen the
secular stranglehold which had reduced the Church to
spiritual impotence. On 10th March 1905 a Moscow newspaper published an article signed by thirty-two priests
demanding ecclesiastical reform, self-government, and the
calling of a national assembly with the view to securing
these. The appearance of this article caused great excitement, and the demand it contained was denounced by
Pobiedonostseff, who was still Procurator of the Holy
Synod. Nevertheless, a majority of the Synod, and, in
addition, the Premier, de Witte, sympathised with it, and
in December of the same year, in accordance with a decree
of the Tsar, a commission of bishops, clergy, and laymen
was instructed to consider what should be the constitution
of the assembly, and along what lines its activity should run.
The subject of the re-establishment of the Patriarchate
was also brought up, and a majority of the commission
proved to be in favour of it. So long as Pobiedonostseff
was Procurator, Nicholas II. refused to call the assembly,
but in 1916 statutes were issued reorganising the Holy
Synod on an electoral basis and reducing the Procurator's
power. What might have taken place after this it is
impossible to say, for the revolution swept the autocracy
out of existence and gave the Bolshevists a chance which
they instantly seized. No sooner did they feel themselves
secure than they took action in a way that no one antici-
pated. They severed the connection between Church and
State. Their decree struck the Church like a thunderbolt
and stunned it for a moment, but it quickly recovered its

composure and set itself to face the new situation. The
All Russian Church Council was summoned to meet in
Moscow on 15th August 1917, and it continued its sittings
till September 1918. It was the first Church Council
which had met since the abolition of the Patriarchate by
Peter the Great, and it was thoroughly representative of
the people. The elections took place in the preceding June
and July, and all adults over twenty-five years of age
were allowed to take part in them. Each parish sent one
priest and four laymen to the deanery Synod. Each
deanery Synod sent two priests and three laymen to the
Diocesan Convocation, and each Diocesan Convocation
sent two priests and three laymen to the Supreme Council.
In addition to 320 members appointed after this fashion
there were 64 Metropolitans and bishops who took their
seats *ex officio*, 9 representatives of Autocephalous Churches,
such as Georgia, Japan, and America, 16 representatives
of the monasteries, and 10 of the Duma.

Civil war was raging at the time, and the deliberations
of the Council were often interrupted by the rattle of rifle-
fire. The deputies knew well that at any moment the
doors of their chamber might be burst open, and that they
might be arrested or shot at sight. Nevertheless, they set
themselves to save their country from the ruin into which
it was plunging. They began by endeavouring to counter-
act the Bolshevist propaganda which was disintegrating
the army. They sent messages to the regiments where
discipline was crumbling, urging the soldiers to remember
their oath to the Tsar and to the country. In the act of
delivering these messages many priests were done to death.
They likewise admonished the clergy to protest against
the pillage and murder which were going on in their
parishes, and, if possible, to extinguish the flame of civil
war. In face of the savagery and bestiality which were
raging everywhere they exhorted the priests to preach the
duty of pity and chastity, and to hold up the ideals of holy
living and self-sacrificing love which are furnished by the
example of Jesus Christ. Many a priest obeyed these
orders at the cost of his life.

Another matter of supreme importance which engaged the attention of the Council arose out of the fact that its connection with the State had ceased. The Church was headless, and the Procurator of the Holy Synod, who was theoretically the Tsar's representative in the supreme court, and who was practically its master, had no longer any reason for his existence. It was inevitable to ask who was to take the Tsar's place. A strong minority feared that if a Patriarch were appointed he would arrogate to himself autocratic powers, to which they were determined not to submit. To meet their views the principle was laid down that as the Church elected the Patriarch, it retained to itself the right of taking him to task and, if necessary, of deposing him and appointing another in his place. His powers and functions were likewise carefully defined, so that the contingency feared became impossible. For purposes of consultation and decision it was resolved to associate with the Patriarch a cabinet in two sections. One is the Holy Synod, with twelve bishops as its members. The other is the Supreme Church Council, also consisting of twelve members, bishops, priests, and laymen in equal numbers. These two courts have independent spheres of administration. It is only when matters of general importance are to be decided that they meet together. After the same pattern, each of the bishops has in his diocese a Council composed of priests and laymen, and the priests in the parishes have an elected committee of parishioners. Other officials connect these courts together, and now for the first time in a thousand years the Orthodox Church in Russia is self-governing as well as free. But the Bolshevists look on its freedom and independence with jealous eyes and are preparing to limit it.

The election to the Patriarchate took place in Moscow on 1st November 1917 while a fierce battle was raging in the streets. The man chosen was Tikhon, and he was enthroned on 4th December. Tikhon was then a man of fifty-four years of age, who had filled many offices of importance. He was the son of a priest in the diocese of Pskov. He has been teacher, inspector, and rector of the ecclesiastical seminary at Kazan. He was afterwards Bishop of Liublin and then of the Aleutian Islands. He became an archbishop in 1905, and from 1913 held the Sees of Yaroslav and Lithuania. In June 1917 he was elected Metropolitan of Moscow, and from that office was raised to the Patriarchate. He is pious, scholarly, courageous, and devoted to the interests of the Church.

As might have been expected from men with their traditions, the Council saw in the violent separation of Church and State nothing but a gigantic calamity, a masterpiece of Satanic ingenuity designed to make the existence of the Church impossible. Their lands and heritages were gone. The accumulated wealth of centuries was gone. Churches and monasteries where venerated relics were reposing had become the common property of Mohammedans, Jews, and heathen. Holy ikons and crosses and vessels used in the most solemn acts of worship had fallen into the hands of mocking atheists. There were no candidates for the ministry, and the training colleges were closed. The Council, therefore, appointed a committee to consider the situation, and in January 1918 Professor Prince Troubetskoi gave in its report. The meeting was held in Moscow in the Diocesan House. " In the broad low hall, with its rising tiers of benches, sat many priests, long-haired, robed in cassocks of grey or blue or black : a few grave, dignified peasants in Russian costume, officials of the Synod, country teachers, merchants, a soldier or two, a few prominent public men, who also happened to be ardent churchmen, and several Moscow professors of philosophy and law who take a leading part in the work of the Synod. On the dais sat the bishops and archbishops in black monastic robes, and two Metropolitans in white caps with a silver cross. Arseny, the learned Archbishop of Novgorod, a middle-aged prelate with an energetic face, was in the chair." [1]

The report detailed the heavy losses which the Church had sustained, and the dangers by which it was surrounded. But it also struck a heroic note, and the members of the

[1] Harold Williams, *Daily Chronicle*, 21st Feb. 1918.

Council thrilled in response to it. After adopting the report, they turned to the altar and sang—a great chorus of men's voices—a beautiful prayer to the unsleeping Virgin. If the time of suffering had come, it was their part to endure. They must labour and fight for their faith, but, above all, they must endure.

Tikhon was well fitted to lead them. He had already proved himself to be a man of courage, and it was not long till he displayed that courage in a way that turned every eye in Russia towards him. In October 1919, when the Bolshevists were preparing to celebrate the anniversary of their *coup d'état*, he sent Lenin and his associates a letter, every syllable of which was fitted to raise their anger against him to white-heat. It begins with the words :

" They that take the sword shall perish by the sword.

" This prophecy of Christ we address unto you, the present rulers of the destiny of our country, styling yourselves the People's Commissars. For a year you have held the power of the State in your hands, and are preparing to celebrate the anniversary of the revolution in October 1917. But the torrents of blood of your brothers, mercilessly killed at your bidding, compel us to speak to you the bitter word of truth. . . ."

The letter goes on :

" Nobody feels safe, all live in constant fear of perquisitions, robbery, arrest, execution. Hundreds of defenceless people are seized daily and lie for months rotting in foul prisons, are executed without investigations or trial, even with the simplified method of trial established by you. Not only are those executed who are found guilty towards you, but also those whom you know to be innocent, and who are merely taken as hostages. Innocent bishops, priests, monks, and nuns are shot on a wholesale, vague, and indefinite accusation of counter-revolution. This inhuman existence is made still harder for Orthodox believers by their being bereft of the last consolations of death, the taking of Holy Communion, and by the bodies of those slain being refused to their relatives for Christian burial. . . .

"You have promised liberty. Is that liberty when no one dares to obtain food for himself, to change one's dwelling, to move from town to town ? Is that liberty when families, and sometimes all the inhabitants of a house, are evicted and their property thrown out into the street, and when citizens are artificially divided into categories of which some are destined to famine and plunder ? Is that liberty when no one dares to state openly his opinion out of fear of being accused of counter-revolution ? Where are freedom of speech and of the Press, where is the freedom of preaching ? Have not many brave Church preachers already paid the price of their blood, the blood of martyrs. The voice of social and State discussion is suppressed. The Press, with the exception of the narrow pro-Bolshevist section, is completely strangled. . . .

" It is not our business to judge of earthly powers. Any power tolerated by God would receive our blessing if it appeared as the judgment of God for the good of the people, and was not a terror to good works, but to evil. . . .

" But now unto you we tender one word of persuasion. Celebrate the anniversary of your coming into power by liberating the prisoners, by ceasing bloodshed, aggression, ruin, persecution of the faith. Turn from destruction towards the restoration of law and order, give the people the longed-for and merited rest from civil war. But now the blood of the righteous which you have shed shall be required of you, and you that have taken the sword shall perish by the sword."

This bold utterance instantly made Tikhon one of those who were marked down for vengeance, and a pretext for proceeding against him quickly came. The mismanagement, corruption, and tyranny of the Bolshevists disorganised the economic life of the country so completely that famine set in, and in 1921 not less than twenty-five millions were threatened with starvation. There was, in consequence, an appalling increase in disease, desolation, panic, and crime. This still continues, and the Soviet *Red Gazette* announced in May 1922 that the Bolshevist authorities in one of the famine districts " for humanitarian and sanitary reasons " shot 117 children afflicted with glanders, which developed after eating the flesh of horses suffering from the complaint. On the ground that they needed money for famine relief the Bolshevists ordered the confiscation of all the remaining Church treasures, and in two months, gold and silver articles valued at three and a half millions, and thousands of precious stones, were seized. The Patriarch Tikhon agreed that the treasures of the Church should be used for the help of those who were in need, but asked for guarantees that the money supplied would reach its proper destination. These guarantees the Bolshevists refused to give. Tikhon also contended that the only organised bodies which could properly carry out the distribution of Church funds were the parish councils and clergy of the Church, which were in close contact with the people and knew the situation. As the Bolshevists were anxious to handle the funds themselves, they refused to admit the force of the Patriarch's argument, and they instructed their agents to enter the churches and carry off whatever was valuable. Tikhon denounced this spoliation and urged the clergy to resist it.

His action gave the Bolshevists the pretext which they needed, and without delay the flood of their vengeance and hatred was let loose.

On 26th April 1922, on a charge of counter-revolutionary conspiracy, fifty-four priests were brought to Moscow for trial. Tikhon also was arrested on a charge of inciting the masses to civil war. The trial ended on 2nd May, when eight priests and three deacons were condemned to death. Six of these capital sentences were commuted to various terms of imprisonment. The remainder were executed, and the trial of Tikhon was postponed. The Bolshevists had discovered that Tikhon might be of more use to them living than he could be dead, and they took measures accordingly. On 6th May he was put into close confinement in the Troitska Monastery, and completely isolated from the world. At midnight on 12th May a small group of "progressive priests," that is, priests who had expressed their sympathy with Bolshevism and had undertaken to support the Soviet Government, entered Tikhon's cell and, after hours of furious wrangling and threatening, forced him to sign a document appointing Agafangel, Metropolitan of Yaroslav, or, failing him, Benjamin, Metropolitan of Petrograd, to administer the affairs of the Church so long as he himself continued unable to do so. Neither the one nor the other got the opportunity of exercising the functions which had been transferred to them. The Bolshevists declared that Tikhon had abdicated, and on 14th May their official organ published a manifesto to the effect that a General Assembly of the Church (*Sobor*) must be called to decide the question of Church administration, and to establish harmonious relations with the Soviet Government. The manifesto was signed by the progressive priests, Vvedenski, Krasnitski, and Byelkov of Petrograd, Stradnik, Kalinovski, Borisov, and Bykov of Moscow, and Rusanov and Ladovski of Saratov.

On 18th May Tikhon was forced to sign another document, under which the whole control of the Orthodox Church in Russia passed, until the creation of a permanent administration, into the hands of a temporary board of progressive priests. This meant that Tikhon divested himself of all his patriarchal authority and handed it over to these renegade clergy who were acting as the tools of the Bolshevists. It meant, in fact, his abdication. On the following day he was taken to the Donskoi Monastery and again shut up in close confinement. The Bolshevists had got almost all they wanted out of him, and they were prepared to wait till the merciless pressure they applied in his solitude finished the process of breaking him down.

Immediately after the key was turned on him in his new prison, the progressive priests, the Initiative Group, as they were called, entered the patriarchal palace and seized the whole machinery of the Church's administration. Their leader was Antonin, who was afterwards made Archbishop of Moscow, and with him were Vvedenski,

Kalinovski, and Krasnitski. These invited others to join them, but the only one who did so was Leonidas, who has become Bishop of Mogilev. On 20th May the Initiative Group began its work of ruling the Church according to Bolshevist ideas, and their authority has been recognised by practically the whole ecclesiastical organisation. Benjamin, Metropolitan of Petrograd, however, definitely refused to recognise them, and declared that until the Patriarch resumed his functions he and his clergy would manage the affairs of the diocese by themselves. He and several of his priests were soon afterwards put to death as conspirators against the authority of the Soviet State.

On 2nd May 1923, the General Assembly (*Sobor*), which the Bolshevists had been carefully preparing for, met at Moscow and proceeded to " reform " the Church. Every one who was admitted to its membership had to give satisfactory proof beforehand of his adhesion to Bolshevist principles, and every one, whatever his rank, who was suspected of hostility was carefully kept out. It was not from any point of view a free and self-governing court of the Church of Christ. It was a packed political caucus masquerading in a religious guise. As might have been expected from its composition, its decisions were unanimous. It formally deposed Tikhon, deprived him of all ecclesiastical rank, reduced him to the status of a mere layman, and assigned to him his original name Bellavin. It abolished the Patriarchate, and vested the whole administration of the Church in a Synod of clergy, all of them of pronounced Bolshevist sympathies. It enacted that all the offices in the Church from the highest to the lowest should be open to all the clergy, married and unmarried alike, and on equal terms, that monks should be allowed to marry if they desired to do so, and that they might if they wished renounce their religious vocation and engage in any secular occupation. It closed all the monasteries and nunneries and turned their inmates adrift. It blessed the whole Soviet regime, expressed its acceptance of the principles of Karl Marx, and set on record its approval of the whole Bolshevist propaganda except in regard to religion.

20

The Orthodox Church as an organisation was by this time helpless in the grip of the Bolshevists. Only one thing more, a finishing touch, was required to make their victory complete. That finishing touch was added. On 27th June 1923, Tikhon published a letter, which he must surely have signed with feelings of utter humiliation and shame. In this letter he formally withdrew his condemnation of the treaty agreement at Brest Litovsk, his anathema published in 1918, and his protest against the confiscation of Church property in 1922. He also declared that he had completely adopted the whole Soviet programme. It would be intensely interesting to know what pressure was applied to him and how long it was applied before he consented to do this, but the knowledge is likely to be withheld. The walls of Russian prisons hide many terrible secrets, and there are probably few who take at its face value Tikhon's further statement that he has been well treated. He is now a broken old man, and the threat of being brought to trial for counter-revolutionary conspiracy is still hanging over his head.

Having in this way got rid of the Patriarch and the Patriarchate, the Bolshevists are now bending their energies to the destruction of the Church. The method of robbery and massacre on a wholesale scale has been laid aside to some extent in favour of other devices which are quieter and slower, but, if not interfered with, not the less effective. The progressive priests and the living Church which they formed have served their turn and are now out of favour, and the movement which they started is withering. The leaders are quarrelling. The adherents are splitting up, and any influence they ever had is disappearing. Meanwhile, all over Russia, the Bolshevists are speeding up the work of disintegration. They have deposed many bishops and left their dioceses with no one to look after them. They have ejected many priests from their parishes and made no provision for the usual religious services. They have turned many churches into lecture rooms, theatres, and music halls. They have closed every institution for the training of priests, in the hope that when the present generation dies out there will be none left to carry on their work and public worship will cease. They have stopped the instruction of the people in Christian doctrine and Christian ethics by ordering that every sermon or religious address, before it is delivered, must pass the scrutiny of the censor. They have made the religious instruction of children by any person except their parents a penal offence.

In this connection they instituted a legal process which drew the attention of the civilised world. Monsignor Budkiewicz, the Catholic Administrator of the greater part of Russia and of Siberia, Archbishop John Cieplak, and the priests under their jurisdiction, denied the right of the secular authorities to interfere with them in the discharge of their religious duty, and continued to say Mass and to instruct children in the principles of the faith in defiance of the Bolshevist prohibition. Budkiewicz, Cieplak, and fourteen others were arrested and charged with counter-revolutionary practices and conspiracy. After a trial lasting for five days, in which there was no pretence of impartiality, sentence was pronounced on Palm Sunday, 25th March 1923. Budkiewicz and Cieplak were ordered to be executed, and in the case of Budkiewicz the sentence was carried out. But the storm of indignation which swept over the civilised world was so fierce that the Bolshevists commuted Cieplak's sentence to one of imprisonment for life. The others were sent to penal servitude for periods varying from three to ten years. The Catholicon of Georgia and the Bishop of Kutais in the Caucasus are now in prison in Tiflis on similar charges.

No attempt is made to conceal the intention which lies behind these prosecutions and executions. The Bolshevists glory in the fact that they are atheists. Having got rid of the earthly Tsar they openly express their resolution to get rid of the heavenly Tsar also. In 1918 the Central Soviet Committee in Moscow published a pamphlet written by Bucharin to the effect that the destruction of religion is essential if the liberation of the workers is to be secured. Bucharin says : " Modern science has proved that the first form of religion was the worship of dead ancestors. When man was little more than a monkey all were equal. Later, the richer and wiser became elders and ordered the others about, and when they died their memory was worshipped. This is the beginning of religion. In course of time the idea of a menacing God who judged, condemned, and rewarded men was developed, and man came to believe that the same order reigned in heaven as on earth. No sooner had men become masters on earth than they devised a God in heaven around whom stand angels and saints, such as St. Nicholas and the Virgin Mary —a sort of empress and the wife of the Holy Ghost—with an innumerable throng of minor saints, cherubim and seraphim, the bureaucracy of heaven. As in this world bureaucrats and their officials must be propitiated, so the worshipper must sing hymns of praise to the heavenly officials and burn candles before their altars. Belief in God is merely a reflection of our vulgar relations, tantamount to a belief in slavery. Those who believe in God are incapable of any struggle, for religion not only throws mankind into slavery but keeps it there. Religion is like opium, it conjures up lovely dreams but undermines and ruins those who indulge in it." [1]

For the purpose of multiplying the number of atheists in the coming years, the Bolshevists have forbidden the teaching of religion in any school (Decree of 23rd January 1918). On the ground that the Church has been completely disestablished, and that education is a national concern, no schools other than those publicly owned and controlled are permitted. Every citizen who has come to years of discretion is said to be free to believe what he chooses, but young people of an impressionable age must be allowed to grow up without any religious bias whatever. In spite of this declaration a strenuous endeavour is being made to fill them with anti-religious prejudice, and a propaganda in favour of atheism is incessant and vigorous. Brotherhoods or social circles have been formed for the purpose of teaching that Christianity is an invention of capitalists, designed to stupefy the proletariat and keep them in bondage. These

[1] Quoted by Hagbert Wright in *London Times*, 25th Oct. 1919.

brotherhoods are the work of Lunacharski. He himself is a pure Russian, but his three principal assistants were, to begin with, Jews who were fanatically antichristian. Under their direction a special attempt is being made to lay hold of the youth of both sexes, and to undermine their belief in the supernatural.

For the purpose of spreading atheism among the masses of the people placards are posted up ridiculing Orthodox ritual and doctrine, and leaflets are distributed in practically every village throughout the land. An elaborate series of official tracts has also been published for free distribution in which " the imbecilities " of the Christian religion are exposed, and there is another series in which the crimes committed by the Christian Churches, and specially by the Russian Church, are gloated over as the fruit of the Christian religion.

The Orthodox Church, on its side, is endeavouring to apply to the defence of the faith the same methods as are used for its destruction. It is, however, labouring under grave disadvantages. As the Bolshevists have seized its worldly wealth it is now forced to depend for its support on the voluntary offerings of its members, millions of whom are in the direst poverty. Even if it had the money it requires its work would be hampered by the fact that it can get nothing printed. The Bolshevists have seized its whole stock of paper, its founts of type, and its printing-presses, and while atheistic posters and leaflets are turned out by hundreds of thousands, the Church cannot publish even a Bible or a book of devotion. In these circumstances it has to rely less on the printed page than on the spoken word. This may in the long run turn out to the Church's benefit. There are millions of Russians to whom print conveys no meaning, but every man among them has an ear and a traditional respect for religion. Unfortunately, here again the Church is handicapped. The Bolshevist propagandists are picked men, trained for their work and familiar with the tricks of debate. The number of the clergy who are skilled in addressing popular audiences is very small. Neither their training nor their cast of mind qualifies them for work of this sort. They can preach a simple sermon, but they have not the knowledge required to expose the economic fallacies of communism. Neither have they the skill needed to expound the evidences of the Christian religion, or to refute the slanders which are hurled against it. The mental torpidity which is the legacy of past generations still clings to them.

Nevertheless, the number of those who can defend the Church's cause is increasing, and the parish priests are being stirred up by conferences and courses of special lectures designed to enable them to answer the questions raised among their parishioners. These are taken advantage of, but the vast area of the country, the complete breakdown of transport, the isolation of the towns and villages, and the general social disturbance confine the influence of this special instruction to limited areas.

The greatest obstacle to the atheistic propaganda, and at the same time the strongest bulwark of the Church, is the religious instinct of the people. The Russian is fundamentally religious, and although his conceptions of Christian truth are sometimes clouded by ignorance, and his creed has little influence on his ethical conduct, he refuses to withdraw from the Church whose services have brought him into contact with things eternal and divine. His attitude is indicated by the complaint of the *Pravda* of 18th March 1923 that the anti-religious journal, *The Atheist*, published by the communistic party, is not being read in the factories. Members of the communistic union endeavour to distribute it, but the adult workmen declare that God will punish those who scoff at Him.

The Bolshevists themselves admit that their campaign against religion is making little progress. The brotherhoods and social circles are falling to pieces, and in many places have ceased to exist. The *Pravda* already quoted says : " The anti-religious circles must not be allowed to continue in this state. If the development proceeds at this slow rate it will encourage the birth of all kinds of new religious sects, which will also be an obstacle to our

campaign against religion.   Why are these circles a fiasco ?
Certainly not because there is no time, but mainly because
we underestimate the importance of anti-religious propaganda.   We must carry on our agitation against religion
just as systematically as we do in political questions, but
with even more determination.   It must not be a recreation,
but part of our daily duties. . . . We must compel suitable
comrades to attend these circles and be trained for the
campaign. . . . This attendance must be a requirement
of party discipline. . . .
    " Although we have declared war on the denizens of
heaven, it is by no means easy to sweep them from the
households of the workmen.   The women especially are
intractable.   They worship before the holy ikons and
impede the progress of the war on religion.   They insist
on having their children christened, and obstruct the
removal of ikons.   It is necessary to work slowly, word by
word, drop by drop, to worm our way and convince the
stubborn that, by the unwritten decrees of the victorious
proletariat, the inhabitants of heaven and all their attributes have been abolished.   With an iron sweeper the
workmen must clear their homes of the last vestige of
all that is holy."
    Under the tremendous pressure which is being applied
to it a certain amount of disintegration has taken place
in the Church, and the little companies who have left it
have formed such new sects as the Living Church, the
Renewal of the Church, the Group of Novikov, the Free
Labour Church, which proclaims the necessity of universal
revolution, and the Union of Communities of the Ancient
Apostolic Church.   In the Ukraine also there are those
who call themselves Presbyterianski.   These, however,
have no influence on the general situation.
    The great fact remains that never before in any part
of the world has atheism, organised, militant, and fanatical,
made such an attack on Christianity as it is making in
Russia at the present day.   In the first Christian centuries
the persecutors of the Church were not atheists, they were
polytheists.   In Reformation times the differences between

Catholic and Protestant were wide and deep, and there was endless suffering, but both of them believed in God and worshipped Him as He is revealed in Jesus Christ. The Bolshevists, however, deny the existence of God, deride the Divinity of Jesus Christ, pour contempt on the ideals which He has set forth in His teaching, and resist His claim to rule over the life of men. By their own confession they are against Christ, they are the embodiment of the spirit of Antichrist, and between them and the Christian Church there can be no compromise. Of their ultimate overthrow both in Church and State there can be little question. Theodore Beza once said, " The Church is an anvil which has broken many hammers "; and the story of its sufferings and triumphs in the past encourages the belief that although the Bolshevists are for the moment a tyrannical force which nothing seems able to overthrow, the ancient prophecy of the Psalmist will be fulfilled : " He that sits in the heavens shall laugh. The Lord shall have them in derision. Then shall He speak unto them in His wrath and vex them in His sore displeasure."

In the years that lie before us there will be confusion and anxiety, but Russia will work out its own salvation. The Bolshevists are only a minority of the Russian people, and cleavages are beginning to appear among them. They are fighting against some of the deepest instincts of human nature. They are endeavouring to destroy a great institution which in spite of many imperfections has been the most vital force and the strongest bond of unity in the nation for a thousand years, and they are endeavouring to root out religion itself from the life of millions who are intensely religious, and who come into contact with religious ceremonial at every turn of their lives. They will ultimately fail. Even already they have been compelled to abandon to some extent their communistic principles and to accept the capitalistic system in commerce and industry. They have long ago lost the support of the peasantry, and are maintaining their authority in the country districts only by the show and use of force by police and Red Army detachments. Their hold on the industrial populations, in which they found their strongest support, is also being shaken by the same means as the Tsarist regime was shaken before the war — by demonstrations, revolts, and other acts of defiance which are steadily becoming more numerous and formidable. In the Church there is a real revival of religious life, which the atheist propaganda is singularly unable to suppress. From the Bolshevist point of view the signs of the times are ominous. On the whole the Bolshevists are easy to explain. They are the inevitable outcome and culmination of the oppression and wrongs, the indolence, superstition, and spiritual stagnation of the centuries which preceded them. But when they have passed, and when liberty, order, and peace have been restored, we may look for a new era of Russian history which works towards the ideal of a purified Church in a prosperous State.

BIBLIOGRAPHY

ALEXINSKI, G. . . . *Modern Russia.* London, 1913.

ANTONELLI, E.. . . *Bolshevist Russia.* London, 1920.

BAIN, R. NISBET . . *The Daughters of Peter the Great.* London, 1899.

,,   ,,   . . *The First Romanoffs.* London, 1905.

,,   ,,   . . "Peter the Great and his Pupils." *Cambridge Modern History,* vol. v.

BEAZLEY, FORBES, AND *Russia from the Varangians to the Bol-*
BIRKETT   *shevists.* Oxford, 1918.

BIRKBECK, W. J. . . *Russia and the English Church.* London, 1895.

,,   ,,   . . *Birkbeck and the Russian Church.* London, 1917.

BLACKMORE, R. W.. . *The Doctrine of the Russian Church.* Aberdeen, 1845.

BURY, J. B. . . . "Russia." *Cambridge Modern History,* vol. v.

CONSETT, T. . . . *Regulations of the Church of Russia.* London, 1720.

CONYBEARE, F. C. . . *Russian Dissenters.* Cambridge, 1921.

CUSTINE, MARQUIS DE . *Russia.* 3 vols. London, 1845.

DEARMER, P. . . . *The Russian Church.* London, 1917.

DILLON, E. J. . . . *The Eclipse of Russia.* London, 1918.

DRAGE, J.. . . . "Russia under Nicholas I." *Cambridge Modern History,* vol. xi.

EPHIMENKO, A. R. . . *A Short History of Russia.* London, 1920.

FLETCHER, G. . . . *History of Russia.* London, 1643.

FORTESCUE, A. . . *The Orthodox Russian Church.* London, 1916.

FRERE, W. H. . . . *Links in the Chain of Russian History.* London, 1918.

GAGARIN, I. . . . *The Russian Clergy.* London, 1872.

GOLOVINE, I. . . . *Russia under Nicolas I.* 2 vols. London, 1846.

GRASS, K. K. . . . *Die Russianschen Sekten.* 2 vols. Leipzig, 1907 and 1914.

HAKLUYT, R. . . . *The Principal Navigations and Voyages of the English Nation.* Reprinted. 2 vols. London, 1907.

HAXTHAUSEN, BARON *The Russian Empire.* 2 vols. London, VON 1856.

HEADLAM, A. C. . . *The Teaching of the Russian Church.* London, 1897.

HEARD, A. F. . . . *The Russian Church.* London, 1877.

HERBERSTEIN,SIGISMUND *Rerum Moscoviticarum Commentarii.* 2 VON vols. Hakluyt Society. London, 1852.

HOTZSCH, O. . . . "Catherine II." *Cambridge Modern History*, vol. vi.

HOWE, SONIA E. . . *A Thousand Years of Russian History* London, 1915.

,, ,, . . *The False Dimitri.* London, 1916.

,, ,, . . *Some Russian Heroes, Saints, and Sinners.* London, 1916.

HOWORTH, H. H. . . *History of the Mongols.* 2 vols. London, 1876.

JARINTZOFF, MADAME N. *Russia, the Country of Extremes.* London, 1914.

JOYNEVILLE, C. . . *Life of Alexander I.* 3 vols. London, 1875.

KARAMSIN, N. M. . . *History of the Russian Empire.* 10 vols. Paris, 1826.

KELLY, W. H. . . *History of Russia.* 2 vols. London, 1902.

KERENSKI, A. F. . . *The Prelude of Bolshevism.* London, 1919.

KLUCHEVSKI, V. O. . *History of Russia.* 3 vols. London, 1913.

KORNILOV, A. . . *Modern Russian History.* 2 vols. London, 1916.

KOVALEVSKI, M. . . *Modern Customs and Ancient Laws of Russia.* London, 1891.

KRASINSKI, COUNT V. . *The Religious History of the Slavonic Nations.* Edinburgh, 1851.

KROPOTKIN, O. . . *Russian Literature.* London, 1905.

LANIN, E. B. . . . *Russian Traits and Terrors.* Boston, 1891.

,, ,, . . . "The Tsar Persecutor." *Contemporary Review,* Jan. 1892.

LEROY-BEAULIEU, A. . *L'Empire des Tsars et la Russie.* 3 vols. Paris, 1898.

MASARYK . . . *The Spirit of Russia.* 2 vols.

MAUDE, A. . . . *A Peculiar People, the Doukhobors.* London, 1905.

,, ,, . . . *Life of Tolstoy.* 2 vols. London, 1911.

MAVOR, J.. . . . *An Economic History of Russia.* 2 vols. London, 1914.

MORFILL, W. R. . . . *Russia.* London, 1890.

MOURAVIEFF, A. N. . *History of the Church of Russia.* Oxford, 1852.

MUNRO, H. H. . . . *The Rise of the Russian Empire.* London, 1900.

M'CULLAGH, F. . . . *The Bolshevist Persecution of Religion.* London, 1924.

NEALE, J. M. . . . *A History of the Holy Eastern Church.* London, 1850.

OVERBECK, J. J. . . *The Orthodox Confession of Peter Mogila.* London, 1898.

PALMER, W. . . . *The Eastern Catholic Communion.* London, 1853.

,, ,, . . . *The Patriarch and the Tsar.* 6 vols. London, 1871.

PASVOLSKI, L. . . . *The Economics of Communism.* New York, 1921.

PINKERTON, R. . . *Present State of the Greek Church in Russia.* Edinburgh, 1914.

POBIEDONOSTSEFF, K. P. *Reflections of a Russian Statesman.* London, 1898.

RAINE AND LUBOFF . *Bolshevik Russia.* London, 1920.

RALSTON, W. R. S. . *Early Russian History.* London, 1874.

RAMBAUD, A. . . . *Histoire de la Russie.* Paris, 1914.

RAPPOPORT, A. S . . *Pioneers of the Russian Revolution.* London, 1918.

RICAUT, P. . . . *State of the Greek and Armenian Churches.* London, 1679.

ROBERTSON, J. N. W. R. *The Acts and Decrees of the Synod of Jerusalem.* London, 1890.

ROMANOFF, H. C. . . *Rites and Customs of the Græco-Russian Church.* London, 1920.

SAMSON-HIMMELSTIERNA, *Russia under Alexander III.* London, H. VON 1893.

SKRINE, F. H. . . . *The Expansion of Russia.* Cambridge, 1904.

SLOCOMBE, G. E. . . *Poland.* Poland, 1916.

SPARGO, J. . . . *Bolshevism.* New York, 1919.

,, ,, . . . *The Greatest Failure in all History.* New York, 1920.

STEPNIAK . . . *Russia under the Tsars.* London, 1885.

,, . . . *The Russian Peasantry.* London, 1905.

STSCHEPKIN, E. . . " Russia under Alexander I." *Cambridge Modern History,* vol. ix.

TCHERKOFF AND TOLSTOY *Christian Martyrdom in Russia.* London, 1897.

THOMSEN, W. . . . *The Relations between Ancient Russia and Scandinavia, and the Origin of the Russian State.* Oxford, 1877.

TROITSKY, S. V. . . "The Russian Church." *Encyclopædia of Religion and Ethics,* vol. x.

WADDINGTON, G. . . *Present State of the Greek Church.* London, 1829.

WALISZEWSKI, K. . . *Le Roman d'une Imperatrice.* Paris, 1893.

,, ,, . . *Peter the Great.* London, 1898.

,, ,, . . *L'Heritage de Pierre le Grand.* Paris, 1900.

,, ,, . . *Paul I.* London, 1903.

,, ,, . . *Ivan the Terrible.* London, 1904.

WALLACE, D. M. . *Russia.* London, 1902.

WILBOIS, J. . . . *L'Avenir de l'Eglise russe.* Paris, 1907.

WILLIAMS, H. W. . . *Russia of the Russians.* London, 1915.

WIENER, L. . . *An Interpretation of the Russian People.* London, 1915.

INDEX

Tilsit, 218.
Timurlane, 61.
Toktamish, 61.
Tolstoy, Dimitri, Count, 257, 258.
Tolstoy, Leo, Count, 278–80.
Traventhal, 174.
Trevor, 3.
Troitska Lavra, the, 55, 63, 74, 85,
  86, 90, 92, 120, 124, 129, 132, 154,
  162, 171, 189.
Trotsky, 285, 289.
Tula, 42.
Tver, 49, 54, 69, 70, 85, 101, 102.

Uniate Church, the, 118, 232.
University of Moscow, 193, 229.
Urban II., Pope, 29.
Uvarov, 229, 234.
Uzbeg, Khan, 41, 42, 48, 49, 52.

Valois, Henry of, 105.
Varangians, the, 2–4.
Varigin, Peter, 277.
Vassian, Bishop, 71.
Vassian of Kolomna, 95.
Vassian, Kossoi, 85.
Vassili I. 57–62.

Vassili II., 62–8.
Vassili III., 80–6.
Vassili IV. (Shuiski), 122, 123.
Vassili the Squinter, 63.
Viatka, 70.
Vienna, Congress of, 219.
Vilna, 58, 59, 117.
Vitoft, 59–61, 73.
Vladimir, the city of, 18, 33–8, 44,
  46, 49–51, 54, 61, 113, 292.
Vladimir the Great, 12–20, 34.
Vladimir Monomachus, 29–34, 42.
Voloss, 18.

Waldemar, 132.

Yaropalk, 12.
Yavorsky, Stephen, 183–6.
Yermak, 108, 109.
Ysevolod, 38, 42.
Yuri Dolgorouki, 33, 34, 87.
Yuri of Moscow, 41, 48, 49.

Zacharias, 74.
Zimisces, John, 11.
Zotoff, 183, 190, 191.
Zozimus, Metropolitan, 74.